THE END OF SCARCITY

The Dawn of the New Abundant World

KRISTEN A. RAGUSIN

This is a work of creative nonfiction. Some parts have been fictionalized in varying degrees, for various purposes.

Copyright ©2022 by Kristen Ragusin
All rights reserved.

Excerpts of talks given by Professor Steve Keen, Ellen H. Brown, and Paul Grignon used with permission. Every effort has been made to trace or contact all copyright holders. The publisher will be pleased to make good any omissions or rectify any mistakes brought to their attention at the earliest opportunity.

The information is in this book is not meant to be, and should not be construed as advice or used for investment purposes. It is not intended to be a source of financial or legal advice.

Final Cover Design by Anthony Morais Front Cover Creation by Maxwell Roth David Aguilar/EyeEm@Getty Images

ISBN 979-8-9862858-0-1 (paperback)

ISBN 979-8-9862858-1-8 (hardcover)

ISBN 979-8-9862858-2-5 (Kindle)

ISBN 979-8-9862858-3-2 (Epub)

INDIGO BOOK PRESS

Published by Indigo Book Press, LLC.
www.KristenRagusin.com

This work is dedicated to my parents, who have been my inspiration to living a life full of curiosity, freedom, and empowerment. Each modeled and encouraged me in their own way, making an indelible impression on me, for which I will be forever grateful. I love you mom and dad.

"There is nothing more powerful than an idea whose time has come."
    -Victor Hugo

FOREWORD

My hope is that this book will bring a profound personal healing to all who read it and to society at large as we come together and employ the wisdom contained within these pages. Reading this book will produce a life changing revelation about money, what money is and what money is meant to be. It will alter how you understand what is not working in this world and why. Not only that, it will heal the conflict growing in our hearts, separating us into warring factions as we spiral into self-destruction losing the battle of "a happy life for all" due to a lack of vital information and a simple misunderstanding about money.

We have come to the point in society where we know that continuing to do what we do cannot possibly get us to where we want to be; to that change we are all yearning for—the peace, the freedom, and the grace of living in abundance.

The great sage Mahatma Gandhi encouraged us to take the initiative and "Be the Change" we wish to see in the world. Suggesting we use the creative power we hold rather than drowning in a sea of self-defeating anger and frustration as we wait for change to happen. Yet when we try to put this into action we find ourselves feeling alone and helpless; in a world full of demands that seem to work against us.

We are missing the most important piece of information about how society works and runs on a money system. We assume we understand what money is and how it works. After all, we use it every day. Yet, money is the single, most powerful instrument determining our life path, what we do, what we value, and, often, even how we treat one another. If we do not understand the simple basics of what money is and how it comes into being we are hopelessly led astray, becoming evermore divided, lost in ever-increasing fighting and endless suffering.

This book is the key to unlock the door of our mutual prison. It is written for the average person. No experience or understanding of markets or the economy is necessary. In fact, the more we think we know the harder it can be to unlearn the misconceptions we have been taught and believe to be true. I encourage the reader to follow the sequence of this book, each chapter builds a subsequent foundation needed upon the other. Reading this book produces a stunning revelation, a new and complete understanding of this mysterious, all-powerful "thing" called money. It will deliver you to a place of peace at how easily we can transform our world, where the liberation of all people is possible, bringing about the abundance, creativity, and joy that we long to express.

INTRODUCTION

I grew up in a world filled with optimism and hope. A world where we knew life was inherently good and, so was our country. We held America deeply in our heart. It was the land of opportunities where those willing to dream and daring to commit themselves had the possibility of success. People who worked hard and did the right thing could find work they enjoyed, a home to call their own, and had the opportunity to raise a family and retire into their golden years. My parents were no different. They were ambitious, lived with high ideals, and inspired me with their good character. In turn, I felt empowered to explore the adventures of life and meet the challenges I would find along the way. Most believed that good things were possible for others too, that they could find the possibility of success they wanted as well, especially if they tapped into the unique sense of divinity within them and contributed to the well-being of others.

This conviction led to a sense of optimism that has flowed throughout my life. Resilient and undying it restored me, time and time again, to a place of knowing that life is always working for our highest good—even in our most difficult and trying times. As a little girl, I earned my allowance explaining to my father how the stock market and interest rates worked. In a way it should have been no surprise that I became a professional financial advisor helping clients invest their money for the last thirty years. But it was not until I saw how much angst, fear, and guilt people had about their money that I grasped how I could help them feel empowered and supported by their money. I believed the markets were an integral part of realizing the American Dream, an accessible way to create wealth and support the collective genius and productivity of our society. I enjoyed the special connection of working with clients and the autonomy of running my practice. It empowered me to question, learn, and grow over the years.

Yet, everything changed as the summer of 2007 arrived. I was completing a Masters Degree from the Fletcher School of Law and Diplomacy at Tufts University and I had been away from the office finishing my thesis paper. By the time I got back to my desk, I noticed some "very secure" investments had sudden losses. As I reached out for answers no one could help me. Financial companies raised curious amounts of money and continued to take on huge quantities of debt. Still, no one could explain this to me or even seemed interested in my questioning. Later that fall, despite being repeatedly dismissed by colleagues, I was convinced something was wrong. I called my clients who didn't need to stay invested for income or other goals and told them I felt it was time to sell. And, so, we did—we sold most everything in sight.

I was working on a second Masters Degree and preparing to attend a course in the Middle East that would take me away that fall for three weeks. I felt I had followed my intuition by selling, and I went off to Jordan with relative peace of mind. While I was away, I watched the market go straight up, every day for twenty-one days, and each night I shut the computer down with a heavy heart. Then, within one week of coming home, the markets began to implode. In the late fall of 2007, the major financial crisis of 2008 began. I thought I would feel somewhat vindicated, but the destruction was so intense, nothing could make me feel relieved. Instead, watching it took my breath away.

It was not "just" a serious downturn. It soon became clear that what I was looking at was the total devastation and decimation of our financial system. What was happening was so far beyond what any of the rules of the game had ever implied. There was a deafening silence while I watched the markets sell off day in and day out, as all the wealth stored in stocks and bonds collapsed and evaporated into nothing. A muted feeling lurked and grew that there was not only something wrong with the markets but wrong with my worldview.

I had to take a step back and find out what I was missing. I didn't know what it was, but I knew I held an assumption that just couldn't be true. I needed to find out how the entire financial system could collapse—seemingly out of nowhere. How all the promises made about the safety of our money could suddenly vanish, taking everything I trusted, and all of life's important decisions down into the dark abyss. I began to read everything I could get my hands on. I researched endless economic analysis about misplaced financial policy and failed strategies. When that proved fruitless, I focused on politics. I examined legislation put in place, regulations removed or not enforced, and I could not find the root of the collapse. Frustrated, I turned to social issues, from racial and gender inequalities to class warfare and, still, I found nothing. Overwhelmed by a deafening amount of information, I had no new clarity. I felt helpless as I watched the world argue louder and louder, endlessly blaming one group over another.

Then, suddenly, something changed. It happened in the strangest and most unexpected of places. I stumbled upon an article detailing how money is created in our world, where it comes from, and how it enters into the economy. Seemingly so obvious, even boring, this was something I was sure I already knew, so much so that I could hardly justify researching the process. But out of ideas, I had nothing to lose. Alas, there it was—the answer I tirelessly searched for—waiting to be discovered in examining the process of how money is created! I was dumbfounded. Here was the source of all economic instability, political confusion and contention, and social and class struggles and, yet, it had nothing to do with economic policy, political perspectives, or human nature. The problem was the way we *create* our money, the actual instrument itself. Money created this way—the wrong way—is a silent, all powerful mechanism producing suffering and destruction in our lives. Without knowing, we believe our money is a simple thing, something we want and need. We spend a big part of our lives focused on getting more of it, and a bigger part of how we live is determined by how much we have of it. Yet, the way it is designed, and comes into existence, programs it to destroy everything we work for and everything we value. I was stunned. It was so simple and incredibly insidious at the same time. I knew that I had found the answer I searched for, but I struggled to come to terms with what it meant, and the grim reality I now faced because of this stunning revelation.

It was the watershed moment of my life. Nothing was the same again. My life and entire world perspective changed. The possibility of the American Dream for everyone was, in fact, an illusion. It was the money, not money in general, but the money we use, in the way we create it that literally made mythic America the perpetual, unattainable carrot for the vast majority. It was forever taunting us as a people to strive, hope, compete, and, in the end, resign ourselves to blame one another. Success was never to be attained or sustained by large portions of the population when using this money. Instead, money was constructed in such a way that failure and distress were programmed to irreversibly come from it.

Understanding this shook my identity. The foundational pillars of my world crumbled. If there wasn't enough money in society to give everyone the opportunity and the potential to design their own dream and realize their hearts' content, how could I believe any of the rhetoric or take pride in what my country stood for? I experienced intense grief and felt disconnected to my dreams. I had little energy to engage in goals or anything that truly made my heart sing. It was hard to entertain and enjoy beauty in a world where every day the structure of the money system excluded and demoralized more and more people. Depression set in. I processed the stages of grief as I finally accepted this deeper understanding of our reality.

To my surprise, as the dust settled, my mind was calm and hope emerged. I was no longer caught up in the dualistic fighting of the left or the right and no longer moved by the perspectives of the "haves" or "have-nots." I couldn't find anyone to blame anymore. No one was right, and no one was wrong. Politically, economically, and socially we looked at a sliver of perspective as we were equally ensnared by the mechanisms of a money system that worked against us. Even more so, one that turned us against each other. Knowing now that our political, economic, and cultural issues were mere symptoms of the real problem which kept us emotionally entangled and distracted from identifying it, I had new energy as my confusion and exasperation evaporated.

It was then that the quest for a solution took over. I was compelled to learn how we could create money the right way. I set out on a journey to find out how to recreate money in a way that supports communities and serves us rather than rendering us, and all of life, its indentured servants. For seven years, I searched, read, and tracked down economists, money reformers, and brilliant new thinkers. In the end, a solution so simple, elegant, and powerful emerged. One that enables communities who come together big or small to implement new systems of exchange making it possible to create and sustain a life worth living for all. So easy, every community near or far can do it. So powerful, every community can reclaim its inherent wealth and change the world as we know it.

There is no need to deprive ourselves by limiting everything we do to as little as possible to sustain life. Nor do we have to remain unconnected and unfulfilled, unconsciously driven by rapacious consumerism and materialism. Instead, the time has come for balance—to return to our natural empowered state. Simply by recreating the way we do money, we can join the rest of nature coming home to our true state of abundance. This is who we are.

The time for fighting and blaming has come to an end. Our despair and confusion has only grown as we imagine politicians and economists can save our world, leaving us only further disempowered and divided. We must put down what we think we know, and look with an open mind and heart, so that we can find the deeper truth that waits so patiently for us to discover it. This journey begins when we let go of the belief that we are right and the other is wrong. When we do, we make way for the 'Un-radical' revolution filled with grace and poise to unfold. It is here that we find freedom, liberation, and, finally, come together.

There is a greater reality waiting for us—where we determine the trajectory of our lives, where we determine what kind of people we are, and how we want to live as communities. It is up to us. We already have all the tools we need to accomplish what we want. We simply need to know what is wrong in our world and how to change it. Come take this journey with me from heartbreak to liberation, so that the future may be ours together. Together we will find the beauty waiting for us as we unite and create a new world—a world filled with prosperity, thriving creativity and joy, a world that lives and breathes in the heart of plenty.

1
THERE IS NO SUCH THING AS MONEY

It was a blustery day in Boston. Though it was early spring, winter was still hanging on giving hearty Bostonians a run for their money. I was having brunch with Sam in the Back Bay. Long-time friends, we met in the late summer of 2000 at the State of the World summit in New York City. We were birds of a feather sharing a passion for being part of something greater than ourselves, and perhaps to make the world a better place.

As I crossed onto Newbury Street, I spotted him. Sam was tall and handsome, a true gentleman. A native of North Carolina and unused to the harsh cold north, he stood bundled in a red ski parka and a warm woolen hat.

"Well, hi there!" I greeted him.

"Nice to see you stranger," Sam said, enveloping me in a big bear hug as I looked up at his beautiful broad smile. I found myself staring for a moment, remembering how I had forgotten that being in his presence made me feel safe and at home in the world.

"Come on, let's get inside where it's warm," Sam said, with a twinkle in his eye as he steered me toward the door.

"Stephanie's on Newbury" was the perfect place for brunch. As we stepped inside, we were immersed in the bustling chatter, the wafting aroma of pan-fried potatoes, and waiters rushing about with trays of bubbling mimosas. Our table was ready and dressed in style, nestled at the perfect angle to warm up by the fire.

"Americano?" Sam smiled. "Mimosa too?"

"Yes, Americano." I was impressed with his memory, and his charm. "Maybe one mimosa. I haven't slept in a while and I still have much to do."

"So, tell me... what's going on?" Sam prodded with a look of concern in his eye. "No one has seen you for ages."

"I've been buried in research. I've been searching for what caused the financial system to collapse," I answered. "You see, when the markets crashed late last fall, I knew it was different—that it wasn't just a severe market pullback. I knew something was wrong, in a way that I hadn't known before." I shook my head as I remembered the daze, and continued, "Day-by-day, week-by-week, the financial system disintegrated right before my eyes. The devastation was everywhere. I had this feeling—that I was missing something—something important. It began to consume me, and I became determined to find out what *it* was—what could collapse everything—and take everything I believed in with it."

I paused for a moment. I was back in the 'no man's land' I wandered last year, grasping for solid ground. I had had a lifetime of experience working with the markets. For the past thirty years, I loved helping clients invest their money as a professional financial advisor with one of the world's largest and most respected investment firms. As a child, I earned my allowance by practicing buying stocks with my father. Now, everything I trusted and believed in had evaporated; the promises my professional life, and life in general were built on. I felt disillusioned by the scope of the destruction and the injustices left in the wake. I felt confused and betrayed, but not sure by whom or exactly what. I had lost my sense of security and the buoyant optimism I had about the markets, and worse, about life.

I took a deep breath staring silently at the white delicate china cup in my hands. I drew it in tightly, taking some refuge in the magical aroma of the espresso.

"Kristen? Are you all right?" Sam asked attentively.

"I am not sure." I struggled to share with him. "I found the problem, Sam, what caused the financial crisis—the real source of all our financial strife and suffering. It has changed everything, and me— the way I look at the world and how I understand everything. Nothing has been the same since."

"How can that be?" asked Sam. "I don't understand—the financial crisis was caused by greed, reckless lending, and corruption. The same old story we've seen over and over."

"No, that's not true. You are simply describing the symptoms of the problem," I said. "The collapse was not caused by bad economic or political policies, or from weaknesses in human nature. And neither are the economic challenges we face today. But we can't imagine what else it could be, so we are stuck...fixed in our political views, sinking into ever-worsening class struggles, while the *real problem* remains undetected. It creates a system that works against us—and turns us against one another."

"Huh? Okay, you've really got my attention now."

"The real problem is our *money*, Sam," I explained, "not money in general, but the money we use today—what it is and the way it enters our economy and our lives. The critical failure is in the way it is designed and structured. It is programmed to destroy all the good it is meant to create. *It* brings about economic downturns, crises, and ultimately prevents us from having any stability and safety."

"Our money causes instability, economic crises, and destroys the good it is meant to produce? That can't be," Sam said and shook his head. "Come on! Isn't money a simple thing? Didn't we learn how it was created in elementary school?"

"In elementary school? What did we learn? I remember stories of how money was invented as a token to replace bartering, to make life easier for people as they traded goods and services."

"Well, right, that's what I mean. I remember being mesmerized by the pictures of the government's gold stacked in vaults at Ft.

Knox, and the sheets of dollar bills streaming off printing presses. What's the big deal?"

"They are nice storybook images, Sam, but they have nothing to do with the way our money is created. We grew up with the impression that money is a thing that just exists 'out there' as something simple and stable, something we can take for granted, and something permanent that we might be able to earn if we go out and try. This is not the case."

"Really?" Sam said, slowing down, "I guess I haven't thought that much about where money actually comes from. Doesn't the government create it?"

"It did a long time ago. But that's not how it works today."

"What about banks? Don't they lend the money they take in by keeping some aside, on reserve?"

"I think you're talking about fractional reserve lending," I explained. "That's when banks receive deposits from customers, hold back 10% and lend up to 90% of the rest. But it doesn't work that way anymore."

"Where does our money come from then?"

"What we use today as money comes from borrowers. We use borrowers' loans or debt as our money. We *do not* have money today. In fact, we are just using debt. There is nothing separate and stable 'out there' called money. It's actually just debt people owe, masquerading as something that looks like money. It comes into existence from out of the blue when someone promises to repay a loan, and it disappears when the loan is paid. Defying logic, these two seemingly separate things—debt and money—are one and the same thing."

"I'm not sure I understand. You must mean, everyone is in so much debt, that our money is 'just' debt," Sam said. "People have credit card balances, mortgages to pay, and school loans to manage. Many people borrow to make it paycheck-to-paycheck."

"No," I corrected. "I mean our money is debt, one and the same —*simultaneously*."

The server arrived with our omelets. They were stuffed and

overflowing. Sam took a bite, as the cheese hung from his fork. He half-swallowed and urged me to continue.

"When you take out a loan what we think of as money is created."

"When I borrow money, the money I borrow is created, right there on-the-spot?" Sam clarified.

"Yes—see when your bank gives you a loan, they don't lend you someone else's money. They don't have piles of money in the vault, labeled 'money-to-be-lent-out.' It's much less complicated than that. Once they decide to give you a loan and you promise to pay them back, they create the money you borrow, right there and then, by putting numbers in your bank account. At the same time, they enter a debit on your loan statement for the equivalent amount. They give you a payment schedule to pay the loan back in small monthly payments for the next thirty years. Voila! The bank creates what we think of as money when you promise to pay them back. Your debt, and burden to pay them, is what brings 'money' into existence during the period of your loan."

"Money starts to exist when we take a loan, when we 'borrow' it. It didn't exist before. Money is, in fact, debt," Sam said slowly as he digested every word.

"Yes, when we spend the 'money' we get from the loan, that money then begins to circulate in the economy or enter society. If we don't *borrow* it into existence, and if we don't *spend* it into society, then there is no money to use. Since money is created this way, we cannot have any financial well-being *without debt*. The debt we borrow creates our money—the money we use—to buy things, hire others, get jobs, and stay alive in a material world."

"So, without loans and having debt, there would be no money. This means that for every dollar I see, there is the same amount of debt somewhere?"

"If there is $1,000 in your savings account, then that means that someone owes $1,000 of debt to a bank."

"The money in my checking account?" Sam asked looking stunned. "The money I gave my nephew for his birthday?"

"*All* of it is debt owed to a bank, created by someone taking a loan," I confirmed. "Any money you see in the world is debt someone owes a bank. Today, most of our money is mortgage debt, but it doesn't matter what the loan is for. Whether it's tuition, hospital bills, a car, or credit card debt, all this debt creates the money we use to live our lives—And it must be earned by someone to be repaid within a certain period of time."

"You are saying our money is debt, pretending to be something permanent and tangible called money. But it doesn't exist. Instead, banks use double-book entry accounting, recording debits and credits, simultaneously making loans and the corresponding cash?"

"Exactly, let me draw it out. Do you have some paper? Or perhaps, a napkin from the bar?" Sam got up and came back with a full stack of napkins. "I don't think we will need that many!" I said feeling slightly nervous.

He smiled, handing me a pen, and said, "Okay, you're on!"

"Let's start with the idea that you want to buy a ski house in the White Mountains?"

"Oh great, so I can be colder in the winter than I am now? Make sure it has a big fireplace."

"And plenty of room for your friends. Now, let's say you need a loan for $200,000 to buy the house, so you head to the local bank in town. You tell them what you want to do, they run a basic financial check up on you, and decide you pass their test. They prepare the loan documents. You sign the promissory note, and, right there on-the-spot, they create the money and enter it into your account. At the same time, they enter a debit on your new loan statement. Before you leave, they give you a payment schedule to follow to pay them back every month."

New Loan - Your Debt, Your Promise to Pay Paid in monthly payments	New Money Bank creates - Spend to Buy House
$200,000 Plus Interest, paid in small regular payments	$200,000 Paid to seller of house, now starts to circulate and enter the economy as money

I drew a box on the napkin and divided it in two. On the left side, I put the debt Sam promised to pay the bank back, and on the right side, I put the money the bank just created with the keyboard. As I pointed to the box on the right, I asked, "Now where did the money they gave you come from?"

Sam pointed to the box on the left. "From the debt I promised to repay? The loan I just took from the bank."

"Yes, they created it, right there on-the-spot, when you signed the loan documents. As soon as you use the money to pay the seller, the seller spends his new money, which is *really* your debt, to buy the things he wants, and then the money—your debt—travels in the economy."

"Ok, let me see if I got it," Sam said. "I want a loan and agree to pay it back. The bank creates the money for me, on-the-spot, and, at the same time, puts a debit on my loan statement, sending me home with a payment schedule to pay them in monthly installments. Now I take that money—which is actually my debt—and pay the seller who takes that money—my debt—and uses it to buy a trip around the world. In turn, the travel agency pays employees with the money —my debt—and the money—my debt—now circulates in the economy. Without me going into debt and giving the bank my promise to pay back the loan, this money would not exist."

"Exactly! Now the chase is on, because you need to earn enough money to meet the monthly schedule to repay this debt to the bank, that never had the money in the first place, but created it. And you repay the bank with interest. The money created is the debt created, two sides of the same coin, like heads and tails."

"Without people willing to borrow and take on the stress of

meeting debt payments, our society wouldn't have any money in it," said Sam.

"See how *critical* it is that people borrow in our money system? We need borrowers, and lots of them. We need people, governments, and corporations—all of them—borrowing, at the same time, to create enough money for society to function."

"Wow, so when we get the impression the economy is doing well," added Sam, "it is actually because people borrowed more and are spending more debt-money. We may be lured in to join them and borrow too, thinking things are more secure. Yet, because more people need to pay back debt, across the economy, there is actually more risk."

"Yes," I affirmed. "As we borrow more, more money enters the economy. We feel better because we see sales increase, home prices rise, and people finding jobs. But ALL this new money is newly created debt. Loans we take from banks, and *must* manage to repay. We continue to increase our debt burden until we hit a point where we can't sustain it, and people stop borrowing. When this happens, we experience a financial collapse."

"When people stop borrowing the economy crashes because no new money is created?"

"As less debt is created, less money flows. Spending slows, making it more difficult for people to earn money. Challenging people to make ends meet, as it is harder to get paid, spend extra money, get a raise, or even keep a job. Which makes it even more difficult to borrow, and even less money enters the economy. It's a death spiral, that is almost impossible to reverse. It is the key reason we see an economic bust almost every seven-to-ten years."

"We are dependent on borrowers to borrow—to have MONEY—and whether they are *able* to make payments," Sam added.

"Think of our society like a snow globe. The snow circling the village is money circling the economy. New money only enters the economy when someone takes a loan. When there are only a few borrowers, there is very little snow circling the globe. The village looks barren, and people struggle to capture what little money exists. To get more 'money' flowing we need more borrowers. Otherwise things remain tight and worrisome, layoffs begin, and work is hard to find. And, yet, the only way to get the economy going again is to take on more debt."

"This is why there is so much pressure for banks to lend and for people to borrow again." Sam took a breath. "Without this never-ending cycle of borrowing we can't recover. But if economic crises come from having too much debt, how can the way out—the way for things to get better—be by taking on more debt?" There was a slight look of panic in his eyes.

"It's a great question, Sam. When money is debt, no debt means no money. In this system, we need endless borrowers to keep taking loans from banks to create our money. And more and more debt—if we want to increase our standard of living."

"That sounds impossible," Sam said, sounding frustrated.

"We are trapped in an unworkable situation where we are pushed to create as much debt as we can. And if we stop, the economy rips open, and people lose their jobs, their homes, and their lives, just because we can't create enough debt."

"Why would we create a system like this, Kristen? Our money supply is dependent on people being able to borrow and get loans—being willing to take on more debt!"

"Well, understanding this makes it easier to decipher the constant pressure we feel lurking in every interaction, to hurry to make money, and more money. To pay loans, and take out new loans. You can see why lenders need to endlessly indebt people."

"Wait, doesn't the government limit how many loans banks can create, by controlling the number of reserves banks have?"

"It doesn't work that way anymore," I explained. "Fractional reserve lending, or what's often called the money multiplier, is an old methodology. Times have changed. The Bank of England, England's central bank, admitted banks simply create money when they make loans, using the 'double-book entry' accounting process we diagrammed. They let the cat out of the bag when they confirmed that loans *actually create* the money lent. More or less, we use a credit system, like a magic credit card. The amount we promise to repay makes the money appear, right there on-the-spot. They revealed reserves don't determine how much lending a bank can do, not the way it used to. Bank reserves are primarily about clearing checks and settling accounts between banks when we buy things."

"This means the government doesn't control how many loans banks can create?"

"Right. When the Bank of England divulged that bank lending is not on a leash, it stunned people, including mainstream economists. Bank lending was always assumed to be controlled by the amount of reserves the bank had. Instead, the banking system and borrowers are on their own, creating as many or as few loans as the market can handle, without real financial oversight. Banks have a time lag before they settle their books, and any standing reserve requirement can be easily met. If not by deposits, then by borrowing from other banks, or the central bank itself."

"Is there anything that can stop banks from creating an endless amount of debt?" Sam asked as he finished the last of his omelet.

"Banks are limited by two things. They will create as many loans as they can, and as quickly as they can, if there's a profit to be made. But they need willing and capable borrowers to do that. If no one wants new debt or if people already have too much debt, no new loans will be created. And that means—?"

"No new money will be created," Sam answered.

"Banks have to be in good financial standing," I added. "Bank health is measured by something called the 'capital-to-asset ratio.' This ratio needs to be positive. It is the cushion used to protect them from losses. The capital gives the bank insulation if the loans they make fail. But this cushion is usually thin, as banks try to put every resource they have into making as many loans as possible, to boost profits. If loans start to fail, they get into real trouble and they will stop creating new loans. If they stop creating new loans—?"

"They stop creating new money," Sam answered. "I never knew

how dependent we were on borrowing and lending—just to have the money we use—and to have economic stability."

"Our economy relies on the constant debt creation and repayment cycle. People need to be able to borrow, and banks need to be able to stay healthy enough to lend. Consistently." I paused to let the point sink in for Sam and then continued, "The borrowing-lending process has to work, and keep working non-stop. Otherwise, the economy will stumble and stall. If borrowing doesn't start again quickly, it will turn into an economic bust."

Our server arrived. She cleared our dishes as we noticed the restaurant was almost empty. The brunch crowd had faded into the lunch crowd, and even now, they were almost gone. She gave us a look letting us know our check still hadn't been paid. With a faint attempt to say it was no bother, we knew she was ready for us to settle the bill.

"It must be getting late. We should go."

"Wait, I have one more question," Sam insisted, "you said that money is created out of the blue when loans are made, and it disappears when they are paid off. What did you mean that the money disappears? Where does it go?"

"Here is the real problem, Sam." I was impressed with how quickly he was grasping the concept. "Money and debt are two sides of the same coin, inseparably linked. Every time you pay your debt, the principal of the outstanding loan balance is reduced on your statement. It disappears. Likewise, the money you paid in disappears. It doesn't go to anyone. It no longer circulates in the economy, it is deleted. Poof! It Evaporates. Debt and money are created together, and they disappear together, they are both 'destroyed' as the loan is paid."

I picked up the pen and a napkin to create a table showing what happens to the money, or Sam's debt, created by Sam's loan when he sent the bank his monthly payment.

Your Loan Statement - Your Mortgage Debt for Ski House	Your Bank account - Where You Keep Your Money
Your starting loan value is $200,000.	The amount in your checking account is $7,000.
Your monthly payment is $750, of which $400 is Interest, and $350 is repayment of the original $200,000 debt.	You write check for $750 and pay the mortgage bill.
The bank receives your $750 and applies $350 to reduce the $200,000 debt. Your new loan balance is $199,650.	Your new bank account balance is $6,250.
The bank has wiped out $350 of your debt because you repaid it—and keeps the $400 for its trouble or to pay its operating costs. The $400 of interest may continue to circle in the economy, until someone earns it and repays their debt, then it too is wiped out.	The $350 used to repay the principal part of your loan is 'wiped' out or, often referred, to as 'destroyed.' It No Longer exists, and thus No Longer circulates. The economy now has $350 less money in it.

"When the bank creates money by making a loan, the amount of money circulating in society, goes up by the amount of that loan. You can see that when the loan is repaid, the money disappears—back into thin air, and the amount of money circulating is reduced by the amount of that repayment."

"This is unbelievable!" said Sam. "Every time I think I do the right thing, by paying my school loans, my mortgage—my credit card bill, I do not simply reduce debt, do I?"

"No."

"I *actually* reduce the amount of money that exists," Sam added. "I *destroy* the money and shrink the real economy because less money now circulates for people to earn. In fact, doing the 'right thing' with money-as-debt edges us closer to recession, depression, and even financial collapse? Using your 'snow-globe' analogy, there is less snow to circulate in the village?"

I nodded. "Unless someone takes out a new loan for the same amount at the same time you pay your debt."

"That's just to keep the money supply stable, to keep things the same, right?"

"Yes, over time, greater and greater amounts of debt are required to sustain the same standard of living. If money is kept in savings, or doesn't circulate quickly and broadly enough, the general standard of living goes down. People need to be able to earn the money that's stuck in savings to stay afloat, because it is debt they owe. Otherwise, even greater amounts of debt are needed to create money, to make up for what's inaccessible as its stored in savings. Let alone, the greater amount of debt needed to increase our general standard of living."

"What an ugly reality!" Sam remarked.

"We live under constant, artificial pressure to go into debt, repay loans, and begin the cycle again as soon as it is complete. It's a cycle that can never end, if we continue to use money created from debt."

I drank the last sip of coffee, as I thought about what I went through when I discovered this for myself. I remembered how long it took me to get over the sadness and the shock that this precarious, self-defeating system of debt somehow became the money we used, the foundation of our economic system, the stability we built our lives on. Somehow, we ended up using this destructive process, of creating and repaying loans, simply to produce money tokens we required for an economy. Using money-as-debt was a trap. It generated unnecessary pressure on us, our communities, and on the earth, itself, with no way to slow down.

All the booms and busts in the economy came from creating money-as-debt, and, eventually, would make the system impossible to sustain. I wondered whether we would sacrifice everything we had to keep it going, or if we would find another way. I needed to know if there was a way out of this, how we could get off this unrelenting treadmill, and stop living our lives for the debt-machine. If there was, I was intent on discovering it. Perhaps to keep going, I had to believe there was. Maybe we could free ourselves, and secure what we had worked for, while avoiding an economic collapse and societal breakdown.

"If we need continuous and constant debt," Sam processed, "how can most people achieve the American Dream? If money disappears as debt is paid, and is taken out of circulation when people save, then there is less and less money flowing. It gets harder and harder for people to secure the life they want."

"It's a tireless, endless—and losing battle, Sam. We spend our lives chasing the ephemeral carrot called the American Dream, as we run to create debt. Just to create a money system. Creating money-as-debt keeps things tight, brings on extreme competition, and progressively leaves more people out of the race. Not only does this process destroy our economy and create crises, but fighting this battle corrupts every aspect of our lives."

"Money-as-debt undermines how we live?" Sam looked at me intensely.

"Creating our money from debt controls our lives. Money-as-debt determines how we live, and, often, why we live. We think we are free, but we are not. The process of creating money-as-debt makes money our master, and we its servants. I have stumbled on seven ways debt-money shapes and dictates every aspect of our lives. I call them the *Seven Imperatives*," I answered. "These imperatives control us, wreaking havoc everywhere money-as-debt is used."

"How is this possible?" Sam was stunned.

"The seven imperatives are invisible strings which manipulate us like a marionette doll. When you see how they operate you will understand why the debt-money system, itself, is the source of our woe. And, why we cannot solve the pernicious scarcity, and suffering in the world with political, economic, or social change. When we review the imperatives, we see clearly how money-as-debt, seeps into every aspect of our lives, and that *it* is the root cause of scarcity, and then finally we can begin to search for a solution." I paused and saw the restaurant was empty, feeling uncomfortable I continued, "I'll share them with you another time, okay? It looks like they're getting ready for dinner!"

We looked at our watches and smiled at how the time had flown. We put on our coats and headed outside. The sun began to set, as the gas lights came on and the lamp posts glowed up and down the street. The old brownstone mansions looked painted in a rich crimson, cinnamon hue. The fiery orange sky rippled with streaks of gray, and had begun to fade into a dark, smoky midnight blue. The chill had set in, even for me. We pulled our collars tight, and made our way to the Copley T station and started down the stairs.

"I have a work event at the Institute of Contemporary Art tomorrow night, at seven o'clock. Will you come with me?" Sam tugged on my sleeve as my train entered the station.

"I love the ICA," I answered as the train approached.

"Let's start early, so you can explain these seven imperatives."

Sam smiled as I nodded, "Let's meet at Faneuil Hall and, then head to South Station."

The train stopped, and the doors opened, as Sam said, "You know, I'm starting to think if people knew that our money comes from borrowers debt—that we need someone to go into debt for us to have money to use—they may be taken aback and feel very confused."

"Well, more than a hundred years ago, Henry Ford, founder of Ford Motor Company, said, 'It is well enough that people do not understand our banking and monetary system, for if they did, there would be a revolution before morning.'"

The train door closed. Soon, all I could see was a swoosh of bright red of Sam's jacket between the many colors. I thought to myself, "What a world." I still was not sure if I was better off knowing what I knew about money, how unstable and unsustainable the system was, and how vulnerable we were to it all unraveling. Perhaps, it would have been more comforting had I not stepped out of the illusion of safety I lived in, but I would have remained lost in the confusion of the world, not knowing what was really going on. One thing was for sure, there was no going back, and now, I was no longer alone, Sam had come to join me.

2
THE SEVEN DEBT STRINGS

It was five o'clock when I got to Faneuil Hall. The sun was still shining, hinting that spring was on the way. Sam was bundled up, not taking any chances with the wicked force of the wind. He was waiting next to the Carousel, the newest addition to the Rose Kennedy Greenway Park. As I approached him, his face lit up with his beautiful smile, and he handed me a ticket.

"Come on. Let's take a ride! You haven't been on this yet, have you?" Sam laughed. "Where do you want to sit?"

"On the butterflies, definitely on the butterflies!" I said as we hurried onto the platform and took hold of the swallowtail butterfly poles.

Every seat was quickly taken, and each was a work of art, made of magical creatures from the land, sea, and air. Dancing lights circled the top of the canopy as it spun round and round. Swirling, we caught glimpses of the surrounding beauty of the Customs Clocktower, the waterfront park, and the lively scenes at Faneuil Hall. As the music stopped, the carousel slowed and the ride ended. We climbed down and crossed the cobblestone path, making our way to Quincy Market.

"That was a lot of fun, thank you, Sam. I don't think I would have stopped to do that by myself."

"My pleasure," Sam smiled, and then looked at me. "I had a hard time sleeping last night. My mind was racing, replaying our conversation from yesterday—the idea that money and debt are the same thing, inseparable. It is difficult to fully grasp."

"I know," I empathized. "Our whole lives we have been conditioned to think of money and debt as two separate things, totally independent of each other. But, in fact, they do not exist separately. Today, our money is just someone's debt, just someone's promise to repay a loan."

As we walked down the granite slabs of the North Market, a street performer entertained a small crowd. The audience cheered as he pulled three doves out of his hat. Then, he drew a bright fuchsia scarf out of his sleeve and waved it about, as the doves magically disappeared. One minute they were there, solid and real, and the next they were gone, as they vanished back into thin air. The symbolism was not lost on us, as we looked at one another, and then back at the street magician.

As Sam was about to reflect, a little boy trailing his family caught our attention. While busily taking in the sights, the boy casually played with his 'yo-yo.' He tossed it forward, as the bright orange wheel spun out of his hand and sped down the unraveling string. Then, with the slightest tug, it raced back up and squarely landed in his hand.

"Right there." Sam pointed to the little boy. "Money-as-debt is actually on a leash! Money *is* invisibly leashed to debt repayment. Every time someone takes a loan, their promise to repay the bank, creates the money 'loaned,' and the money is yanked out of the economy when the debt is paid. Bam! The bank destroys the amount of debt repaid—along with the dollars that pay it off. The money is no longer circulating 'out-there' in the world. Repaying debt reels in the money with it, and they vanish together."

"The money we use, to keep society going, is vanishing and shrinking with every breath we take because loans are constantly paid." I took a deep breath. "Since we need money to operate, we need a constant flow of new debt."

"We must constantly create loans," Sam echoed as he processed what this meant.

"Yes," I affirmed, "this is the first imperative money-as-debt creates. The more debt we get rid of, though an individual may be in a better position for the moment, as a whole, we are in a worse position. Immediately, less money circulates. It is imperative that new debt be created as soon as existing debt is paid. Everyone, anyone, big or small, must take on as much debt as possible. We can *never* be free of debt. We need to create a continual stream of loans. It is our lifeline."

"The First Imperative is the unrelenting pressure to take on debt, as fast as we can," Sam stated.

"Yes, forever." I nodded as I remembered the moment I first learned about the first imperative. When I realized that using debt as our money meant that we could never be free of debt, I was frozen, almost spellbound. It was literally mind-bending, as my mind reverberated in the confusion, trying to understand that as we reduce debt in society, there was immediate pressure for more debt to be recreated. The concept was difficult to grasp because it flew in the face of the way I understood the world. I believed debt was something separate from money, and that it was something that could be helpful when used wisely.

Now, I had come to see it *was* our money! I never, in my wildest imagination, would have thought that debt was actually all there was, and that money, itself, was an illusion. This meant that we had to create reasons *to create debt*, and to manufacture the desire and willingness to go into debt. This went far beyond commercialism or materialism, it meant that, as a society, we manufactured the desire for commercialism and materialism in order to create debt—just to be able to use something as money.

I was angry at how creating money this way put tremendous pressure, unnecessary pressure, on us, and our world. I thought about the beautiful ride on the carousel, Sam and I enjoyed, and the contrast of our reality. We were all trapped in this system, as we ran on an incessant treadmill, trying to keep up the pace, and having no way to get off. Creating money this way was more than self-sabotage, it was a slow form of collective suicide.

"Everyone assumes as we get rid of debt that we have more money. But when we get rid of debt, we ALSO get rid of money," Sam said as I tuned back into our conversation.

"It's true. Getting rid of debt doesn't give us more money. It gets rid of the burden of being personally responsible for the loan. So, one person capturing money and repaying debt, is in better shape for the moment, in that his debt is settled. But if new loans are not taken out, there is less money for others to earn. When this person pays off his loan, there is a momentary feeling of satisfaction, but he is blind to the bigger picture. He can't see the system, as a whole, has less money."

"There's less money for everyone, so someone has to go with less?"

"Yes."

"This is a win-lose game. If someone wins, someone has to lose. Isn't it possible to make the pie big enough so we can all get a piece?"

"No," I said, shaking my head. "The only way to expand the pie is to take on even greater debt, and this means people have to handle a greater burden of debt."

"You could say each dollar has an expiration date on it, right?" Sam suggested.

"I guess so," I mused. "When a loan is made, the debt has a date by which it must be paid. Since the dollars are 'destroyed' when the debt is paid, you could say the dollars have an expiration date. In this game, when someone wins others are left to aggressively compete to catch dollars to pay their bills before another does."

"We can only hope that someone takes on more debt to create more money, and that we can earn it—before someone else does."

Sam and I sighed as we continued through the marketplace. As we came to the corner, we noticed a crowd gathering around two jugglers. 'One potato, two potato then, three potato' circled 'round their heads. They juggled in perfect rhythm. The crowd stirred and began to applaud and cheer as the performers put blindfolds on, they continued without skipping a beat!

"I feel like I've been blindfolded," Sam said. "I never realized when I judged others for being in debt, or spending more than I thought they should, the extra debt they created actually created more money for me! They were willing to juggle more debt, and I reaped the benefit of them adding more money to the overall system. Money that I could earn, and even put in savings."

"We haven't been able to see the system as a whole. So, it has been easy to judge others as irresponsible. The system would fail if people did not amass debt."

"Not only that, Kristen, I blamed myself for not doing as well as some guys I know. I thought there was enough money for everyone to develop their talents, get out there, and earn. At times, I wondered if I wasn't good enough. I never thought the underlying system was squeezing us like this."

"Yes, it is interesting when we see the greater context. There certainly is something deeper at work here—a deeper reality. There is a mechanism operating, one that pits us against each other."

We went up a few steps to the food court building. Sam took hold of the thick iron handle and pulled the heavy door back, as waves of heavenly scents swept over us. We headed straight for the New England clam chowder. His stomach was growling, and we had at least two hours before we would eat at the ICA. And worse, I had discovered I was wearing the wrong shoes and already looked forward to sitting down.

"Starving!" Sam said as he devoured a large spoonful of creamy chowder.

"Oh, my feet!" I grumbled as I kicked my shoes off.

I regretted I ventured to break in a new pair of shoes that evening. Yet, it was a poignant reminder that when something was wrong in my body, no matter how small or seemingly trivial, I was captured by it and suffered as I focused on what hurt. Even though each organ was separate with its own function to perform, our bodies were a comprehensive system. The pain made me aware of how I took my body, and its magic, for granted.

I considered our money system and what it would be like if our bodies acted with its same principles. If our heart, liver or lungs competed with each other for resources, hoarded blood and refused to let it flow? If there wasn't enough blood, to carry oxygen and nutrients to every cell, what would happen to the system, as a whole, and to everything in it? It would breakdown, die, and disintegrate. And, yet, we were using a system to create money—the currency or life flow of our society—that demanded we compete against one another, hoard our resources, and ignore those unable to keep up.

We finished eating and headed down the stairs, as we wove through the crowd of people coming up. They carried all kinds of enticing things to eat, and Sam was still hungry. While he took stock of every tasty bowl of pad thai, lobster roll, and steaming piece of lasagna, I noticed the people streaming by looked serious and intent on getting somewhere. In the main hall, the food vendor stalls were still packed. Customers herded into long lines, defending their turf as they impatiently waited their turn. They were not the only ones focused on getting what they wanted in a hurry; as we got outside we saw more of the same.

The traffic was gridlocked with cars inching forward to shut out others wanting to change lanes. Sam and I quickly discovered pedestrians attempting to cross the road became instant enemies of the fiercely focused drivers. We made it back to the greenway, and saw a small group of children playing a game of musical chairs. Sam and I stopped for a moment to watch.

As the music played the children ran around the chairs, and the moment of truth arrived when the music ended. Each time there was one chair too few, and one child left scrambling. The competition was intense even though it was a game, the pressure was on. As I observed, I remembered playing as a child. The adrenaline ran through my body, as I tried to make sure I had a seat and didn't lose. It seemed fun then, but reflecting on it now, I saw how much the game was filled with panic and fright.

"Did you play that when you were a kid?" asked Sam.

"Yeah, we did a lot. How about you?"

"I never liked it very much. I got tired of it after a few rounds." Sam contemplated, "When I look at it now, I see these little kids are rewarded to run and compete for a place to sit, a chance to rest before they must run again. The more the game continues, the less seats there are for everyone. It's got a conflicting message, 'Run and compete as fast, and as hard as you can. If you don't, there won't be a seat left. Forget your buddies. There's no time to think of anyone but you!'"

"Ha! That's the foundation of our debt-money system, isn't it?" I pointed to the children and said, "They are being conditioned to accept the Second Imperative: 'Our time does not belong to us. Time is money.' Chop! Chop! No time to lose with each tick of the clock, we move closer to when loan payments and bills are due. Hurry up, earn money in time pay off your debts and quick, start again, new debt must be created."

Sam and I stayed while the children finished the game, as the last child stumbled about and realized he had no chair. I continued explaining the second imperative.

"Monthly scheduled payments must be met to pay our loans. The schedule entrains the rhythms our lives. There is no rest for the weary, the sick, or even to simply explore our inspirations. All that comes second or third or who knows if ever—for most people. We constantly need to produce, compete, and earn to repay loan payments and meet bills. We cannot break from the pack and live to the beat of our own drum. We exist under this pressure to meet monthly debt payments and bills. We need to make sure we have enough money coming in to make our payments *on-time*."

"Wow," Sam remarked. "I never stepped back far enough to see this. Like the children's game of musical chairs, monthly-scheduled debt payments send us running. We are tense, forced into the game of competition. This structure of having to repay something every month keeps us in-line. Even if we don't have debt, the bills we owe, are owed to people who have debt, and the system determines when everything is due."

"We don't even recognize we are being driven by the debt-machine," I said, "demanding we slave to feed it. We are increasingly less human and less alive, as our time, energy, and attention are restricted by the need for money. The need to get paid, to meet the relentless demands the loan schedule, becomes our 'do or die' ruler."

"All this pressure and activity to pay bills or meet a payment schedule created by banks. We are not free to be inspired or creative," Sam said with a tone of anger.

"It is crazy when you think about it," I agreed. "No wonder humans are so stressed out. We live with an intensity that makes earning money the most important thing in our lives and keeps business 'serious.' The punishment is severe if we cannot keep up. We lose our homes and the money we put down as collateral—all going to the bank which created the money as our debt right there on-the-spot. Because we agree to repay them for money they didn't have! This payment schedule sets the pace we live by."

"I guess no one is alone in this," Sam remarked. "If people cannot keep up this non-stop pace, and begin to fall behind, then they are less able to take on new loans which means there is less money circulating for all of us."

"That's right. The less people can run non-stop as the second imperative demands, the less money there is in our economy. We all suffer, unless people can keep up, and live their lives according to the debt-machine's clock."

"Interesting, it is a grand metronome in the sky, ordering our lives," Sam said. "The Second Imperative: Time is money. Our time does not belong to us. Nope, we belong to it."

Sam looked at his watch, and saw we still had an hour before the festivities started at the ICA. We walked through the winding parks of the Greenway toward the Boston Harbor Hotel, as we passed the Aquarium. I thought about how debt engulfs every aspect of our lives, without us knowing the scope of its power and control. And yet, at the same time, all of nature was waking from winter's long sleep. The trees along the path shimmered with the red glow of budding leaves ready to burst through the branches. Glorious pink and gold banners waved over head as we crossed the hotel's grand atrium, and we gazed at the harbor. The sea was a solid medium blue. Suddenly, Sam stopped and turned around to pick up a copy of the Boston Globe on a nearby bench.

"Look, good news! Jobs increased this month for the first time in almost a year," he said, pointing to the article.

"Yes, I guess it is. I just can't look at it that way anymore," I said with some resignation.

"What do you mean? You don't think it's good more people are going back to work?"

"Well, in a debt-money system, people have to have jobs. If they don't have a job, how can they earn money? How will they race to pay debt and take on more debt, so we can have money! I mean *any* job is considered a positive. No matter how destructive that job is to society or to the person doing it. The system requires as many able bodies working, as much as possible, for as long as possible. We don't need 'jobs' to create our living we need them to service the Debt-Machine generating the money we use."

"Interesting. Do you know where the word *job* comes from?"

"No, where?"

"Originally it meant petty, piddling work. Then, it was used to mean a theft or planned crime. Either way, it was the unpleasant things people did as a lucrative affair or just to get by."

"Taking work and reducing it into a low form of a job, just for pay, is very useful to a debt-money system where people are reduced to numbers," I replied. "When work becomes a job done, just for pay, our vision for our lives becomes limited. Our inner voice and greater purpose are drowned in the busyness of getting a job, and trying to keep it. Even though we hate doing it—we do it. And, we start to die a little, then a lot. Our lives are wasted doing things we don't want to."

"So 'a job' isn't a true vocation," Sam clarified. "It's not a person's real work as a contribution, or an expression of their gifts and talents to the greater whole."

"Yes, Sam that is exactly what I mean." I smiled. "So, where does the word vocation come from?"

"Vocation? Ah, you're testing me now," Sam teased. "I'm prepared. It comes from the Latin *vocare* which means to call. It's a calling. A trade or profession which one feels is one's purpose in life. A strong feeling of suitability for a particular career or occupation."

"That is beautiful. Yet, the vast majority of us have lost our connection to a deep sense of purpose in our work. Often, because, the work we do isn't connected to a deeper sense of purpose. Many of us have lost touch with our internal compass, and no longer know what makes us feel alive. We don't know what we want to be part of, beyond having our basic needs met. True work or vocation is infused with purpose and deep meaning. There is a sense that the work we are about is greater than us, greater than our individual contribution and compensation. It connects us to the web of life, tapping into something eternal beyond our own sense of mortality."

"Now *that* is beautiful, Kristen. When you put it that way, I wonder how only so few of us live that way. Or how we lost touch with something so vital to our happiness, and ended up not only with a 'job,' but celebrating that we got one."

"It's true, Sam. The concept of a job has denigrated work as something we do for pay. It is as if money could make up for the lack of connection, opportunity to explore, express and experience who we are in the world. When we permit ourselves to do work for money or see a job 'as a paycheck,' we violate ourselves at the deepest level. We live inauthentically. We set foot on the path of drudgery and our hearts begin to grow cold as resentment sets in. Rather than seeing challenges, opportunities, or impetuses for new ideas, we let our hopes and dreams slip through our hands."

"It's troubling. I feel like so many people are stuck in that situation." Sam paused, then said, "Hey, look at this." Sam pointed to the lower right side of the newspaper. "One-fifth of Americans are on anti-depressants to cope with stress. The highest level ever reported."

"I wouldn't be surprised if the unofficial number is much higher. Most Americans, if they are fortunate enough to have a full-time job, work forty-plus-hour weeks. Spend hours in mind-numbing traffic. With families and homes to manage, there is little time for living. Chasing debt-money preoccupies people, unable to express themselves, and be available for one another. Who wouldn't be depressed? Dealing with tension, stress, and low-grade pain, people find themselves suppressing what they naturally want to do. People's lives have dwindled down to making a paycheck, spending it, and trying to find some meaning in between. It's easy to see how life has become a battle, instead of an adventurous miracle or mystery."

"Well, Kristen, how many parents are going to tell their kids to do what they love? Not many. They need to tell their kids to make money. Even knowing the price they paid, they are still too afraid to encourage their children to step out against reason. Parents have instincts to protect their children, that, and the pressure to meet the cultural standard of being a good parent. They are worn-out—living in a world of scarcity and competition. Most believe they should dismiss their children's imaginations, and down play their dreams, for their survival."

"This is especially sad because it is true. But it doesn't work. True work and passion call us home. No matter how far we wander, the call remains forever strong and steadfast. We try to convince ourselves that money, or the stuff money can buy, is enough. But truth rattles and stirs within us. Even though our hearts are stifled, and we cannot easily decipher what we would love to do, the yearning for something more continues to call us. It calls ever louder, until one day, we come face-to-face with it."

"But we need a job," Sam objected. "How else are we going to pay the bills? Especially if the money is constantly being destroyed, as people pay their credit card bills and other loans. We need new debt as soon as the old debt is paid. It is relentless. If we don't all try to get a job and spend that paycheck, the system will crash, and we will be in line waiting for the soup-kitchen."

"The drive to earn a paycheck is shared by almost everyone," I agreed. "This leads us to the Third Imperative of debt-money: 'Everyone must get a job, any job.' We need a job to keep the debt-machine rolling. We tell ourselves it is okay to take 'this' job because we need it, or it's just a paycheck. But, we cannot separate ourselves from our work. When we try, we become vulnerable. We are willing to believe the money we get in return can be a vindicating payoff. We compensate for this lack of fulfillment, connection, and inability to contribute by creating all sorts of imbalances in other areas of our lives, from addictions, to any number of horrible things. This tension wears on our relationships, our families, our health, and society, as a whole. And, yet, we want more jobs! Do we really need more of this in the world?"

"I totally agree, Kristen. But, tell me, what *is* the alternative?"

"The important thing to know is that debt-money drives this third imperative into our world. It makes us want a job, so desperately, as a direct result of creating money-as-debt. We are lost in role reversal. Instead of money being at our service, helping us to manifest our gifts and contribute to society, we are used as fuel for the debt-money system."

"Maybe that's why zombies are so popular? People are like the living dead. When they dress up and go to these mass zombie parties, they get to be real—instead of pretending to be alive—when they are dead inside."

We entered the hotel, and a beautiful, young woman, a fashionista to the max, charged through the door. Every ounce of her body was adorned in full glamour regalia and she was overloaded with shopping bags. As she bowled through the door she almost knocked me over, but Sam caught me before I could fall. With the gusts of her commotion, her receipts streamed from her bags and wafted through the air, as they landed at our feet. I quickly picked them up and began to scan her transactions.

"Whoa, are you all right?" Sam questioned, looking me over. "I thought you might be the first casualty suffered by shopping bags speeding through the exit of the Boston Harbor Hotel."

"Well, that woman is certainly doing her part to keep the debt-money system going. She fed the debt-monster a good dose of fuel by putting all that on credit cards. She is the living embodiment of the fourth imperative in towering Jimmy Choo heels. The Fourth Imperative is we must consume, and consume everything in sight."

"Is that why politicians tell us what we can do for our country, is to 'Go out and spend money'? It's how we can serve as good Americans," Sam reflected.

"That's sadly true," I agreed. "Consuming, as much as we possibly can, is the primary way we keep our debt-machine humming. To keep churning the inexhaustible wheel where more is more, old is out, and next is best."

"Maybe that's why politicians talk about people less as citizens, and more as consumers."

"That makes sense, Sam. 'The consumer' is an all too familiar label we use to describe ourselves. It is our role; we are consumers. Ironically, shopping has become the new freedom. American ideals are built on liberty, yet we have lost much of our freedom. New policies, laws and executive orders threaten the basis of the US Constitution, and are justified over and over in the name of fear and security."

As we walked through the halls of the hotel, a large TV screen broadcast breaking news. It was the latest report on how much consumer spending was up last month. The *Consumer Confidence* numbers had just come in, the index used to gauge how consumers feel about spending money. The reporter said the data would move the stock market when it opened and the Dow futures already started to react.

"Breaking News! I see what you're saying, Kristen. American freedom today means being able to go to Walmart, and get as much for as little as possible. Or going on vacation to Disney World or on a cruise around the Caribbean, or the right to decide if we want the blue car or the red one. We are free to choose what we buy, but meanwhile we are losing our freedom and personal liberties."

"A debt-based money system doesn't need citizens. It needs consumers."

We both paused for a moment. It was a powerful revelation. Sam and I continued to walk. I thought about how we let our real freedoms quietly slip through our hands, while we suffered the non-stop barrage of advertising enticing us to consume at every corner. Trying to convince us, that we had achieved some kind of victory, when we got more for less. We headed down toward South Station, passing a storage center to our right.

"There's a recession-proof business." Sam pointed to the self-storage garage. "Our homes are stuffed to the gills with stuff we don't need. People say they want to purge but they just can't seem to pull the trigger."

"True, and those that do, often find they carry in new stuff just as quickly as they carried out the old. A debt-money system needs consumption and passionate unconscious consumers. It couldn't function if people were clear-minded and centered. It defines our cultural norms and values. The system insists we consume whether we need to or not, and whether we want to or not. Desire and need are manufactured."

"And if we stop mindlessly over-consuming, we can be sure what would happen. The debt-money system would come crashing down. The Fourth Imperative: Debt-money drives us to non-stop over consumption," Sam said somberly as we headed into South Station.

We went down the escalator to take the Silver Line to the Seaport District. A couple of years ago it was a barren flat tundra where the frozen wind would barrel in off the sea, chilling anyone to the bone in three-seconds flat. When we got out of the station we could barely see between the towering buildings and endless cranes ready for construction. More million-dollar condos were cropping up here than anywhere else in the city. The clear majority were sold even before builders broke ground.

"Look at this place. Every time I come down here it is like a new neighborhood, hardly recognizable from a few months back," Sam remarked, reestablishing his bearings. "I can't believe how fast this all changes, it seems to come from nowhere."

"They build on every scrap of land where they can make a profit," I said. "The new buildings here are beautiful, but it is scary how fast it grows, and when there's a downturn how fast it all stops. There are only two switches on this action: on and off."

"I have a feeling we're on to the next imperative, aren't we?" Sam smiled mischievously.

"We are, Sam. The Fifth Imperative is the growth imperative. The debt-money machine needs endless growth. If there is no growth, the whole system comes crashing down. Everyone and everything is caught in the pressure to create endless growth. No matter what role we happen to have, big or small, we are all under pressure for the same thing. Growth."

"So, society has the virtual pedal to the metal," he added. "Without new growth, there isn't enough demand to create new loans. We have to manufacture reasons for people to spend, so they will be motivated to take out loans, earn money and pay debts."

"It's the bad ride we can't get off."

"Look at these beautiful condos and new restaurants," Sam said as we scanned the expanse of the new development. "They can shut down just as fast as they popped up. Everything is precarious when we are dependent on keeping this borrow, earn, shop, spend, repay and borrow again cycle going."

"It's a losing game." I looked down and shook my head.

We rounded the corner toward the ICA. The seaport was congested with cars, trucks and everything in between pushing to get business done. As we took a step onto the street, a speeding car flew through the intersection just as the light turned red. The wind blew us back as we caught our breath and shook off the fright.

It reminded me of the 1994 movie *Speed* with Sandra Bullock. She was forced to drive a bus non-stop at high speed to avoid triggering a hidden bomb. It was set to explode and kill her, and everyone else on board, if she slowed down. As she drove, she burned through the gas and brought their imminent demise closer. The movie was an uncanny representation of the foundation of our economy. We were all on that bus. At any moment, slowing growth could trigger the latest and greatest bubble to burst.

As I looked at all the beauty and glamour surrounding me, I couldn't help but wonder where we were going with all this endless 'growth.' Our need for growth, created to keep the money-as-debt scheme going, was instigating booms and busts, and devastating our financial stability. Worse, it had become a cancer corrupting every industry. The need for more and more growth, no matter how destructive, superseded all other values and concerns. It was our unquestioned religion.

Corporations did anything to beat quarterly earnings and forecasts to protect the value of their stock, which usually required laying-off workers and reducing the quality of their services and products. The race to the bottom was everywhere, and in everything. It was in the degradation of our food supply, water, healthcare systems, education and, even, entertainment. We had to research the safety of our banks, interest evaporated on our savings, and investing was often infiltrated by gamblers. In the end, the incessant need for growth corrupted us. We sold everything we believed in and stood for, in exchange for the illusion of safety and a sense of temporary comfort. But what were we to do? Our survival was at stake. I often felt sad, as I saw through the flashy veneer of the latest and greatest enticements. We were unwitting participants creating our demise.

The beautiful white domed roof and large glass paneled windows of the ICA stood before us. We arrived shortly before seven o'clock, just as the waitstaff prepared to circle with trays of posh and elegant-looking hors d'oeuvres. It was a private event, sponsored by the architecture firm where Sam worked. We checked our coats and started to explore the exhibit. Sam made sure we didn't stray too far from the waiters with the appetizers. I had forgotten that we hadn't eaten much, and, luckily for Sam, there was a sit-down dinner to come.

"I wonder if any of these contemporary artists will ever become as famous as Pablo Picasso?" Sam questioned, holding a plate filled with bacon wrapped scallops in one hand while taking almost a half dozen mini Swedish meatballs from a serving tray with the other.

"In 2004, didn't his painting, *Garçon with Pipe*, sell for $104 million at Sotheby's auction?"

"Yes, it did," Sam answered. "Since the financial crisis, fine art prices have soared. Most people are still trying to recover, and yet a few are doing very, very well."

"The first five imperatives of our debt-money system encompass and impact every aspect of our lives. It's impossible to get free of their enormous undertow but there is *one* ticket that offers a break from the relentless treadmill, sometimes for a little while and for a few— seemingly a lifetime."

We walked over to the bar to get a glass of wine.

"What's the ticket?" Sam asked curiously.

"It's the Sixth Imperative: A debt-money system requires big risk-taking, or what's called speculation."

"You mean betting money at high-risk? Putting some money down on something where you might lose it all, but you could win big? Like high-stakes gambling?"

"More or less."

"Why is that an imperative of the system?"

"People can't take out enough loans to keep the system running. We just can't handle all that debt the money system needs."

"I see where this is going," Sam interrupted. "Creating money-as-debt drives society to run at an inhumane pace. You cannot get sick, or have life interfere with your ability to play your role generating food for the debt-machine. Depending on where the money flows, not everyone is in a place to be able to earn it. The more people who fail to keep going, the less money circulates, and the dominos start to fall."

"Yes, and risky lending creates fast and unusually big new loans," I added, "which generates lots of money-as-debt, filling the Debt-Monster's tank when humans can't. Responsible lending is slower. It takes time for investments to create profits, while producing something good. A money-as-debt system doesn't have time for that."

"People who take these risks win huge payouts. The excess money gives them a rest from the debt-money treadmill."

"They capture large sums of money as they extract wealth from society. Typically, people who produce the real things we need in society, pay the price."

"Our culture glorifies the super wealthy as super heroes," Sam pointed out. "Putting them up on a pedestal because they are rich, quietly sending the message that it is possible for us to be just like them."

"But when money is debt, it's a long shot," I responded. "What's worse is risky bets usually fund things that do a lot of harm to everyone else. Creating loans for risky investment does not invest in the real economy. It doesn't put money into industry or innovation. Instead, it is like eating candy for breakfast, lunch, and dinner. It pumps sugar into the system, void of nutrition."

"You never get that part of the picture," Sam remarked. "You just hear how smart these successful investors are or what foresight they had."

"These people 'win' big gains by making risky bets. They don't contribute to the real economy. Instead, they get a pile of money they can use—to acquire what actual contributors produce. They gain the ability to extract wealth legitimately created by others. They are takers. It is not earning money. It is not investment. It is Speculation."

"Money-as-debt mandates speculation to keep the system running. As it rewards its minions for doing its bidding. Amazing," Sam remarked.

It was time for dinner, and to our surprise there was an accompanying dance performance. The dancers took the stage just as the food was served. It was a contemporary rendition of *The Wizard of Oz*. It was already a full night, and we still had one more imperative to uncover. But, I welcomed the reprieve to escape into the magical land where anything was possible, where all our problems could be solved. I hadn't seen the story for ages and it was wonderfully entertaining to watch while we enjoyed our dinner.

We picked up our coats and headed back on the Silver Line, inbound to South Station. Within a few minutes, the train pulled into the financial district. As we crossed Atlantic Avenue, a towering gray, and somewhat ominous, building stood before us.

"Is that the Boston Federal Reserve Bank?" Sam asked as he craned his neck up to capture the full magnitude of the building.

"Yes, it reminds me of a fortress, don't you think? That's where our 'Wizard of Oz' lives, working some kind of magic behind the curtain." I winked. "The Federal Reserve system is in charge of our monetary policy, leaving us to rely on the Wizard too."

"Isn't he just a man behind the curtain?" Sam half-heartedly laughed.

"Yes, but money-as-debt creates the Seventh Imperative which requires a small group of people hold the most meaningful power and control in our society. Not very different from kings and queens of feudal regimes, money-as-debt interferes with the ability for our Constitutional Republic to viably function. Even though we feel like we are free citizens, the defining parameters of our lives are determined by those who control the flow of our money. We don't get to vote for them, unlike the president or congress, all of whom are virtually powerless in comparison. The real power is held by those who dictate policy about how easily our money flows and its quantity grows."

"And when we pull the curtain back?"

"No magic, no real power to fix anything. We find a system that creates money-as-debt driving the population to keep up on the treadmill—at the service of producing debt as money as its master."

"What do you mean they hold more power than everyone else?" Sam asked sounding frustrated.

"They determine how much our mortgage or car will cost, whether jobs exist and what the stock market will do."

"I thought we voted for people to make these kinds of decisions."

"Well, using money-as-debt lacks any stability of its own. It is a fragile arrangement, you know? The system is entirely dependent on the perpetual cycle of loan creation and repayment to generate money-as-debt. Perhaps to have faith in it, we have to believe in our magical wizard who can solve our problems."

"Any slow-down in loans threatens the entire economy. Someone has to save the day."

"This maestro maintains the illusion that he can keep the system humming. He needs to make up for debt-money's incompatibility with human nature and nature's limitations, but the truth is he cannot. When 'debt is money' he can try to slow down the economy by making the price of borrowing money more expensive, you know... by raising interest rates. But he can't get an economy going again. The wizard can only say things to help people believe the economy is getting better. If people are so strapped with debt they already have, trying to make ends meet, they can't spend more or take on more debt."

Sam agreed. "No matter how cheap it is to borrow, if you cannot handle any more debt, and you cannot repay what you have, you can't take on more debt. No new money can be created to jump start the economy again. The wizard is just a man pulling levers behind the curtain. Maybe this is the reason, after so many economic downturns, countries spiral into violence, and suddenly end up in war."

"It is a suspicious pattern, isn't it? The money-as-debt system's instability remains hidden as we focus on the heartbreak of war. War generates tons of new debt, which is money. When it begins to circulate, it gets the economy going again," I agreed. I yawned suddenly. Embarrassed, I smiled as I said, "Well, we did it. We uncovered all seven imperatives controlling and destroying our lives. It's late—and we have work in the morning, I better head home. Thank you for a lovely evening."

I gave him a big hug as he said, "Let me walk you home, it's dark."

"It's only a few blocks, Sam. There's light from the lamp posts the whole way. Go catch your train, and let's talk tomorrow."

We smiled at one another, and I went on my way. As I got to my door, I looked back, and I could see Sam waiting to make sure I had made it home safely.

3
ARCHITECTS OF OUR OWN DEMISE

"Hey, good morning! How are you?" Sam's voice greeted me as I answered the phone.

"Good, thanks again for yesterday. You know, I'm feeling a lot better now that I have someone to share all this with, especially you, Sam."

"Do you have time for lunch? I'm working in the Back Bay today. I can meet you at Sonsie's at noon if it works for you?" Sam asked with his irresistible charm.

"That works, I'd love to. See you soon."

It was a little warmer out. The bitter chill was starting to lose its edge. As the wind brushed my face, it carried the softness of spring in the air. Sam was already reading the specials as I arrived.

"They have a spot for us right by the window. Do you like it?" Sam pointed to a table for two with a prime view of the street.

I nodded and put my keys on the table as Sam pulled out my chair. I sat down, as he handed me the menu. "I bet you know what you are going to have already, don't you?"

"Yes, ma'am, you know me well." Sam patted his stomach. He had always been a big lover of food and never shied away from finishing an extra plate or two.

"I saw you last night waiting for me to get home safely. Thank you, that was sweet."

"Of course. It goes against my gentlemanly upbringing not to see a lady home. That's the least I could do," he said as he fiddled with the keys, spinning one on the table. "Something dawned on me as you walked home under the light of the lamp posts last night."

"Really? What was that?" I asked curiously.

"Have you ever heard of the parable, 'The Old Man, the Traveler, and the Lamp Post'?" Sam looked at me with a prolonged stare.

"I'm not sure. Why do you ask?"

"Now, that I have a deeper understanding of what our money actually is, my whole perspective has changed. This thing, money, that we all want so much—in the form it comes in— is actually our enslaver. It is clear to me that it is the *root* of our strife. Creating our economic, political, and social struggles with its seven imperatives, stealing our lives. And our freedom."

"Sam, it is sinking in, isn't it? It's amazing. The key to our problem is our money." I felt grateful that he understood so quickly, what I wrestled with for so many months on my own. I had no one to talk to or consider these ideas with and now, that had changed.

As he picked up the key, he said, "The key to our problem lies undiscovered and hidden in the dark. While we are lost, arguing and pontificating, staunchly holding onto our own views, we do not realize there is another place to look for answers! Examining how money is created is new territory we must search. If we could just stop fighting with one another, we would have a chance to discover the real problem."

Stillness swept over us for a moment, as we sat looking at each other. Then he continued, "As I watched you walk down the street under the light of the lamp posts, the parable started to play in my head."

"Tell me about it."

"Well, it's a story of two men. But it's not just their story, it is our story. It's the story of how we are lost. Lost, looking for answers, trying to solve our money problems, big and small."

"I like it so far." I smiled. I thought I knew the story, but I wanted Sam to share it.

"Ok, here we go," he continued in a deep voice as he announced the title and began:

"The Old Man, the Traveler, and the Lamp Post:

> *It was late in the night. In the dark shadows, a traveler noticed an old man hunched over searching for something lost under the light of a lamp post. Sympathetic, the traveler walked over to the man. Tugging at his collar to shut out the sting of the cold night air, he asked the old man, "What are you looking for?"*
>
> *Dusty and forlorn, the seeker raised a heavy brow to peer at the traveler with one eye and grumbled, "Lost my keys...can't leave here, can't go anywhere 'til I find my keys." The traveler, feeling for the old man's predicament offered to help and join the old man in his search under the lamplight. He believed surely together with enough effort, they would find what he was looking for under the burning light of the lamp post.*
>
> *Time passed. Diligently searching, the men grew weary. After scouring every square inch under the stretch of the light, they were no better than at the start, only that much more depleted and daunted. Disbelief, confusion, and frustration prevailed, and finally, the traveler stopped for a moment. He bid the old man, "Are you sure this is where you lost your keys?"*
>
> *The old man abruptly looked up with a shock of surprise and gruffly replied, "What? No, no, I lost my keys two blocks down to the east."*
>
> *Dumbfounded and amazed, the traveler, with anger rising and feeling betrayed, yet not completely sure by whom,*

spit out "What? Why? Why are you looking here if you know they cannot be found here?!"

"Because," the old man boomed in a clear matter of fact tone, "there Is light here, I can see here. I can see where I am and what I am doing. Down there, there's no light and I can't see nothing!"

"We are just like the old man," Sam said. "Searching for the answers to solve our problems, looking for ways to find enough money. We believe the reason there isn't enough is political incompetence or corruption, mismanagement of 'The Economy' or that something is wrong with other people or, worse, that something is wrong with us. Examining and arguing about these ideas tirelessly, going around and round—and getting nowhere because we pursue the solution where it does not exist. We are lost without even knowing it."

Sam smiled a big smile and my eyes began to tear, I was grateful for his insight and his companionship. All the research I uncovered had challenged the foundation of my life and the core of my identity; I was not fully aware of the toll it took on me. As I sat with Sam, it struck me how alone I had been in the last year. I saw that I had not had any compassion for myself.

Then, suddenly, loud, aggressive voices shouted at each other. The restaurant manager had switched on the TV over the bar and the volume was turned all the way up, left from the night before. Refined and polished-looking people viciously argued with one another, each trying to dominate the other with their point of view. No one was interested in listening to anyone else, and I felt unnerved by their hostility.

And yet, I saw the echo of their anger and violence in all of us. At one time or another, we were lost in the same rigidity and obstinance, fear and scarcity were pervasive in our world, so much so that it was easier to blame others when their values didn't match ours. Divided by political ideology, believing the other was wrong, we were lost searching for answers where they could not be found.

Having the same conversations, covering the same points with the same people, we felt somewhat better—and, remained trapped. Though we sensed a pointlessness to it all, there was some comfort in reinforcing our familiar ideas. Even when anger, exasperation, and helplessness took over, we still found some security in our point of view.

I wondered if we would hold onto our beloved beliefs and stay at war with one another, pacing like the old man, as our problems got worse. I hoped that we would somehow search for answers where we had not looked before even if it made us uncomfortable.

I had heard this parable almost twenty years earlier, and it was something I never forgot. It haunted me, as I felt I never understood it. As I learned about our money system, my understanding grew, and I had new empathy for the old man, and for us. We were moths mesmerized by the incandescent glow of the familiar light of the lamp post. Bound by our beliefs, blinded by them, we were lost divided—blaming and fighting, while the real problem waited quietly, patiently for us to find it two blocks down to the east.

I believed that as each one of us learned about the money system, our hearts would soften, and our minds would open. The system was creating the scarcity that we condemned each other for. As we started to recognize it, we could move beyond the illusions of our division and find unity in our shared affliction.

Sam and I finished lunch and paid our bill. As we left the restaurant, the sun was shining, and the air was brisk and refreshing. Sparrows sang in the Magnolia trees as they hopped from branch to branch. The flowers were budding, ready to welcome spring back to Boston. We walked for a few blocks enjoying the afternoon sun.

"You know, Sam, it amazes me how we are born into this world just accepting money, like air and this radiant sunshine. We unconsciously accept money as a fact in our lives. We think of it as a force of nature and we do not think of questioning it, or even, that it can be questioned."

"We don't. We assume it's a good thing and more of it will make our lives better."

"But as a society, we create money and decide to use it. Money is a 'social-agreement' that we 'make-up.' We are the ones who actually determine how it should work."

"That's true, Kristen. It is not a law of nature we have to deal with."

"Then there must be very specific choices we can make when we design money. Ways that we construct it to help everyone, and serve us."

"And other choices that make our money a tool of enslavement, or our *master*."

"Right, money controls everything, and our current system of scarcity spreads fear and hostility. To find a better way, maybe we need to change our worldview because it is rooted in lack and separation. It is too divisive."

"Kristen, isn't this what Albert Einstein meant when he said that we could not find the solution to the problem with the same mindset that created it?"

"I think so. Our current perspective is embedded in scarcity and fear, and we cannot see that the money we use creates our suffering."

"Perhaps, we need to see something else is possible. That more for everyone is possible."

"Yes, Sam, and maybe this is why the key waits for us in the dark. Not only do we need to discover our money is the problem, but we may need a new mindset to see new possibilities—so we can find a *new way* we haven't thought of before— then we will be able to design money in a way that works for everyone."

"You know, I'm doing something like this tomorrow. I'm flying up to Grand Rapids, Michigan in the morning, to attend an architectural design conference focused on the principles of biomimicry. We're taking a look at nature to see how we can apply its genius to create better designs. Nature does have a thing or two to teach us."

"How interesting. Sam, maybe you will learn something to build a better money system."

"Nature thrives on interdependence and doesn't create self-sabotage. You can come with me if you'd like," Sam added with a big smile.

"Did you say Grand Rapids?" I said, tempted to join him. "That's not far from Thompsonville, is it? Professor Steve Keen is speaking there Thursday night. He is one of my favorite economists. He's the head of the School of Economics, History, and Politics at Kingston University and the author of *Debunking Economics* and *Can We Avoid Another Crisis?* He is one of the few economists in the world that predicted the financial crisis. Maybe I could fly into Traverse City, Thursday. If you want, we could drive up to Thompsonville and go to his lecture together."

"Kristen, you're on! I'll see you in Michigan. This is turning out to be an adventure, isn't it?" Sam winked as he took my car key out of his pocket and put it in my hand.

4
GOLD IS NOT THE ANSWER

I ended up on a midday flight to Traverse City. My flight had been delayed by an early spring snowstorm in Michigan. I walked out of the gate into the most beautiful airport terminal I had ever seen. It was paneled in rich cherry wood, with blue and green stained-glass windows, and copper light fixtures overhead. At the end of the concourse, there was a towering stone fireplace complete with a lit fire. It felt like a north woods lodge, not an airport. Without skipping a beat, Sam was there waiting for me.

"Welcome to Michigan," he said as he took my bags and gave me a hug, "you made it!"

"This is beautiful. Is it really an airport?"

Sam explained, "This is the sophisticated beauty of Frank Lloyd Wright's Arts and Crafts design. It's meant to capture the vast openness and natural beauty of the North Michigan landscape."

"It captures it well. I want to stay here and curl up by the fire."

"Come on, we better head to the car. Your flight was late, and it's a long drive, so we need to get going if we don't want to miss Professor Keen at the conference," Sam said as he led the way to our rental car.

The roads were icy, and the driving was slow. We had about an hour and a half ahead of us before we got to our destination. Sam was comfortable driving, and all I had to do was sit, relax, and enjoy the scenery. It was the best way to travel. As we got onto the highway, we passed a small strip mall with a jeweler advertising 'Cash for Gold' on a large sign.

"Kristen, wasn't our money backed by gold at some point? Wouldn't it be better if we went back to gold as people did long ago, when barter exchanges were replaced with metal coins?"

"That is a great question, Sam. Money has a long and checkered past. Using gold as money failed over and over throughout money's history. Most people do not really understand why it failed and, of course, what is wrong with the money we use today. So, the idea of going back to gold as 'sound money' or the right way to do money resurfaces repeatedly. When, in fact, going back to gold-money would only make things worse than they are now."

"Really? How did it fail in the past?"

"Gold is limited in supply, or at least kept that way. Whenever kings or governments used gold-as-money, the amount was too small to meet all the needs of the people. Yet, those in charge maintained their power by keeping the money supply too small, which created intense competition among the people—unnatural competition—as most people had too little access to too little money. Eventually, gold money systems broke down as revolutions rose or those in charge capitulated to demands to print more money, beyond the amount of gold they had."

"So, gold isn't better than creating money-as-debt?"

"Gold is another form of debt-money. It doesn't cease to exist when debts are repaid, like the system of debt-money we use today. But it is 'scarcity' money. It is always in too little supply to meet the real demand for money. It works for a while—for the few who have it. But in the end, those in charge are forced to create more money than there is gold, or 'dilute' the gold-backed money."

"I read a story of how goldsmiths in the medieval markets

diluted their gold-money. Written by Basil Moore, an Australian economist," Sam enthusiastically interjected. "Since gold was impractical to carry around, heavy and got attention from robbers, goldsmiths offered a safe place for people to store their gold for a modest fee. In return they gave the people paper receipts as proof of their deposit, like a claim-check you get at a parking garage."

"Interesting," I smiled. "Tell me more."

Sam carried on, "The local people felt secure that they could get their gold back at any time. Before long merchants accepted the paper receipts as payment for all kinds of services. In essence, a new paper money, backed by gold, was developed. The gold was safe in the vault and could be claimed at any time by anyone presenting the receipt. People bought and sold from each other with their new paper money, spared from lugging bags of gold coins around. The paper receipts were an advancement in the way money was used."

Sam winked at me as he kept his eye on the road. Encouraged by how impressed I was, he continued telling the story.

"Soon enough the economy was thriving, and people wanted to start new businesses, but there wasn't enough gold to go around. There was all this desire and readiness to be more productive, but there wasn't enough money to make it happen," he paused, "isn't that called 'pent-up demand'? Growth ready to burst into action like buds on a tree but without enough money, it becomes artificially suppressed?"

"Yes, legitimate growth is artificially suppressed when there isn't enough money flowing."

"People went to the goldsmiths to borrow gold, so they could do more business. The goldsmiths noticed that only about 10% of depositors came in for their gold at the same time. The rest of it, 90% of it, just sat there in the vault collecting dust. So, the goldsmiths drafted new 'counterfeit' receipts and lent them to people who then spent them as money. In fact, they drew up nine times more receipts. The goldsmiths wildly increased their income with the fees and interest they charged by lending gold which already belonged to others. The economy grew everywhere the paper gold receipts were accepted. No one noticed the goldsmiths were engaging in foul play until it became suspect how much more money they were spending relative to what they should have been able to spend. They had significantly increased their 'purchasing power'?" Sam stopped again.

"Yes, the ability to buy things. It is how much money you have or how much more you can put on your credit card. That's your 'purchasing power.'"

"Ok, their purchasing power had increased so much that others started to talk. It dawned on the townspeople that the goldsmiths were simply printing up receipts and using them as money. They started to worry that their gold wasn't so safe after all. They descended upon the goldsmiths' door, clamoring for their gold back. The goldsmiths were caught empty-handed. The people had more claims for gold than what was in the vault. The whole thing collapsed," Sam recounted the story with a glimmer in his eye.

"But that wasn't the end, was it Sam?" I quizzed.

"True, it wasn't. They came up with something remarkable," Sam continued. "They weren't ready to stop creating money out of thin air. They decided to let others in on the game— you know, to keep them 'interested.' They offered depositors a cut of the fees they took in. They paid them interest for keeping their gold in the vault with the understanding that ten percent would be kept in savings. This way there was always gold available when people wanted it."

"You explained it beautifully, Sam."

"Well, thank you, ma'am." Sam smiled mischievously. "You have to say those goldsmiths were pretty shady characters. But with all that money to print up at their fingertips, I guess greed took over."

"There's another way to look at that," I stopped and explained, "The goldsmiths witnessed a functioning economy, as you said, with lots of pent-up demand, many more people willing and able to buy and sell things, but with no gold to do so. We see this happening today with not enough money easily flowing, and throughout history. There is too little money circulating creating recessions and depressions.

"The goldsmiths saw how much gold was sitting there, how much purchasing power was not being used. They saw how much demand there was for it, how much need there was for more money to circulate. They created the additional money and spent it in the marketplace, providing people access to more money.

"They effectively created the missing money, and bridged the gap separating buyers and sellers. They created money to fund the real productive capacity that was artificially suppressed, with too little money in circulation. With this keen insight, the goldsmiths discovered the fundamental principle that money must be elastic—where the quantity in circulation expands more or less to match the supply of the actual productive capacity and the demand of the people—thereby allowing the right level of exchange to take place."

"This gives me a whole new perspective," Sam said with a pause. "Without the goldsmiths, the productive capacity of the people would have remained suppressed."

"Right!" I agreed. "The goldsmiths were innovators. When the real capacity of the economy was greater than the amount of money in circulation, they created a way to increase the money supply to meet its legitimate need. The value and quantity of money should be determined by the amount of work, real products and services, people contribute to one another. Bright ideas, earth's resources, and elbow grease is what makes money real, not scarcity or gold we lock up somewhere. The lesson is a priceless treasure."

"So, it is not what backs money, like gold, that makes it 'sound' or good money. It is the right quantity of money circulating, that matters?"

"Yes. Now, the goldsmiths could have easily taken this too far by creating more paper money than the real economy needed. But the lesson is that the amount of money in circulation needs to be elastic, more or less fluidly changing, equal to the real demand in society. The quantity of money circulating in the economy is the most important factor determining whether the economy thrives or fails.

We need the right amount of money circulating, equal to our actual productive capacity. These two sides of the equation must balance—then, we have a solid foundation."

"We clearly need more money today to meet the real demand. Why doesn't the government create more money and spend it into circulation as the goldsmiths did?"

"Technically, the government could, Sam. But today, people believe that the government doesn't have the power to create debt-free money as the goldsmiths did."

"What about all the country's gold reserves?" Sam questioned. "Could the government issue dollars backed by *that* gold and create more money society needs, and regain control over managing the quantity of money in circulation?"

"Not so easily. After the run on the banking system, in 1933, when depositors found their banks were out of gold, the government gave up its right to issue currency backed by gold."

"The banks ran out of gold—did that mean the government was bankrupt? Is that why it stopped issuing money backed by gold?"

I shared with Sam that, effectively, the United States was bankrupt in 1933 due to all the sovereign powers it gave up. After an aggressive seventy-year campaign to constrict the money supply, 'legal tender' was limited to gold, which ultimately led to the loss of the nation's power to create and maintain its money supply. The driving was difficult, but it didn't deter our conversation. We wound along the curves of the road as we followed the twists and turns of our money history, as it slowly unfolded before us through the black night air.

Previously, the American people had more access to money as money was 'bimetallic,' both silver and gold. They were suspicious of abandoning silver as money, and replacing it with gold as the only form of 'legal tender.' They believed silver money was necessary for prosperity. Silver was the people's money, widespread and readily obtainable. Gold was the bankers' money, limited in quantity and available to only a few. Productive people speculated that if money was only backed by gold, the money supply would be too small and would bring on slave-like economic conditions. Their fears were confirmed as the Coinage Act of 1873 stripped silver of its legal tender status. It was dubbed the "Crime of '73," rumored to have passed through corruption. It facilitated the manipulation and reduction of the money supply. It made it easy to consolidate power into a few hands. Farmers' loans were called in early, before harvests were ready, as productive people lost everything, especially their power. For the rest of the 1800s, the contentious battle to bring silver back kept on, as the money supply was reduced further, continuing to lessen people's control over their economic destiny.

Nebraskan Congressman William Jennings Bryan relentlessly championed for silver money but ultimately failed as President McKinley signed the Gold Standard Act into law in 1900. Gold, now the explicit legal tender, was the official means of payment and the sole basis for redeeming paper currency. Soon after, in 1913, President Woodrow Wilson signed the Federal Reserve Act creating the Federal Reserve Bank, allocating the nation's right to produce and control its money supply to a small group of bankers. The Federal Reserve Bank was, and still is, owned by commercial banks.

Sam had a hard time fully grasping that the Federal Reserve Bank was privately owned. He wasn't alone, most of us did. Especially after years of watching bank officials testify before Congress or the President appoint bank chairmen with official pomp and circumstance. Who would think to question who owned the institution?

"Are you sure the Federal Reserve Bank isn't a government agency?" Sam insisted, "You can't be right, it is simply independent of political parties, but it is the government's central bank."

"That is what common sense would tell you, but no—the Federal Reserve Bank is about as Federal as Federal Express." I smiled. "In essence, it's a private bank, with some governmental auspices, which controls the monopoly of our greatest national power—the power to produce and control the money supply. The

Federal Reserve Bank is owned by shareholders, all of whom are private commercial banks, in fact, the banks it regulates."

By 1933, the country was in the midst of the Great Depression, just twenty years after the central bank was created, as the quantity of gold was too scarce to support the economy. Franklin Delano Roosevelt, FDR, became president as thirty-seven states suspended their banking operations and people feared the system was imploding. Unable to keep up with panicked customer demands, banks were incapable of returning customer deposits. Just like the people who went looking for their gold from the goldsmiths, depositors were left empty-handed. To stop the ever-growing collapse, FDR issued a bank moratorium which prevented banks from redeeming dollars for gold. Banks could no longer "pay out, export, earmark, or permit the withdrawal or transfer [of gold]..." Only one month later, FDR issued a nationwide 'gold recall,' which required Americans to surrender their personal gold holdings to the government; any gold coins, bars, and paper gold certificates they had in their possession. They were forced to accept the nation's new paper currency: Federal Reserve notes. And, thus, the current money-as-debt system was born.

Though it is hard for most of us to imagine, not even one-hundred years ago, the government banned silver as money and then confiscated our parents, grandparents, and great-grandparents' gold as this debt-money system was put in place. It happened as their money was suddenly taken away and something new was installed. This could easily transpire again, bringing something even worse as the current system fails.

"People were forced to accept Federal Reserve notes when they took silver, and then the gold away?" Sam asked.

"It's when the current money-as-debt system took over," I emphasized. "The Federal Reserve Bank has the government sanctioned monopoly to make our currency. People think the government creates its money by decree or that we use Fiat money, but the government borrows Federal Reserve notes, just as we borrow from banks. Our money is created as bank credit or debt made by loans

issued by commercial banks, the shareholders of the Federal Reserve Bank."

"So, to transform this debt-money system," Sam shared as he pieced all the information together, "by returning to a gold-backed currency, the money supply would not increase, nor would it become elastic or flexible to meet the changing needs of the economy. Instead, it would make the money supply very small, and create perpetual recessions and depressions. There wouldn't be enough gold to invest in innovation, and to develop new things in the economy. Not only that, but when we use a scarce commodity like gold-as-money, wealthy people can buy up most of what's on the market, and easily gain control over everyone else."

"That's right. That's why gold has always been the choice of the super-wealthy, keeping hierarchical systems intact. Opening up access to the money supply, as silver money did, allowed the masses to participate and dilute their power."

"Gold quickly becomes a tyrannical way of doing money."

"Yes. The important point to remember is that *the quantity of money should be elastic*. It should never be too limited in quantity or be kept scarce to be 'valuable.' The amount of money in circulation should be large or small, depending on how productive the people are at any given time. The amount of wealth people want to produce and consume is what determines how much money needs to be available. Gold and money-as-debt are scarcity tools, keeping the actual productive people hustling to get enough money to get by. The scarcity fortifies established players and their position at the top, rather than empowering society to flow."

"This clears up my confusion around gold. Many people argue that gold is the right way to do money, but it is never explained in this context. Limiting money to gold shrank the money supply and cleared the path to instate our current money-as-debt system. We need money in the right quantity to empower people." Sam slowed down on the road and entered the campus.

"Look at how full this parking lot is! I guess we're not the only ones interested in discovering how money and debt really work. Right, Sam?"

"That's for sure. Hopefully, we will still be able to get some seats." Sam found a lone spot far from the entrance. "Let's hurry up and get inside. Just be careful with the ice."

5
NO ONE IS SAFE

It was late by the time we pulled into the convention parking lot. We wasted no time as we got out of the car and headed through the pitch-black night toward the door.

Sam looked at me knowing I would be disappointed if we missed any of the talk. The seats were almost all taken, but luckily, we found two together in the back corner and quickly sat down. Professor Steve Keen walked toward the platform. Vibrant and fit with his boyish good looks, he was full of energy.

"Sam," I whispered, "Professor Keen warned of the coming financial crisis ahead of time, and, yet, mainstream economists didn't see it."

"How was he able to do that?"

"Professor Keen is one of the few economists who understands how money is created. He knows when more debt is created, more money is created which brings on optimism which eventually leads to dangerous bubbles in the markets."

"As more debt produces more money to buy more houses?"

"Yes, the loans create gobs of instant new money which fuels the prices higher. The houses aren't worth more, but they sure are more expensive."

"Until, they rise too much…"

"Then the whole thing collapses, housing prices bust, loans are no longer created, and so new money is no longer created, and sales fall and people lose their jobs. A financial crisis ensues because the debt—creating all this hot new money—was used to buy things and inflate prices. It was not invested in innovation and productive activity, so incomes cannot keep-up with the higher loan payments."

"Other economists didn't see this?" Sam asked, incredulously.

"Mainstream economists tend to hold onto the old model of how money is created. Thinking that the money lent is actually someone's savings rather than understanding it is brand new money just created. They do not acknowledge that this new money is now available in the economy, which adds fuel to the fire, and is readily available to buy things. Nor do they recognize that when loans are repaid that new money is taken out of the economy."

"How does Professor Keen forecast that a crisis is brewing?"

"He tracks loan growth. Particularly how much private debt increases. He follows how much new debt is created, and how quickly, and compares it to the amount of income people have to sustain the payments and keep the cycle of debt expansion going."

"Oh, he can track and forecast when the bubble might burst?"

"Yes, Sam, that's it. Professor Keen says the perception of economic stability leads to instability, and often unseen risks. Legendary economist, Herman Minsky, suggested that creating money-as-debt means that 'stability leads to instability.' We feel things are stable and full of opportunity, and we buy more and take on more debt. But, we miss the fundamental concept, that money circulating is really debt, so we don't see that our optimism is fueled by increasing amounts of debt—creating increasing amounts of pressure to keep this precarious house of cards functioning."

The moderator greeted Professor Keen on the platform and began with his first question.

"Professor Keen, we have heard you say that economists do not include how much debt banks create when they make predictions about the economy. This cannot be right. We must have missed something here," said the moderator as the audience chuckled.

Professor Keen answered with his distinct Australian accent, "What's very hard for people who haven't studied economics to imagine is that mainstream economists ignore the role of banks, and how much debt, and money is in the economy. I know that sounds like an outrageous statement, but they study the economy in such a way that they completely leave banks, money, and debt out of their equations. They make their predictions about the economy, as though the amount of money and debt don't matter, and they perfectly ignore *this* like 'being on the Serengeti Plains and ignoring an approaching herd of Wildebeest.' It is just beyond belief that this is how they operate, but it is. That's the fundamental reason they didn't see the latest crisis coming. They had no idea why it happened."

"How can mainstream economists ignore how much debt banks create and how much money there is? Especially as failing debt began to explode during the financial crisis," insisted the moderator.

Professor Keen underscored, "They completely ignore the role of banks, debt, and money, and yet they give advice on how to handle a monetary system! They think money is already in the system as a lubricant. Like looking at an engine and assuming there's oil in it. Fully ignoring how the oil comes about. They ignore that when loans are made money is created as debt—increasing the amount of goods and services people are willing to buy at certain prices, and equally important when people reduce debt rapidly, as they did during the financial crisis, that that rapid reduction of debt destroys people's ability to keep buying at higher prices. They ignore the major factor that causes the ups and downs in the global economy which has people like me pulling my hair out in exasperation."

The room was quiet as everyone had their full attention on Professor Keen. The moderator continued, "Money created in the lending process is new money which drives up the demand for products and services, or the price of houses. It puts gas in the tank. But when people pay down debt rapidly there is less money, so the gas runs out quickly, and the economy hits the skids. The Federal Reserve and their mainstream economists ignore this?"

"Yes, they completely ignore it, and say banks, debt and money don't matter."

"Mainstream economists deride you, calling you a radical because you point this out, as you believe the amount of debt created is important." The moderator held up Professor Keen's book and asked, "Is this why your book *Debunking Economics* is subtitled *The Naked Emperor Dethroned?*"

"Yes," Professor Keen answered, "banks, money, and debt do matter to what is happening in the economy. People rightly expect economists to know about money, but they do not. They run forecasts of the economy as if we barter goods and don't need to include banks, money, and debt."

The audience was stunned.

The moderator went a step further, "Professor Keen, you say that not all bank lending is good for society. You suggest that about 80% of bank lending undermines capitalism and creates parasitic loans rather than promoting investment. Will you explain the difference?"

"Let's start with the positive role of bank lending," Professor Keen began. "Bank lending provides investment funds for corporations and working capital. Banks provide funding for increases in productivity, new technologies, the iPads of the world and so on. That's the good aspect of debt; it creates credit to fund innovations. But, the vast majority of lending is made to people gambling on rising house prices, encouraged by banks. This plays a negative role because fundamentally, banks are financing Ponzi schemes. They are giving us money to gamble on housing prices, but the money they are giving us to gamble with is actually what causes the prices to rise. That is the parasitic behavior. When debt is used to fund pure speculation, rather than new investment or working capital, it doesn't increase an economy's productive capacity. And when debt grows much faster than incomes for an extended period, it leads to bubbles that ultimately lead to a financial crisis."

The moderator probed, "when banks lend to businesses creating new things, banks extend legitimate credit to entrepreneurs who develop new technologies, and jobs with real wages for people. This contributes to a stable foundation for the economy."

"Yes, that is right," Professor Keen agreed.

"On the other hand, when banks create loans, providing money to speculate or gamble on housing prices, the loans they make available actually cause the prices to rise, and fast?"

"Yes, that is right," Professor Keen affirmed again.

"Since there is no investment in the real economy, incomes can't rise as quickly as housing prices rise. When housing prices rise, people want to jump on the bandwagon to make some fast cash. They fear they will get left out and priced out, not able to buy a house if they wait. This creates a giant bubble."

Professor Keen nodded and explained, "The danger is that monthly payments need to be made to repay the mortgage. People need to be able to earn enough money to stay afloat—and the next bloke buying the house at a higher price has to earn even more! Otherwise, the explosion in this speculative debt, driving housing prices to all-time highs, collapses."

The moderator listened intently as Professor Keen continued, "The simple problem with banking is that banks profit by creating debt. The process of debt creation costs them almost nothing. Banks are always willing to create more debt to finance speculation. That gives banks a vested interest in Ponzi Schemes: lending people money to buy houses, which in turn makes houses more expensive."

The moderator interrupted, "Professor Keen, just to review the concept, a Ponzi Scheme is a scam disguised as an investment opportunity, in which the initial investors are enticed by the promise of making a quick profit. But early investors' profits actually come from the cash that subsequent investors put in, and investors coming late to the party lose all they invested."

"That's right. See, Ponzi schemes work up to the point,"

Professor Keen answered, "where the price of a house, relative to the income earned, becomes too high for new people to buy houses so the demand stops. The bubble bursts and we have an economic crisis. The key factor that allows Ponzi Schemes to work in housing markets is the 'Greater Fool' promise. The idea that a stock bought for a dollar today, can be sold for ten dollars tomorrow. No interest rate, no regulation can hold people back from piling into what such a promise foments, and that's what created the now 'almost forgotten' folly of the dot com bubble."

The moderator clarified, "People continue to buy houses because they cannot see an end to the rising prices. Until it is too late, then the whole scheme comes tumbling down. The average price of a home has gone up dramatically because banks make loans available. A home used to be three-times annual salary. Today, it is twelve-times or more in major cities, taking a huge part of our income to pay for the mortgage—leaving us with less and less money to spend on other things."

"Yep," Professor Keen confirmed. "You get to the stage where you can't stay alive, buy food and whatever else, and *pay your debt on your mortgage at the same time*. If you don't make your mortgage payments, then your house gets repossessed. This prevents you from consuming other things because there's a shortage between what your income is and what you need to spend to maintain your minimum lifestyle."

Professor Keen explained further, "Our standard of living goes down the drain. We struggle to buy a home in a system that schemes to push up prices by its own design. The money we earn gets sucked up by bigger mortgage payments, we are left with less to buy things, and businesses end up with fewer sales and have to cut expenses like wages or even start layoffs. Thus, creating a recipe for disaster and self-sabotage. Housing should be a place to live, not something used for leveraged speculation. It's risky speculation has distorted our capitalism. Turning our investment industry-based economy into a speculation gambling economy."

Sam whispered, "Let me get this straight, the debt-money

machine is partial to creating debt for speculation—as we saw with the sixth imperative. The need for endless growth and debt encourages this parasitic lending—and that's why 80% of bank lending is parasitic."

"It creates a system that pushes prices higher by its own design. Putting ever-more pressure on all of us from home buyers to renters as we use more and more of our paycheck just to have a place to live," I whispered back.

Sam continued, "And at the same time, it diverts lending away from productive investment in industry and innovation, which is the foundation of capitalism. Wages and income cannot rise. Instead, they decline as more people compete for fewer jobs."

"Sam, when you think of it, creating our money-as-debt works against us in *both directions*. It drives the price of housing up while it pushes our incomes down. Prices rise, debt burdens increase and there is no solid foundation for us to earn an income. We can't sustain the pressure of rising costs and things inevitably implode. Money-as-debt wreaks havoc."

"We find a similar dynamic in school tuitions," Professor Keen started, "student loans are a source of short-term profits for banks and are readily available. These loans drive up tuition prices exponentially by making it impossible for students and families to pay. Putting incredible pressure on them. I have seen this as an economics professor with my own students. They focus on trying to pay debt rather than staying focused on their education."

The moderator added, "Student loans in America have exceeded $1.5 trillion, an unbelievable number. These kids are crippled with debt, as they can't even think about buying a house. If students cannot find good paying jobs to pay off their loans when they graduate, their loans can get bigger as the interest compounds. These loans hold our young people back instead of moving them forward. Students are becoming indentured servants."

"It is actually counterproductive debt," Professor Keen replied. "The sheer amount of this debt and inability to pay it off takes the economy down."

The moderator asked, "Since money is debt, created as a 'double-book entry' by banks, every dollar of debt repaid extinguishes the debt—and extinguishes the dollar used to repay the debt. When everyone is so indebted, the amount of money we have can only shrink, and it cannot grow, right?"

Professor Keen answered with a grave look on his face, "That's right. Escaping from the debt trap we are now in will require either a 'Lost Generation' or policies that run counter to conventional economic thought and the short-term interests of the financial sector."

"Mainstream economists apply the wrong fixes because they don't understand how money is created."

Professor Keen shared, "If we leave it to bankruptcy, the basic mechanism by which capitalism eliminates excessive debt, a slow-grinding process of paying the debt down will ensue. To get back down to the level of debt that the system actually needs could take something like twenty years."

"This is terrible," the moderator continued. "We will need to wait for enough people to go bankrupt, until the level of debt is reduced—enough for growth to start again? Meanwhile, we keep interest rates low to take pressure off borrowers, and we starve savers and make it impossible to retire. If pension funds falter, with no growth in the economy, people will be stunned when their pension checks are cut in half. Is there a way out of this?"

Professor Keen answered, "When we examine history, we find societies in this situation wiped out debtors' debts to keep society going. It was called the 'burning of the books of debt,' a regular activity in pre-capitalist societies, where they actually wrote off the debt completely. Liberating people who were cast into debt-slavery. Without that escape valve, none of those societies would have lasted."

"Is this similar to Biblical jubilees—where they wiped out the debt and started over?" the moderator pondered. "Can we wipe out the debt?"

"If it was easy to do, yes," Professor Keen answered. "But, it's not. If we had the situation of the 1930s where the banks owned all the debt, and if you wrote the loans off, the banks were the ones who would directly suffer, it would be easy. The trouble is the banks haven't simply created far more loans to the debtors than they should have, they've also bundled the loans as securities and sold them to pension funds and individuals."

The moderator looked stunned. "These loans are investments—such as bonds—in pension, 401Ks, and retirees' savings accounts. If we were to free society from this death spiral of debt, people's retirement accounts and savings would be destroyed?"

"Yes, that's right," Professor Keen continued. "It's far too interconnected to do it in the old-fashioned way of a jubilee. You could not do it without causing as much destruction as you're trying to prevent. What we need is a modern-day jubilee, we need one that simply bails people out instead of the banks. We need to wipe out debt by giving a small amount of debt-free money to everyone to start with. Those with debt would have to apply it to pay down debts owed, those without would simply receive money. This would stop us from declining into the abyss."

"Whoa," Sam whispered. "People who took mortgages and student loans were keeping the debt-machine going. Banks were too, but they were responsible for making sure the loans were legitimate. It seems that the banks and their bankers already got a jubilee, and, worse, that these unpayable loans are now in retirement accounts and pensions. It's not fair to wipe out retirees and stop younger generations from retiring."

"We have to face reality," Professor Keen started, "My colleague, Dr. Michael Hudson, has a simple phrase that captures it best. 'Debts that can't be repaid, won't be repaid.' It sums up the economic dilemma of our times. This does not involve sanctioning 'moral hazard,' since the real moral hazard is found in the behavior of the finance sector creating this debt in the first place. Most of this debt should never have been created since all it did was fund disguised Ponzi Schemes that inflated asset values without adding to society's productivity. Here the irresponsibility

—and Moral Hazard—clearly lay with the lenders rather than the borrowers. The only real question we face is not whether we should or should not repay this debt, but how are we going to go about not repaying it. Otherwise, we will endure personal and corporate bankruptcies and slow repayment of debt in depressed economic conditions."

The moderator suggested, "It seems unless someone gets rid of this private debt or adds lots of money—without debt, we are in a hopeless situation."

"Yes," Professor Keen confirmed, "we should be writing off large parts of it, and I would actually write it off by the capacity of the government to create debt-free money. That would be using what I call the modern debt jubilee. It would be quite feasible to do that on a grand scale. Preventing a future crisis will require redefining how loans can be made to eliminate leveraged speculation that leads to this Ponzi lending. I have a detailed outline on my blog."

"Are you hopeful?" asked the moderator. "Do you think our policy makers will learn that debt is money, and issue a Jubilee to the people?"

"No," Professor Keen plainly answered. "What we'll do is let people go bankrupt and hound those who can't pay their debts, and force them to pay debts which are unsustainable, like what is happening in Greece right now. Rather than people being able to spend money, they'll be forever paying off their debt with whatever income stream they have, and by doing it will depress demand in the economy."

"Incomes will fall, leaving us stuck in recessions, waiting for all the unpayable debt to go through bankruptcy," said the moderator. "Is this why the Occupy Wall Street movement drew such a wide scope of people in its movement? When you think about their outrage, it wasn't polarized to the left or the right."

"That is correct, that's one of the positives to me," Professor Keen shared. "This Occupy Wall Street movement was very broadly based. Very much youth-based, but also particularly in America, large numbers of people who were laid off, industrial workers, some laid off financial workers. People who wouldn't normally sit in a tent at the bottom of Wall Street."

"This was different. It shows people, regardless of their perspective, lot in life or side of the fence they come from, were willing to come together?"

"Yes, a major part of their attitude," answered Professor Keen, "was they felt their trust in society was betrayed. They wanted to bring about a harmonious society. They weren't socialists in the old-fashioned overthrow-capitalism style of previous protests. They were emphasizing that they believe society should be something we can actually trust in and that's been destroyed by what's happened with the financial sector. They were trying to rebuild that trust, not quite certain how, it was a very vague movement, but they were looking for answers."

The audience was fully engaged as Professor Keen's interview came to an end. I looked at Sam, and he was wide-eyed intensely following the conversation. I nudged his arm as he glanced at me.

"This is sad," said Sam. "The two things we want most, a home and an education, are used to create Ponzi schemes or parasitic lending. Debt desperately needed to keep the money system going, inflating prices, and running our lives as we try to afford them."

"Take student debt for example," I added. "Kids are raised to be ultra-competitive. They compete for grades, test scores, and fret to develop the perfect resume to get into the best colleges. Parents compare their children's success with one another, reinforcing competition. Family events come second to sporting competitions and other extra-curricular activities. Our culture is built around getting kids into the best schools possible, no matter what. If families don't get caught up in this, they are considered social misfits."

"The message is drilled into us from day one. We are told we must get into the best school, to get the best job, to make as much money as we can!"

"The true value of the college education is never compared to its price tag. Maybe there is some quiet conversation about it at home, but there is too much social pressure to talk about it openly.

Parents would be 'doing' the wrong thing not to put 'education' first."

"Yeah, Kristen, and when these kids get accepted the price tag is outrageous. It is literally suffocating, but lenders swoop in to save the day."

"I know. It may be easy to say they shouldn't go to college unless they can afford it, but everything in society is structured to put these kids and their families into debt. Without explaining the costs of these loans, how they compound, and grow relative to the value the education provides. As high-quality jobs dry up, these loans just keep the debt-machine alive."

"Right," Sam agreed, "the loans are made easy to get. Of course, the lenders who make these loans are just doing their job, they aren't bad people."

"It's not like they wake up saying 'Let's go get some families into debt.' They want to keep their jobs and pay their bills. They probably believe they are helping kids get an education, without connecting the dots, as to how much these kids might actually earn when they graduate—let alone, be able to do something that makes them happy. Now, with heavy debt burdens, following their hearts and choosing what they want to do for work becomes impossible. We end up with more sad workers fueling the debt-machine instead of vibrant, creative, and empowered kids."

I paused for a moment, and thought about how the average American lived with unfathomable amounts of debt. The idea of using credit cards was marketed to us everywhere we turned, and at an earlier and earlier age. Not only had the debt-money system corrupted home ownership, education, and narrowed our career paths, but it seeped into every purchase we made. The result was that we owned nothing, and put all our resources into renting what we had, by making minimum payments.

It was hard to imagine a strategy to educate children about how loans worked and interest accrued because schools no longer taught anything on the subject. Perhaps a few children still had parents who could prepare them, but most did not. Our lives had changed.

Many children had unstable families, and most parents were exhausted from chasing money.

Every retail store pushed customers to open store credit card accounts. They enticed shoppers with 10% or 20% off purchases, with promises of more 'perks' to come. Of course, there was never an explanation of how paying the minimum balance would not pay down the debt. Compounding at 17% to 24% plus interest, unpaid balances doubled every three-to-four years, if not sooner. Employees pushed store credit cards with monthly quotas to fill, requiring a certain amount of these cards be opened. If they failed they found themselves with worse schedules, ineligible for raises, and looked upon with general disfavor. There was a coordinated system, recruiting us to create more debt, as its primary motive and all else was secondary. I took a breath and looked at Sam, and saw that he was deep in thought too.

I said, "The debt-money system gets us to enlist ourselves doing its bidding, in the name of capitalism itself."

"Think of it—as people try to make their lives better, they play their part in a system—completely unaware that the money they want to make things better— is actually the money that makes things worse."

"You know, Sam, I think the most frightening thing I learned tonight is that all these bad loans people struggle with and fail to repay, are in retirement and pension accounts. And that even letting banks fail won't get rid of them, without destroying retirees and savers across the board. This shows how vulnerable everyone is in the debt-money system."

"I don't think people with savings or pension accounts understand that their safety is dependent on the success of people struggling to make ends meet."

"Consider the Occupy Wall Street movement and the people who came together united as the struggling 99% of the population oppressed by the 1% with the money and power. I understand the perspective, and it always made sense to me. But, the more I see how money-as-debt has no stability, the more I see that *no one* is safe, not even the 1%. As borrowers edge closer to bankruptcy, unable to pay their loans, the loans are in pension and retirement accounts—which come closer to failing. The idea of safety is an illusion. Regardless of which category we are in, we are in this mess together. The truth is we are the 100%, each and every one of us."

It had been a long day, but it was worth the effort. I was ready for bed, and as I walked to my hotel room I thought about the ethos of the Occupy movement. It was evidence that we, as a society, were beginning to rethink fundamental questions about money, and who we were. Yet, the more I saw that money was simply debt, that it did not exist at all, I understood that we were actually the 100%—not the 99%, unbeknownst to most. There was no one to fight against.

Money had no reality of its own. It was just a temporary token circulating in the economy until the debtor earned it, paid his loan, and then it ceased to exist. I could see the illusion that those with lots of money lived in as they believed and assumed money had an independent existence, unattached and unaffected by those struggling to get it. It seemed reasonable to believe that even if things got worse, having enough money or a steady pension would keep life calm. But this was not the case.

I stared at the ceiling for a while with the shock of the revelation that no one could be protected or insulated by creating enough money in a debt-money system racing toward its end. I found some comfort remembering that crisis always carried the medicine we needed hidden deep within its storm. The solution we were looking for had to be in the problem, waiting for us to have new eyes to see it. I took refuge in the fact that we were irreversibly in this mess together, and that as we recognized this, we would find our way out of it together.

As I drifted off to sleep, images from a storybook fable from my childhood, the *Five Blind Mice,* came to mind. The blind mice stumbled upon an elephant. Each one crawled on a different part of the elephant—one on the tail, one on the leg, another along the trunk, one on the ear and the last along the elephant's back. Never having experienced an elephant before, they argued with each other. Each one declared he knew what they found—thin like a rope, round as a column, curly like a snake, wavy as a fan, and broad like a vast boulder. Each stood their ground and argued with one another, sure he was right and the other was wrong. Yet, each one was right *and* wrong. Their experience was too small, too limited by their isolated point of view. They each only experienced the part of the elephant they were on, not the whole animal. Only when they came together, and shared their experiences, did they see what was really going on.

We were just like the five blind mice, limited in our vision by our own financial position. The person struggling to make ends meet easily believed the person with lots of money was greedy and insensitive, causing the lack and hardship he suffered. The person watching taxes and prices rise saw the person with ever-increasing amounts of debt as irresponsible, lacking in self-discipline, or lazy, and as the reason her standard of living decreased every year as government debt and welfare costs grew. Each believed the other was doing something wrong, and from a narrow vantage point, felt justified. But in reality, it was the wheels of the debt-money machine grinding away. The debt-monster, working behind the scenes creating scarcity and risk for us all, was the "whole animal" waiting to be discovered.

I knew that as we started to see the greater picture we would no longer stumble about blind. We would discover we were all doing the best we could, each in our own way. Doing the best we could, in a system engineered to bring out the worst of what we could be. Our vigilance and our unforgiving points of view would ease, and we would begin to have compassion for ourselves, and, even, for one another.

6
TO DIVIDE AND CONQUER

The warm sun streamed through the window as I stretched and adjusted to the bright light. The sky beamed in a pure turquoise blue in stark contrast to the crisp white snow. I fumbled around as I looked for the clock, realizing I had no idea how long I had slept. It felt late and a little too quiet, like the world had already gotten up. Sure enough, it was after eight o'clock. I quickly jumped out of bed knowing Sam would already be downstairs having breakfast.

"Good morning sunshine! What a beautiful morning." Sam greeted me with his forkful of hash browns. His plate was loaded with buttermilk pancakes, scrambled eggs, and several links of sausage smothered in butter and pure Michigan maple syrup.

"Well, good morning, Sam. How did you sleep?" I smiled, looking for the server to find some coffee.

"It took a while to settle down and sleep. I thought about how the endless debt machine, with its voracious hunger for more debt, influences every aspect of our lives. What really stuck with me was what you said about the Occupy Wall Street movement, that actually everyone is the 100%. Most people think people with money are safe in this mess—that there isn't any risk to their savings. But it isn't true."

"Not when money *is* debt, Sam," I agreed. "As more and more people become bankrupt or pushed out of the economy, the money system itself becomes unstable."

"Besides inequality, what makes people angry is that they believe those who have a good amount of money in savings will make it while everyone else sinks. But, that's not the case in the long run."

The server arrived with my coffee, and an omelet stuffed with local raclette cheese and vegetables. Before she left, I asked for an order of buttermilk pancakes. Looking at the sweetness of the maple syrup drenched on Sam's plate was too tempting to pass up.

"Truth be told, I ordered the omelet to cover up the fact I just want to eat the pancakes soaked in sugar—albeit natural sugar—but sugar!" I smiled mischievously.

"Good call, it's worth every bite," Sam said as he put a flyer on the table. "Look, Dr. Michael Hudson, Professor Keen's colleague, speaks tonight at a monetary reform conference in Chicago. He discusses how debt and lending destroy capitalism. He wrote a new book called *Killing the Host, How Financial Parasites and Debt Destroy the Global Economy*."

"That sounds interesting. Tonight, Sam?" I asked. "I guess we could be back in Boston in time for work Monday. How long is the drive?"

"It's a decent road trip. It's about five hours to Chicago. I think we should go, after all we're in the 'neighborhood!' If we leave after we finish eating and get some gas, we will make it no problem."

We both laughed, enjoying our spontaneity. We were on a daunting adventure to unlearn everything we knew about money and debt, one we would have never stopped to take. We thought we already understood money. We knew how to make it and how to spend it. What else did we need to know? Life reinforced our ignorance and misconceptions about what money was, but luckily, we were waking from the stupor, and discovering we were determined to find the key to set us free. And, we were having a lot of fun along the way.

Sam pulled into the gas station as we rounded the pump. There was a long line of cars, and the cold wind was coming down off the Great Lakes. As we pulled up to the machine, Sam got out to pump the gas, and I headed into the convenience market.

"Get some snacks!" Sam shouted with a smile as he unwound the gas cap. I was back in just a few minutes with a small paper bag. I came up behind him as I noticed there was a kerosene pump.

"No putting kerosene in the car!" I teased.

"You can trust me. Regular unleaded ma'am," he assured. "I hope you have something good to eat in that bag. We've got a long way to go."

"Nope, sorry, Sam," I explained, "we need to find a deli where we can get some sandwiches. There was nothing in there but sugar." Sam looked disappointed as I added with a wink, "I did get some water though."

As we made our way back to the highway, Sam turned his head and glanced at me for a moment and said, "You know, my younger brother is a medical doctor. I always assumed that doctors had to undergo extensive training in nutrition. After all, getting the right nutrition seems essential to keeping the body healthy, but it turns out he spent just ten hours of four years in medical school studying nutrition. Some of his other buddies got about twenty hours, but no more than that. He said if he wanted to learn more that it would have been necessary to go somewhere else for his education—as in somewhere else other than medical school!"

"Really?" I asked surprised, "Isn't most chronic disease related to nutrition and diet? You would think that medical doctors need to learn the relationship between food and illness."

Sam shared, "I couldn't help but think of this while listening to Professor Keen speak about mainstream economists last night. They are powerful, and influence how we handle our money, and they never study how money and debt come about! No wonder our economy is a massive Ponzi scheme with endless booms and busts.

Economists tell us these booms and busts are a normal part of capitalism, and yet, they lack the basic education of how money and debt are created."

"We trust our experts," I reflected. "Having good health and money creates stability in our lives. Economists do not acknowledge that easy lending drives up housing and tuition prices, and diverts investment from salary paying work. Instead, they champion rising housing prices and tell us that this means we are doing well."

"Right Kristen, this is the kerosene we use to fuel the debt-machine. With the easy Ponzi lending, we shoot up into flames and burn out."

"Are you familiar with Ambrose Bierce, the famous short-story writer, who said, 'Debt is an ingenious substitute for the chain and whip of the slave driver'? Ponzi lending leads to debt-enslavement."

Sam looked to see if it was clear to merge onto the highway and said, "I am stunned that risky bank loans are now in our pension and retirement accounts. It is unbelievable that banks can sell off the risky loans to pension funds. This removes their incentive to make sure they make legitimate loans."

"I know. Money-as-debt forces banks to get these loans off their books, so they can make more loans. Pension funds and retirees are so hungry for income that they are willing to buy these loans or bonds because they pay high-interest rates, so they have some money to live on. The loans can be packaged to make them look safer than they are. But, in the end the debt-machine's need for more debt drives this behavior."

"So, in a way, Kristen, everyone is innocent and responsible for this mess at the same time. All doing the best they can, all fueling the corruption—no matter how unwittingly."

"The truth is this is a dysfunctional way to create a money system. Our ability to make legitimate investments is destroyed. When we create money-as-debt, where debt doesn't represent real productivity, it becomes a virus. Just like eating sugar or using kerosene to fuel the fire, easy money creates Ponzi lending and burns hot. It lifts the prices of stocks and bonds as people chase them. When it runs out, stocks crash, bonds go bankrupt, and people have to start over again—never making any headway."

Sam interjected, "People aren't really investing, are they? *Everything* is speculation."

"The markets rise because of this easy money, not because of legitimate investment. And, many of the bonds, in pensions and retirement funds, are the loans that borrowers struggle to repay. So, investors' and borrowers' fate hang in the balance of whether the debt-machine can continue to keep the bubble going."

"So, what can people do?"

"Not much," I answered as I stared out the window, "we are *all* the 100%. No matter where our money is—it is someone else's debt."

"I don't think people know that. People, with and without money, are completely inseparable, just like two ends of the same stick."

"I think you're right, Sam. People with money or pensions don't know what actually makes them 'safe.' It's not having money. It's borrowers' ability to repay and borrow again. And, people struggling don't know how fragile this illusion of safety is."

"Well, Kristen, there's a silver lining here. This predicament demonstrates that we are inseparable from each other. We cannot have safety in our money without the well-being of those trying to earn money to repay debt. Just like we cannot have a buyer without a seller or a business without customers, and customers without businesses."

"I thought about this as I fell asleep last night. Coming to grips with the shock of what we're living with, I have some courage that we are all in this together. I think there may be something beautiful waiting to be born from this."

I heard the car door shut as Sam got out to refill the gas. I had not realized I had fallen asleep as the hours flew by. We were just outside Chicago, not far from Roosevelt University where the conference was. I looked about remembering how beautiful

Chicago was, but it seemed I always had the off luck of being there when it was still cold.

"Hey, did you have a good nap?" Sam asked closing the door, "We're only about fifteen minutes away. I think we can valet the car nearby."

"Thanks for driving, Sam. You make it easy to relax and enjoy the ride."

We pulled into the garage and the valet handed Sam a claim check for the car.

"Last name?" mumbled the attendant with his attention on a car stuck leaving the gate.

"Bailey," Sam answered.

"What is it?" asked the attendant again.

"Bailey, the name is Sam Bailey," answered Sam trying to keep his attention.

"Oh. All right, you are all set. Leave the car here," the attendant said as we gathered our things and headed out of the garage.

We made our way into the antique building. It was beautiful with its old-world charm. There were two curved, red-velvet carpeted staircases on either side of the hall. They led to the mezzanine level where the vaulted ceilings, covered in truncated panels with ornate crystal chandeliers, echoed with the drama and grandeur of the turn of the twentieth-century when the building was built. Sam and I registered as we were consumed by the dazzling ambiance and took our seats in eager anticipation for Dr. Hudson's talk.

"Please welcome Dr. Michael Hudson, President of The Institute for the Study of Long-Term Economic Trends, a Wall Street Financial Analyst, distinguished research professor of economics at the University of Missouri, Kansas City, and author of his latest outstanding book, *Killing the Host*. The conference director opened the program as they both sat down on the platform.

"The middle class seems like it is dying, and America needs any hope of growth to return to its economic health of, say, fifty years ago. Tell us Dr. Hudson, what is destroying the economy?"

"Debt is what's destroying the economy. The American economy has now slowed down, and the Eurozone has turned into a dead zone, largely because it is drowning in debt. If Americans have to pay their debt, and the Europeans and other countries must pay their debts, there is no way that these economies can grow further. Because all the money is basically going to be spent paying the financial sector, not for goods and services, but rather to pay debt.

"And America is drowning in debt. If you add it all up, only about one-quarter of the average American family's paycheck actually goes for goods and services—for clothes, food, transportation, other basic needs that they have. What that means is that even if you give American workers all their clothes and all of their food for nothing, they still couldn't compete with foreign workers because they have to pay such a big nut out of their paycheck every month for housing costs that are vastly inflated by the banks.

"A house is worth whatever a bank will lend. And as the banks lend more and more relative to the value of the house, on easier and easier credit—on junk mortgages—housing prices continue to rise," Dr. Hudson began with great intensity.

The moderator asked, "So, why are average citizens so helpless? Why can't they get anyone in power to help?"

"Because, beyond this, there's a deeper phenomenon: the generalized financialization of the economy. We have moved into a central planning economy—exactly what the free market people warned about as they fought against socialism. Our economy is being planned. Not by government, and not by elected representatives, but by Wall Street, by the financial firms. They are now in charge of allocating where the economy's resources go. Wall Street and the banks don't lend money for the same things that governments spend on. Governments spend money on building infrastructure, social programs and doing the things that governments do. When banks lend money, they do not spend it into the economy for goods and services. They lend money to buy assets, and that means to inflate the price of housing. The more banks lend for real estate, the higher real estate prices go. The more they lend students to pay for their education, the higher universities are able to raise their tuition rates, because students can now get the money. Then, when they graduate they have a lifetime of debt peonage. So increasingly, the economy is having to pay off the debts that have run up, and more of the money in the economy is drained out to pay debt. The way to recover is indeed to wipe out the debt."

The moderator probed, "So why is wiping out people's debt so radical? We do it for the banks. We've seen other countries in history do it like Argentina or Germany after the Second World War. Where did this concept of the sacredness of debt or the 'sanctity of debt' come from, the idea—that paying debt regardless of the suffering it imposes—is more important than people, society and the quality of our lives?"

"Other countries, for thousands of years, avoided falling into debt peonage or enslavement by canceling debt out by wiping the debt slates with jubilees. Until the Roman Empire came on the scene. The Roman Empire conquered any new region led by its financial class, the Publicani knights, and they descended on rich regions and stripped the whole economy, reduced one-quarter of the population to debt-bondage or outright slavery and brought on feudalism and the dark age. That is what happens when you don't cancel debt. Rome was the first society not to cancel debts, and we know what happened: the whole of western Europe was plunged into a dark age.

"This practice continued until capitalism began to emerge. When capitalism developed in England and France in the 17th through 19th centuries, the major political fight of that era was to free industrial capitalism from feudalism, to create a banking model that invested in industry and innovation. But the model was slowly pushed toward lending on assets and the predatory model of banking we know today.

"In the mid-1900s, the Chicago School developed a new economic curriculum that wiped out thousands of years of economic theory and inserted this new predatory debt model. This was done in the name of prosperity and greater independence for

Americans, but it led to the financial sector stealing the government. When Adam Smith, John Stuart Mill, and the classical economists talked about "free" markets, they meant an economy free of rent, free of interest, free of parasitism. Today in the United States —thanks to Ayn Rand and the Chicago school (to name just a couple culprits)—the whole idea is that a free market is free *for* the parasites."

Sam and I absorbed Dr. Hudson's talk with his extensive knowledge of history and understanding of how investment capitalism had morphed into financial feudalism. Debt-money corrupted the basis of our lending institutions, transforming them from partners in our communities into robotic automatons producing mountains of debt. Now, forty percent of Americans were so indebted that they were unable to handle a $400 emergency. And, nearly half of all Americans could not afford the basics of middle class life, like rent and food. With unbound destructive lending, free-market capitalism capitulated into neo-feudalism as debt became the overlord and people, working to meet debt-repayment schedules, became serfs.

Not only was our free market corrupted by debt-money, but so was our government. No longer ruled by the people, of the people, and for the people. Financiers determined who received loans, and how much. Dr. Hudson articulated how they directed the distribution of resources, not markets, and—not people. Money-as-debt reduced banks to caretakers of the debt-machine, doing its bidding, creating debt to sustain it, extracting resources from the people who created the wealth of a nation.

Sam tapped me on the arm. "Since the 1950s, market capitalism, meant to empower and protect the freedom of productive people, has been contorted, used to promote finance-capitalism. To put the *Debt-Machine,* in charge."

What Sam said was true. In the past, banks helped communities become stronger as they extended legitimate loans, and maintained them until they were repaid as they shared in the risk. Banks were partners in the success or failure of businesses and of the communities at large. Today they won no matter what. Easy lending fueled housing and education costs, and drained investment from industry and innovation. We were less able to afford the essentials of the American Dream as our salaries stagnated and fewer good paying jobs existed. In the end, as we created our money supply through loans, primarily mortgages and college debt, we rented what we once owned. We lived as modern-day serfs, working to pay the lender monthly fees for our keep.

"What is happening isn't obvious at first," Sam added, "we see rising prices as a chance to make money in housing markets or borrowing for an expensive college education as the ticket to land a high paying job. We don't consider the years of debt payments or how much of what we earn must go to pay for these rising prices."

"We are all unwitting participants in our own demise," I agreed. "History and our understanding of what money is, and how it should operate, has been slowly erased. We thought we were getting ahead, or that others needed to catch up, only to discover we have a terrible system running our lives, and there is no winning in it."

It was late, and we had had another full day and were ready for a good night's sleep. We found our coats and headed straight to the garage. Sam had the claim check ready and handed it to the valet.

"Good evening, Mr. Bailey, I'll be right back with your car," said the attendant.

As we waited for the car, my mind drifted to George Bailey, the hero of the 1946 film, *It's A Wonderful Life*. He was the neighborhood banker who brought the community together by investing in people delivering real goods and services, contributing to the greater good of all. At first, it seemed almost romantic to think of, like dreaming of a by-gone era, but the movie was just as applicable today. Money was not meant to be about creating debt or leveraging what we had, to get as much as possible. Instead, money was our collective credit—the credit we gave each other—to invest in the good we created *for* one another and *with* one another.

In his darkest moment, George Bailey forgot that trust and the capacity to create are the foundation of money. His guardian angel, Clarence, appeared to remind him that our faith in each other is what makes prosperity possible. Yet, today lending was manipulated, creating the evils propagated by the money-as-debt system, eroding our faith, our communities, and destabilizing everything we had.

We left the garage and headed towards the hotel. As we drove past the empty city streets, I reflected on how much the world had changed in such a short period of time. Today a horde of the nation was speeding toward bankruptcy. Money-as-debt destroyed the lives and opportunities of all, rich and poor. Perhaps we, too, were circling our darkest moment. Knowing the money we used was a hidden virus, my heart sank wanting to find a new way, one that would work for us all. Staring silently out the window as I watched the streetlights cast shadows on the buildings as we passed by, I prayed for answers.

I hoped there was a greater intelligence working through us, prodding us to wake from dreaming a life too small. We assumed life was hard and filled with scarcity. And, why wouldn't we? Our daily lives reinforced it as an almost unquestionable fact. But it was an illusion, an illusion created by our money system. Our system not only generated the scarcity we tried to solve, but it was a system *we had the power to change*. But how, I wondered? Most didn't want to let go of it, most thought we needed it, and worse, most were caught in the trance, obsessed with winning the self-sabotaging game. And maybe, just maybe, without the pain, we would not be able to discover the real cause of our unsolvable problems. Perhaps our suffering was helping us, that without it we could not begin to see that there might be a greater reality waiting for us.

7
FINANCIAL FAIRY TALES

It had been a full week back in Boston. Sam and I both worked late taking care of everything we left behind. Friday arrived, and we met after work to run along the Esplanade. We still had a few hours of sunlight now that spring was here to stay. Everything and everyone celebrated life again. Sailboats sauntered carelessly along the Charles River, as rowing teams in racing shells zigged and zagged across the water with razor-sharp focus. The magnolia blooms faded as apple blossoms took their place. Daffodils and tulips blushed with a hint of color ready to reveal their vibrant yellows, pinks, and red. Chipmunks and squirrels scampered up and down the trees and darted between us as we ran on the path.

Sam had always been an athlete. Throughout his years at Harvard he was a talented runner and I couldn't remember a year he had not run the Boston Marathon. Luckily for me, he did not mind my slower pace. We started at the Fielder Footbridge near Arlington Street, and wove up and down the winding paths past the Hatch Shell where the famous Fourth of July celebration took place every year. We crossed on to Massachusetts Avenue and headed toward Cambridge. We looped back up to Memorial Drive and finished across the Salt and Pepper Shaker Bridge. Sam barely broke a sweat and looked like he was ready for more. I was just thankful we completed the run, as he handed me a water bottle and walked toward the Boston Garden.

"I want to go to New York City tomorrow," I said still a little out of breath, "I think you should come with me. It's going to be beautiful weather in the city, and one of my favorite authors is giving a talk at Pace University...David Graeber, have you heard of him?"

"David Graeber?" Sam asked, "His name sounds familiar. Wait, isn't he the one who started the Occupy Wall Street movement?"

"He helped the movement emerge. He is one of the most brilliant thinkers of our time. He wrote the bestselling book called *Debt: The First 5,000 years*. I read it twice, almost three times!"

"Interesting," Sam paused. "Of course, I will go. Do you want to take the train? It's the best way to get to the city, it goes along the coast."

"Great! I was hoping you would say yes. I think we should try to catch an early train around seven o'clock. I'm not sure if we can still get tickets on the Acela, otherwise the regional train will take longer. We can meet at Back Bay station?"

"I'll be there," Sam assured, "with coffee, and I'll make yours an Americano."

"You're the best, Sam. Come with me to my car. I brought David Graeber's book for you, in case you want to look at it tonight."

At a quarter-to-seven I walked through the big orange doors of Back Bay station. I found Sam sitting on a bench deeply engrossed in David Graeber's book. He jumped as I tapped his shoulder.

"Oh, sorry stranger!" I laughed. "I didn't mean to scare you."

"The book is so good that I haven't been able to put it down," he said gathering his things. "Here's your Americano. Let's head down to the tracks—I think the train should be here in a few minutes."

The train arrived, and we boarded taking two seats on the left to make sure we rode ocean-side. I wanted to surprise Sam, so I brought two piping-hot chicken calzones and ricotta filled cannoli straight from the North End for the ride.

"What do you think," Sam asked, opening the bag to find his calzone, "about the experience that prompted David to write this book about debt?"

"It's an amazing story," I shared. "He engaged in a conversation at a garden party and shared with a woman that he had just come from Madagascar where 15,000 people died as a result of cutting back health programs to repay massive debts to the IMF."

"The IMF is the International Monetary Fund, right?"

"It is a global banking institution that makes development loans, typically to third-world countries. The local people of Madagascar aggressively cut their budgets to meet the repayment schedules. They went without healthcare necessities and as a result, almost 15,000 people died, half of them children."

"It's sad," Sam said, shaking his head, "especially the way the woman responded is shocking. Saying it was *'simply too bad they died, but they had to repay the loans.'*"

"Her reaction stunned David too," I added. "That's what prompted him to write about debt, to discover how people have handled it throughout history, and to examine its strange and powerful hold on us."

"And," Sam continued as he finished a big bite of the calzone, "the woman understood, like most heavily indebted countries, the people of Madagascar didn't borrow the debt themselves. The money probably went straight into a dictator's Swiss bank account."

"Or that the people already paid back the original loans twenty-times over, thanks to the magic of compound interest."

"David had to point out to her that making development loans involves risk. Profits are meant to be the reward for making wise investments or prudent loans. Yet, using the model the IMF imposes on the world, the one where they get paid back no matter what, the incentive for making well-advised loans is gone."

"Despite knowing all that," I remarked, "and that 7,000 babies died, the woman maintained that the people owed debt and it had to be paid back. No matter how unjust or unfair it was!"

"Yeah, that's what left him dumbfounded, Kristen. David thought in what other context would she think of justifying letting these people die? And his mission to explore the power of debt began."

"The woman was captured by the 'sanctity of debt.' What Dr. Hudson spoke about in Chicago. The idea that debt must be repaid, regardless of the cost. Somehow this notion of the 'sanctity of debt,' makes good people legitimize unthinkable consequences, demanding, that no matter what, unpayable and unjust debts be paid."

"It's as if something happens to us."

"We become suddenly vacant and brainwashed, Sam. We lose touch with the sanctity of our humanity. Instead, the need to pay debt becomes the ruthless arbiter over all."

"You have to wonder if the debt-money machine pushes us so hard to compete and to try to earn money that we just become desensitized. David discovered that humanity has grappled with this question of debt, what we owe and how to repay it, since the beginning of time." Sam paused for a moment and then looked at me as he said, "It makes me stop and think: Who are we really in debt to?"

"To everything and everyone, to all of life," I said. "We are in debt to one another. In reality, there is no separation between us, and we aren't merely individuals. It's this uncomfortable ambiguity that drives us to flesh out strict financial rules around debt, and our sense of morality. We imagine we can put a number on what we owe each other or even, on one another's worth."

"I guess it is an attempt to draw firm boundaries around what we contribute and what belongs to us, and not to someone else," Sam added. "A way to meet our obligations of what we owe others. But it never seems to work."

"We calculate what we give others and what we get back, and make sure we get our fair share. But this is a dangerous narrative as it distances us from our humanity."

"It lets us judge others when we see them suffer, as a way we can protect ourselves."

"I agree."

"Wisdom teachings and holy books throughout the ages point to the dangers of defining our worth in numbers."

"But, it is the road we've taken." I continued, carefully enunciating each word, as if it would help me to have a better understanding even as I spoke. "Creating a political, economic, and social system that lives and dies on the dictates of a money-as-debt system. It has left us morally bankrupt, confused, and harboring shame. Because when it is all said and done, being right is not what brings us true happiness, living in love does."

I paused for a moment and watched the still, pale blue water of the ocean roll by out the window. I reflected on how interesting and also confusing it was to me to see how we tried to use the exchange of money to draw firm boundaries around what our obligations were to each other. Regardless of the relationship, from the most casual to the most bonded, we endowed the payment or gifting of money with a mysterious power of finality around our sense of obligation. Even in our day-to-day interactions, we often treated each other in unconscionable ways that we would never otherwise because somehow the payment of money excused our behavior.

Yet, we were multi-faceted beings imbued with deeper perceptions and feelings. Even if we made excuses when we degraded or took advantage of one another, we remained physically, emotionally, and spiritually connected. Any lack of respect or dignity did not go unaccounted for, and in the end, we were all dishonored and disheartened. Though we tried to separate ourselves instead of embracing the paradox of our reality, we were dependent on each other for everything, from food to shelter to life itself. If we stopped to see what we did for each other, every moment of the day, what we received from others' work, an overwhelming sense of vulnerability and gratitude softened these hard lines we drew.

It was all too easy to slip into arrogance, to live with our hearts closed, feeling we had paid our dues or debts to others. I found myself falling into this many times in my life. Yet, as I felt deeply grateful for what someone had done for me or recognized all the things I could never accomplish alone, the contradiction immediately humbled me as it exposed my unacknowledged hypocrisy. Those moments were gifts, whisperings of a higher knowing opening me up to access my true humanity—to really live which required an open and grateful heart.

Sam had gone back to intensely reading the book.

"Sam, did you get to the part where David revealed people did not use the barter system?" I asked, nudging his arm. "The idea that townspeople went to the market to trade a cow for forty chickens is made-up! It is not the history of how money was invented at all."

"That floored me," Sam said. "We all believe the inconvenience of bartering is what caused money to be invented, right? David gently calls it a pet peeve, a story that won't die, one that continues to show up in economic textbooks. He's too nice. It is an out and out lie!"

"Anthropologists searched for over two-hundred years to find one group of people who used barter before money was invented, and they have yet to find one. Adam Smith made it up."

"People simply ran accounts with each other. They tallied-up 'giving and taking' while they used rough estimates of fair play. They did not haggle 'tooth and nail' trying to get the most while giving the least, like we were led to believe."

"It really is surprising, Sam."

"Not only that, Kristen, but that people made sure they gave less or more back. That they left everyone 'in-debt' to each other, as they acknowledged the sense of community and their general indebtedness to each other."

"We were taught fictitious stories about the history of money," I added. "In essence, these credit systems were used for ages, then coin money arrived later and was rarely used. People used coins with those whom they didn't want relationships with, like heavily armed soldiers or questionable looking travelers."

"David revealed that the kings created coin money to sustain massive standing armies," Sam enthusiastically explained while he scanned the section in the book, "The kings didn't know how to feed their soldiers. Instead of employing thousands of people to haul-in supplies, the kings simply minted coins and put their own pictures on them. They compensated the soldiers in the coins and required the townspeople to pay a tax in the same coins. People quickly set up markets next to the armies to sell their goods and get the coins. Like magic, the kings discovered an effortless way to maintain armies. Only after this did people start using metal coins as money with any importance."

"Ingenious and amazing! With the need they created for the new coins, the kings accomplished a self-sustaining way to achieve everything they wanted. Without any force, they changed and drove the behavior of the people to take care of the armies."

"It *was* ingenious, Kristen. Now the people were easily controlled because they needed this coin, and the kings controlled the quantity that circulated. They tightened the noose by reducing the supply and heightened competition. Or they lengthened the leash by adding more coin, and provided the people the ability to make more things as they did the unseen bidding of the kingdom."

"We were told that people instinctively bartered and haggled, and tried to get as much as possible while they gave as little as possible. Led to believe that money was invented to maximize our getting, and minimize our giving. It's fabricated."

"The Hobbesian point of view," Sam declared as he put the book down and handed me a cannoli. "How many times have we been told that man is a savage trying to survive in a jungle, each man for himself in a dog-eat-dog world? By making money a specific token people need, and keeping it in 'too small' supply, they produced the Hobbesian jungle. Keeping people at each other's throats, and acting in barbaric ways."

It was stunning and heartbreaking to think of all that had been withheld from us. We were taught falsely constructed narratives, to make artificial scarcity seem like a necessary struggle. Graeber demonstrated that the anthropologic record proves that early people used gift-economies, which relied on women to divvy-up resources among families in the community. Beyond that, they extended credit to each other and gave each other what they needed, knowing they would receive help in return.

Our distant ancestors understood that we were mutually indebted to each other. That our indebtedness to each other was the basis of community. Yet, as empires grew, and kings took over foreign lands, systems of debt-money were imposed by bankers. As the debt invariably choked the masses, debt-forgiveness or jubilees were proclaimed to keep societies functioning.

"Did you know," Sam asked, "that the colonists were heavily in debt? They were in search of financial freedom. It is the main reason they left England—this piece of information is curiously left out of textbooks."

"It is strange, Sam. Did you know that since the 1980s companies have focused less on making products and more on making loans or financing available to buy their products."

"I guess that's the wheels of the debt-machine turning. Grinding away, looking to create debt as our money as companies focus on developing loans instead of products."

"Look at General Motors," I suggested. "GM didn't go bankrupt for making bad cars or not keeping up with the marketplace. Their primary business wasn't making cars. It was making car loans or financing available for car purchases. When the banks collapsed from bad mortgages in 2008, GMAC, GM's financing arm, took

GM down because GM had become a bank, making endless bad car loans to sell cars, and well, to make money from the loans."

"Profits came from collecting the finance charges, Kristen. Maybe more than from actually selling cars."

"This is the reason so many stores push customers to open store credit cards, and entice them to use them. That is where stores really make their money."

"When debt is money we need lots of debt. It is the lifeline of the economy—no debt, no money. Not too much else matters."

"Sam, did you come to the part where David points out that societies in the past were subject to these money-as-debt systems, but ours is structured in an even worse way than theirs?"

"I did. This time there is no escape valve, or no safety net, to free borrowers without destroying savers."

Still feeling somewhat incredulous about this idea, I wanted to review it with Sam and see his reaction.

"All other societies, from Mesopotamia to the Middle Ages, had a way out, when the debt levels became unsustainable and threatened their collapse. Yet, today, our global institutions, like the IMF or the World Bank, protect lenders not the borrowers. In the past, borrowers were protected. The only escape route people have today, to combat the inequity and virtual slavery, is a revolt. That is unless we can change the system, or create a new one."

"That doesn't seem fair. Through this debt-money system, Kristen, we've set up the world to make people run at an exponential pace, an inhuman pace, manipulated by the seven imperatives that drive our lives—and demand that no one should ever default."

The train slowed, and the lights came on as we entered Penn Station. We got up quickly and gathered our things. The time had flown and it was shortly before eleven o'clock. We had about an hour to get to Pace University where David Graeber was speaking. Sam stretched while he put David's book in his knapsack. I had a feeling that if I wanted my book back, I was going to have to buy another one.

The auditorium was packed; full with a mixed crowd of all ages and walks of life. It was a friendly crowd as most were familiar with David's work and were his fans. David took the podium, a good-looking man in his early fifties. Well-spoken and provocative, he was skillful at prompting people to look at the world in new and insightful ways.

David began, "After Occupy Wall Street was evicted from Zuccotti Park, we tried every conceivable way of setting up a public place where we could gather. City officials changed the laws every day to outlaw everything we came up with. Basically, the First Amendment in the United States is now gone—quite an amazing reaction to a few guys sitting in the park. This shows you how afraid they are, how threatening real democracy is. We were democracy in action.

"We had time to consider our lives, the problems we experience and how we live as a community. We thought about the topics we would examine in a free society, and the topic of debt and money came up over and over. When we got down to it, we saw that the concept of money is just a promise we make to each other. It is the idea that we will make good on helping each other.

"This brought us to the fundamental question of what we owe each other. We concluded that we need to completely reimagine what we believe we owe each other. Thinking about what money is an important way to start that. The Bank of England wrote a report admitting that the mainstream economic point of view, that there is only so much money— not enough money to take care of society —is untrue. This philosophy, that mainstream economics promotes, is the basis for enforcing austerity and other devastating community cutbacks.

"The Bank of England turned conventional economics on its head when it acknowledged that money is created by banks when they make loans, that there is no limit to the money supply as having some finite quantity that makes us scrape by and live at its mercy, as we take away fundamental services from people. Yet, no politician that I know of has acknowledged this. There is a complete disparity in the way those who make laws talk about money compared with the way those who actually run the money system talk about money. They are totally opposite to each other.

"People who want to think about and create a viable economy need to talk about money as it actually works, not the way we have been led to believe it does. Once we admit we can create money as we choose, we have to ask ourselves what we want to do with it. What do we want to fund? It really is our choice to decide what kind of society we would like to create and support. We are not restricted by 'hard' choices and backed into corners as politicians tell us."

Sam poked my arm and whispered, "We don't have a limited amount of money like our politicians tell us? We don't have to make hard choices about what kind of health services, social security, and other social services the government can fund?"

I answered, "When the Bank of England let the cat out of the bag a few years ago, they acknowledged that governments who create their own currencies like the United Kingdom, or the United States, can create as much money as they want. So, no, we are not restricted by some finite number, instead we need to make sure that we create money for real work and the real services we want in society. Then, it's valid and legitimate."

"Why don't our politicians acknowledge this?"

"Good question."

We turned our attention back to David, who spoke of what happened to the quality of work in our society.

"We have to ask ourselves what kind of a society do we want to create. We see capitalism breaking down all around us. We can see this as a huge percentage of the workforce is sitting somewhere actually thinking, 'I don't do anything, I hope no one figures it out.' I estimate 20-30 % of all working people are thinking, 'We write up reports and have meetings about these reports.' These people don't actually *do* anything. And of course, there is a huge number of people employed doing things like making lunch, dry-cleaning clothes, or cleaning bathrooms for this huge number of people who don't do anything. Think about it, we have this huge number of people supporting a huge number of people who actually don't do anything! How can we have dignity in labor?

"Factory work is gone and hasn't been actually replaced by service work as we are told. Yet, administrative, and clerical work has quadrupled. One must ask oneself what is valuable in work to begin with? Paperwork and its bureaucracy have replaced value. You can see this in a Soviet society where they made up jobs to have a full employment number, using the bulk of people to 'make up' jobs to keep people working, we can understand it there. But capitalism is supposed to be the total opposite. How is this happening in capitalism? Private firms shouldn't be hiring people who don't do anything."

The crowd laughed an uncomfortable laugh at the irony. The fundamental tenants of capitalism were breaking down, and the root of its destruction was money-as-debt. There was an explosion of administrative jobs. Beyond doing busy work or having meetings about meetings, we spent our energy complying with ever-increasing regulations. With mind-numbing regulations as hoops to jump through and legal documents to comply with, companies tried to insulate themselves from lawsuits as the quality of products and services declined. It was the race-to-the-bottom to capture profits that no one won, as business became a riskier and riskier venture. It was no wonder stagnating administrative jobs dominated the workforce as we tried to cover our bottoms, as we set out to meet our bottom-line.

Worse, we as workers felt uninspired, unable to put creative energy to good use. We found the ability to think for ourselves and make heartfelt decisions corralled systematically. Employing common sense to the situations at hand seemed like a luxury, as the demands for rigid, robotic legal compliance to corporate rules dominated us with an iron fist. It, of course, was reinforced by the fear of losing our jobs. Where *was* the dignity in our labor? The possibility to engage in real work, work that fed the soul, connected us to life and to one another, had been destroyed. Work existed to feed the endless debt-monster driving our lives. Money-as-debt turned capitalism into neo-feudalism creating communist style labor. True work was good for the soul. Contributing to one another was important for our well-being. I couldn't help but think we were losing our souls, and for what?

David prepared to finish his talk and paused briefly to emphasize his last point.

"People say today, 'Oh, no, no one is going to have to work anymore,' complaining robots are going to take work away. Now, think about it. If there is ever a sign an economy was stupidly organized, this is it. What are we investing our lives doing? We need to unleash popular creativity. We need to set out in the direction pursuing a set of principles. The technology we need will emerge around that. I emphasize democracy as a way to define what we want. It's a means where we can decide for ourselves how to unleash creativity. To think about what sort of economy we would like to live in. We act as if ideas on this are scarce, that people are not imaginative. But this is not a normal, natural way to think. This is a result of a thirty-year campaign against the imagination. Why are we not hearing new ideas on how to recreate our society or solve our problems? Because 99% of people with new ideas are told to shut-up all the time. Once we are no longer told to stop thinking, the rest will take care of itself."

Sam and I joined the room in a standing ovation as David concluded. His unencumbered common sense was a breath of fresh air. We felt inspired and motivated to reimagine what kind of world we wanted to live in.

As we walked backed toward Times Square, I thought about David's point that we were not limited to the amount of money politicians kept telling us we were. Threatening us, day-in and day-out, that social security and healthcare were not sustainable and that we would eventually run out of money. Yet, the Bank of England, and even Alan Greenspan years before, disclosed this was not the case. This was something that I wanted to explore with Sam in greater detail.

"Look at Times Square," I said. "It's had a revival."

"I guess, Kristen," Sam said with some resignation in his voice. "It is not a revival. It is commercialization or the 'Disneyfication' of Times Square. Before the area became so depressed it was a center for theater, art, and entertainment. Making it more accessible is great, but it has become a car-free zone where millions of tourists are captive to advertisers. Zoning laws actually require billboards to cover all the surrounding buildings."

"Interesting, I see your point. The energy of these electric billboards is amazing—mesmerizing. Look there's an ad for Wells Fargo mortgage company flashing over the NASDAQ ticker."

Famous economist John Maynard Keynes warned about lending losing its moral intent. Oil tycoon J.P. Getty often repeated one of Keynes' quotes, "If you owe your bank a million dollars, you have a problem. If you owe your bank several hundred million dollars, your bank has a problem." Creating money-as-debt means if our big banks have a problem, we all have a problem. I shared this with Sam as the lights lit up our faces.

"It's true," Sam agreed. "Any money in savings is someone else's mortgage debt, college debt, car debt, or credit card debt, and the debt machine needs us to endlessly churn out more."

"All the money in savings," I added, "whether it's in secure state bonds, used to finance roads, or, in highly rated Ford or Walmart bonds, in pensions—it is someone else's debt. Stability and safety are dependent on the probability of others' ability to repay, which eventually becomes an impossibility. We are the 100%."

"Except for the billionaires, they are safe with enough insulation," Sam said with a smirk.

"Well," I said, "when the whole borrowing-repaying cycle fully breaks down, I think everyone with wealth in our dollars will be at risk. Everything starts to default, go bust, as the flow of the economy breaks down. Even the ultra-rich, the .001% of our population, are not excluded, no amount of money or power can protect them from the pitchforks."

Sam's face dropped as he looked at me intensely. I shared with him I was alluding to an article wealthy entrepreneur, Nick Hanauer wrote called, "The Pitchforks Are Coming...For Us Plutocrats." The article caused quite a stir as he described the undeniable inequity throughout our society. Worried, Hanauer urged his super rich counterparts to make an effort to get more money circulating. He feared, that sooner or later, the sheer numbers of people left out, enraged by the injustice, would revolt and attack them.

The problem was, of course, that money-as-debt created an unsustainable system where money did not flow where it was needed. As money concentrated into the hands of the few, even businesses with great products could not continue to sell their products because customers would simply lack the money to buy them. All businesses would suffer, even those run by the ultra-rich. They, too, lacking the understanding of how money-as-debt works, did not know *why* we were dealing with pernicious inequity. Instead, they could explain it with notions that they were smarter, created better luck for themselves, or merely dismiss other people's discontent as 'a case of sour grapes.' But the truth was that we each only had part of the picture in the money-as-debt scheme. In the end, we were all in debt to one another. Without people who bought our goods, we had nothing to offer. Likewise, when we focused on what life had not given us, we had yet to consider how much we benefitted from and depended on the work of others.

Sam looked sullen and his light-heartedness hadn't returned. His growing understanding, of how creating money-as-debt undermined the optimism and opportunity central to our cultural ethos, was taking a toll on him. He turned away from the billboards and adjusted his watch.

"It doesn't sound very hopeful, does it?" Sam sighed. "I can't imagine what will happen as inequity continues to grow."

"As it reaches new levels of disparity, the idea of pitchforks is something that will make very rich people pause and take another look at the system."

"It seems like we've been trying to save or fix a system that is working against all of us." Sam added, "How will we create a new way?"

A bright flash on the jumbo screen above One Times Square suddenly caught our attention. The screen filled with wobbling eggs. An Easter bunny hopped around and stopped to check them out. There was a small crack in one egg, then in two, and then they all started to rumble. Little beaks pecked their way through the shells and within moments the screen was filled with new baby chicks. They were shaking off their old world, venturing to explore the new one surrounding them. Sam looked at me as we shared the recognition.

"Look," I said, "to the baby chick, the shell is everything it knows, its source of well-being. It bumps up against it, finding something wrong with the order structuring its life. The chick tries to work around it, turning and repositioning. It doesn't want to lose its shell but each day the little chick grows, facing a troubling reality. It must peck, chipping away at all it ever knew. Otherwise, it will die. The nutrients that kept it alive have turned to toxins, as impending death looms compelling the chick to strike. Yet, the desire to live overrides any fear that could hold it back. Soon, the little bird finds himself in a new world."

"Right," Sam nodded. "The chick is equipped with what it needs to grow until it is ready to propel itself to the next level. If we tried to help it, it would die. It must be ready to come out on its own. Breaking the shell and pushing itself out strengthens it, makes it healthier, and resilient. No matter whether the shell is protector or terminator, it plays the key role in the chick successfully becoming who it is meant to be—unfolding perfectly in its own time."

"Sam, we are growing too, getting ready to break free into our new world. Maybe this is the maturing process life takes us through. As we begin to embody that we are both individual and inseparable at the same time, the 100%, we recognize our financial system is meant to self-destruct. It is meant to disintegrate because it is built on a worldview of imagined separation, using money-as-debt mechanics that cannot be sustained in a world where we are connected."

"Yes, as we step out of this old perspective and unleash our creativity, we can envision the kind of world we want it to be and our new systems will follow," Sam said, taking a deep breath as the sun began to shine brightly through the clouds.

8
DEBT TERRORISTS AND REVOLUTIONARIES

FAO Schwarz, the grand toy retailer, stood before us. This glorious high-end toy store first opened its doors in 1862. Sam and I ventured in and were immediately surrounded by a world filled with our distant childhood memories. A life-sized Indiana Jones, made from Legos, greeted me as I fondly examined his hat. Within moments Sam and I were lost in the candy cafe, spanning six thousand square feet, swirling with endless gummy bears, sweet n' sour fruits, and chocolates in every shape and size. As I lifted my head from the sea of display cases, I saw Sam motioning me to join him on the jumbo floor piano. Before I knew it, he and I were trying our own rendition of chopsticks. We were not very good, but we had a great time. We lost each other again until I found him at the cash register.

"What are you getting?" I asked.

"Monopoly. It's the eightieth-anniversary edition." Sam smiled and held up the game. "I always loved playing as a kid. My whole family did. I remember spending lots of nights playing the game."

"Me too. We played it a lot. I would beg my sister or anyone else I could find to play with me. My sister would usually humor me and play for a while until she couldn't take it anymore." I laughed remembering how I loved counting the money, and I just had to be that Scottie dog.

"You know, Charles Darrow, the inventor of the game, created it during the Great Depression," Sam shared. "He received a patent in 1935 and went to Parker Brothers to see if they would sell it. They turned him down saying it was too complicated, but FAO Schwarz was willing to sell it. It was such a hit at Christmas, that Parker Brothers went back to Darrow and signed him up. Before long, Monopoly was a raging success. Darrow was a heating repairman who lost his job during the Depression. He got the idea for the game, and worked day and night perfecting it. He ended up becoming a millionaire in the 1930s! In fact, Parker Brothers became a major player in the gaming industry on the profits they raked in by selling Monopoly. You know, Darrow's story, of how he rose from rags-to-riches, is a testimony of what has always made America the great land of opportunity."

"Well, Sam, it's a great story…but the only great invention in that story is that story itself," I said sadly not wanting to take the wind out of his sails.

"What? Are you serious?"

"Yes." I explained, "In fact, the game was created in the early 1900s by a woman named Elizabeth Magie. She was a highly educated, brilliant thinker, and money activist. She created the game to help people learn what happens when monopolies soak up all the money and destroy investment that would have gone into invention and innovation."

"Wow," Sam processed, "so the original game was created to teach us how monopolies destroy capitalism."

"The original version was called The Landlord's Game. In fact, people taught each other how to play, making their own versions using a piece of linen or oilcloth and simple crayons to draw the streets. It was something Elizabeth Magie took pride in as she didn't create the game to 'make money.' Instead, she hoped it would be a powerful tool to educate people and she encouraged them to pass it on to one another."

"Interesting. More families had electricity in their homes and had more time at night, so board games became very popular."

"You know, our great-great grandparents and their great-great grandparents understood how money is created and who was meant to control it. They knew how important this knowledge was."

"In just a short hundred years, people have long forgotten this..."

"Elizabeth Magie's game provided players two ways of playing," I explained, "either as monopolists or as competitors, as monopoly or as prosperity. When monopolists won monopoly, the rest were left bankrupt and when competitors won prosperity, wealth was created for everyone. She took out several patents and talked to Parker Brothers over the years. They were not interested in buying it until around the time they also bought Darrow's game. She sold her game to them for $500 with no future royalties."

"Boy, that doesn't sound like a good deal. Especially when you consider the fortune Darrow made."

"True," I agreed, "but she was happy at first because she thought it would be widely distributed and help people learn as they played."

"What happened to The Landlord's Game? I don't recall ever seeing it. Let alone hearing about it."

"In 1932, Parker Brothers purchased the rights from her, under the condition that they would continue to publish her game alongside Darrow's Monopoly. But they didn't put the official rules for prosperity in the game. People buying the game, who wanted to learn to play it as prosperity, had to contact Ms. Magie directly for the rules."

"Weird. Why would they market two similar games like this at the same time?"

"Good question, Sam, I guess we'll never know, but who knows how much they wanted to promote it because they almost immediately recalled it and pulled her game off the shelves. Sadly, almost every unsold copy was destroyed."

"That's terrible. That must have destroyed this woman, what a tragic irony."

"She became angry. She told newspapers that Darrow had appropriated her idea, that he basically stole it from her. Her work and dedication were lost for almost forty years. That is until in 1973, when an economics professor at San Francisco State University, Professor Anspach, created the Anti-Monopoly game. It was based on Elizabeth Magie's rules. Players could choose to be either monopolists or competitors, and see what happened. Parker Brothers didn't like that very much and sued him for copyright infringement. He spent the next ten years of his life fighting them in court. The case went all the way to the Supreme Court, and in the end, Professor Anspach won! Through his valiant efforts, Elizabeth Magie's work and her teachings were brought back out from the grave where they had been buried for years."

"Kristen, we played the game for hours and hours as children, as did those before us. Generation after generation we were encouraged to dominate others, the market place, and shut out the competition. We learned that this was the way to succeed in our capitalist system and that rising real estate prices were good, and that charging rent others paid us was king."

"Instead, monopolies destroy capitalism. They steer money away from innovation and starve industry. They leave little money to invest in real productivity. Rents and housing prices increase, and power is redistributed up-the-food-chain."

"Less money to put in infrastructure or things like education and healthcare," Sam added.

"Yes. Monopolies consolidate power. A few people can own the most important resources, everyone needs access to, privately. Producing neo-feudal societies, where a handful decides for everyone else."

"So, we have seen our economic textbooks written with a particular slant and our history rewritten repeatedly. Now, we see the games we played were retrofitted to teach a certain point of view?"

"Elizabeth Magie created other games too," I said, "and Parker Brothers bought them as well. In those days, there was even a popular game called Finance that circulated before Monopoly took over."

"Think about it, Kristen, the types of games people played, at the turn of the century, were games about prosperity and finance. They had a grasp on basic math skills. They were keenly aware of the impact borrowing money had on their lives, way more than we do. Today, people don't understand how credit cards work. That paying the minimum balance due every month does not get rid of the actual debt they owe. Instead, it encourages debt to grow. These basic skills aren't taught in school or reinforced in our culture anymore."

"It's a terrible contrast with what kids play today. Video games with sophisticated graphics, mesmerizing them and putting them in a trance. Encouraging them to fear, defend, and kill. They become desensitized to life. Their brains are overstimulated with chemicals these virtual world dramas generate, making real life less interesting."

"Meanwhile, there's so much social pressure for kids to play. If they don't join in the war games, they lose out on socializing with their friends. But, while they play, their attention spans are chopped into little bits, and undermine their ability to focus and concentrate. They need these skills to consider important issues which affect their lives!"

"One lesson everyone needs to learn is 'The Rule of 72,'" I stated emphatically.

"What is that?"

"It calculates how fast debt or savings double, based on the rate of interest earned. It is an effective tool to understand the power of compound interest. If you owe $10,000 and your credit card charges 18%, simply divide 18, the rate of interest, into the number 72. This shows that the $10,000 you owe doubles or becomes $20,000 in 4 years."

"Let me get this straight," Sam recounted, "when you divide the rate of interest into the number 72, you learn how fast debt will double. If you owe $10,000 at 10% interest, it will double in 7.2 years?"

"That's how it works. People need to know this when they carry a credit card balance. It can easily get out of hand with the power of compound interest, especially when interest rates are as high as they are on credit cards. But, of course, you have to wonder with a money-as-debt system running our lives—how dangerous it would be if people knew this tool."

As we walked along Bryant Park, we admired New York's beautiful Public Library. It was starting to get dark, and people were sitting outside enjoying the weather, ordering drinks and some casual, fun food-fare. It was festive leisure at its finest. We walked toward Penn Station to catch the train back to Boston as we came across a billboard-sized clock. It was rapidly rolling numbers higher and higher, up into the trillions, with the words 'Debt Clock' written across the top.

"What is that?" Sam looked at me alarmed.

"A wealthy real estate developer put a debt-clock here to show how our National Debt grows bigger—every second of the day. It gets a lot of attention and it's often displayed on TV, especially when politicians want to point out how broke the country is."

"That's pretty disturbing to watch," Sam said as he seemed uncomfortable witnessing the numbers count higher, one after the other. "Someone had to be pretty upset to put that here."

"It is meant to be alarming."

"No wonder everyone is so agitated by the national debt—and at the government." Sam grimaced. "Aggravated enough to put a big clock up there and ruin a pleasant walk."

We stood there for a moment, and stared as the numbers rolled higher, one after the other. It was unnerving to watch. It reminded me of the non-stop ranting we heard over the years and how it had only gotten louder. David Walker, former US Comptroller General, went on endlessly, about how broke we were. Telling us we needed to raise taxes to levels we had never paid before, that we needed to cut total spending by unthinkable amounts or further mortgage our children's future.

Sam and I found some humor in the irony that no one in Washington agreed on anything, except for the debt. Then they echoed each other with one warning after the other. Sam and I took turns sharing some of our favorites: "The government's big debt problem is irresponsible" ... "We take out a credit card from the bank of China, in the name of our children, driving up our national debt" ... "A government that spends more than it takes in doesn't add up" ... "It's immoral" ... "The debt burden is America's biggest problem."

But there was so much more to be said about the national debt and it wasn't easy to accept because it went against everything we heard before. So, I took a breath and began to share the truth with Sam.

"Well, it certainly does seem to make sense," I started. "After all, you and I have budgets, we have a certain amount of income and we need to make sure that we are not spending more than we bring in. The city of New York has the same issue, as does F.A.O. Schwarz. Our surpluses, or money in savings, and our deficits, or debts, matter to us. So, when we think of the federal government, why wouldn't we think it would be the same thing? *But, it is Not.* This ranting on the national debt is a misunderstanding of the money system and how it works."

"Are you saying the debt clock and our politicians are missing something? It's not true?"

"Yes. In fact, all these people, no matter how sincere or well-intended they may be, act as debt-terrorists. They do a good job of scaring us. All of us. Their argument makes sense, and it sounds rational because we think of our own lives. But, this idea is flawed, and built on a misconception of how a sovereign federal government works. They terrorize the public into believing the federal government is broke. This poisonous impression creates some pretty terrible things. Like attempting to get rid of social security, making healthcare impossible, or the student-debt issue unresolvable. Of course, rebuilding our roads, bridges, or other infrastructure, like securing our energy grid, becomes laughable, an impossible luxury, within the context the 'national debt problem' is framed."

A few years ago, Congressman Paul Ryan questioned Alan Greenspan, then chairman of the Federal Reserve Bank, about the need to privatize social security. He suggested that the country would run out of money and not be able to fulfill its commitments to retirees. Ryan looked for Greenspan to agree, to say the government would not have enough money for social security. But, in fact, to Ryan's chagrin, Greenspan told him the opposite. He informed Ryan that the United States Government would always be able to create as much of its money as it wanted. Greenspan suggested the real question was *how* the money created was invested. He urged Congress to question whether the money created was invested to develop industry and productive capacity, so when people received their social security checks, there would be goods and services available for them to buy.

This is what David Graeber referred to when he pointed out that the politicians, who make our laws, and the people, who run our money system, contradict one another about how much money we have. Sadly, we are subjected to politicians endlessly telling us that the country is limited by its tax revenue and can only borrow so much before going broke. But, Greenspan affirmed the opposite when he told Ryan the country could always create as many dollars to pay off any loans it owed in dollars, running out of money was not the problem. The real issue was what we did with the money that we created. Was it invested it in a productive way?

This idea was new to Sam, as it was to most of us. He wanted me to clarify.

"Our politicians say the government has a finite amount of money to use, which it gets from taxes. To spend more than that, it must borrow," Sam stated, "and it can only borrow so much before it goes bankrupt?"

"This would be true if we were limited to some amount of gold,"

I answered. "They say the government is limited by the taxes it brings in and to spend more it must borrow from someone else."

"This clock is ticking down to Doomsday," Sam checked, "to the day when the debt is unpayable?"

"Yes. It suggests if we don't pay the debt down, the interest payments will strangle us. Therefore, we must tax more, spend less, and give up the social services we need and want. Otherwise, life will get worse for the generations to come."

"If we follow Walker's advice," Sam reasoned, "we will have less money to live our lives with, even though it is already a struggle for most, and we have to get rid of our social programs and safety nets just because we owe debt. That's truly frightening."

"The entire idea is frightening," I agreed. "It takes me back to a time when I was seven years old. It was a late summer afternoon, school was out, and I found my favorite cartoon, *The Jetsons*, was coming on TV. Jumping with joy, I ran into the kitchen to get a big bowl of ice cream before it started. Midway, I overheard my father on the patio discussing the national debt with his best friend from high school. As I heard his friend say, 'Well one day the debt will be un-payable.' I stopped in my tracks. My heart started to pound, and I thought to myself, 'What? What will we do?' I was stunned and completely forgot about *The Jetsons*. Then, I heard my father laugh in a gentle, reassuring way and say, 'We will pay it off. We owe the debt to ourselves, we will create the money and pay it off. We will recognize it is all in our control and we will simply pay it off.' I relaxed, breathed again and went on to get that ice cream."

"But, we don't owe the money to ourselves, we owe it to China," Sam said.

"We hear that all the time, don't we?" I offered. "We never stop to think what the national debt is. We only hear what a destructive thing it is and yet, the national debt is United States Treasury bonds. These bonds are safer than bank CDs, which are Insured by the Federal Deposit Insurance Corporation, or FDIC. Treasury bonds (pieces of the national debt) are purchased by the most conservative investors, who are either wealthy enough to not need a lot of return on their savings or pension and insurance funds which need to invest in the safest investments possible. China owns only about 7% of the treasury bonds, which means China only owns 7% of our debt. The vast majority of treasuries are owned by US Investors, insurance companies, and retirement funds."

"Wow, I've gotten such a different picture from the news and politicians screeching that China owns us. I had the impression they owned at least 90% of our debt."

"Our beliefs about the government's money contradict one another. First of all, we think the government makes fiat money, meaning it creates as much money as it wants by decree, or just by issuing it. Despite this idea, we believe the government is a household like you and me, that it is limited by the revenue it takes in from tax dollars and beyond that, it has to borrow its money supply. Now, these are conflicting ideas because essentially if the government has a printing press in the basement, why would it need to borrow money?"

"I always thought the government had the power to create unlimited money just by deciding to," Sam stammered with a confused look on his face.

"Technically speaking, the government could do it but remember that power was given to the privately owned Federal Reserve Bank in 1913. That's when the government's ability to create money debt-free was transferred to our privately owned central bank. Instead of creating debt-free US Dollars, we borrow Federal Reserve Notes from the Federal Reserve Bank. The private bank lends our money to our Government. In essence, we, as a people, rent our money supply from private banks."

"Why would the government, representing the wealth and work of over 330 million people, borrow its money supply from a private bank instead of issuing it itself?"

"A good question, Sam. It is critical we reexamine the role the government is supposed to play in the economy, what its debt is meant to be, and how it is utterly and totally different from any debt we are familiar with."

"How is the government's debt different from our debt?"

"We understand sound financial advice that suggests you and I should save and not spend more than we earn. We are taught to take as little debt as possible and do our best to pay it off as soon as possible. It seems like common sense to apply this same advice to our national debt. But, applying this advice to the government is applying it to the wrong model. Government debt doesn't work this way."

"Government debt doesn't work that way? What do you mean?"

"The government isn't an equal player in the game of the economy," I explained. "It is the inventor of the game. It makes the rules. Even if we feel like we've lost the government's power to corporations, the Constitution exists. It is up to us to make sure it is followed. When we don't give our power away to special interests, we, the people, as a collective, are the government. We could, in fact, pay the debt off or any portion of it with dollars we create, anytime that it gets too burdensome. No one could stop us. We are the only ones who could stop ourselves."

"But, isn't that inflationary?!" Sam interrupted abruptly.

His reaction gave me pause. We are so conditioned by the debt-terrorists, that most of us react the same way Sam did. We hear the "inflationary argument" so often, that we repeat it ourselves, even without deeply questioning it. More often than not, we hear it accompanied with condescending laughter. The ridicule works quickly and effectively to shut down these conversations. We are left afraid to entertain new ideas about the government debt for ourselves, instead we resign ourselves and defer to pundits. This same cultural shaming has been used to stop people from examining what money is and our money system, itself. I thought about how difficult it was to unwind these concepts; as Mark Twain said, "It's easier to fool people than to convince them that they have been fooled." Sam wanted me to answer his question and was growing uncomfortable at the implications of what I suggested.

"So, what are you saying?" Sam asked. "That our politicians lie when they tell us we are hostage to the debt, that we must find a way to pay it down?"

"I believe most politicians don't know any better," I attempted to reassure Sam. "But, if there are politicians who do understand how government debt works with our money system, and if they tried to share it with the American people, I think they fear being run out of town, chewed up, and spit out as people attack them for being idiots. Let's get on the train, and look at this idea of inflation a little later. It will be easier to understand when we go back and look at what the founding fathers knew about debt and money."

Penn Station was crowded already. We joined the pack of people clustered on the central floor and fixed our gaze on the display board overhead. We waited for our train to arrive, and within a few minutes, the board flashed 'Track 17 East Boarding Boston.' We hurried down the escalator to the platform. As we entered the car, we found seats with a table and opened Sam's new edition of Monopoly. Sam set up the board and handed me the Scottie dog token, while choosing the top hat token for himself. He assumed the role of the banker and dealt us each seven neatly stacked piles of colored Monopoly money.

"Look, Sam," I pointed out. "See how the game is set up? The money is supplied and issued first—before the game begins."

"There isn't any debt either," Sam said, "the money is ready to fund our accounts to get the game going."

"The colonists understood this idea. As you mentioned earlier, they were heavily indebted and were in search of financial freedom. They came to America to get a fresh start."

"What did they use to trade goods and services with one another?"

"Well, they needed money but metal coins were scarce, there weren't any established mines and England forbade them from forging their own coins. What few coins they had went to pay debt payments owed to British merchants. So, they drafted beautiful parchment certificates called Colonial Scrip and issued them."

"They created money without debt to the British Crown or any foreign bankers?"

"Yes," I answered. "The colonial governments printed up the Scrip or bills and declared them legal tender. Colonists could make purchases or use them to settle obligations amongst themselves. The most successful Scrip were distributed from land banks owned by the governments."

"How did they disseminate the Scrip?"

"Land banks were chartered in all of the colonies. First in South Carolina, in 1712, and last in Virginia, in 1755. The governments used land as collateral and to determine the quantity of Scrip needed. Whether someone owned a piece of land and wanted to have money to use, or whether someone wanted to borrow to buy a piece of land, the quantity of paper scrip money was issued in the amount equal to the value of the land."

"Sounds like a simple concept."

"Yes, it was an excellent way to begin a new money system, to fortify faith in the new money, and temper how many to release, as it was tied to real value that existed. They were no longer stymied by a lack of gold or silver coins. Benjamin Franklin liked the system because the value of land did not fluctuate much in those days, and the paper currency couldn't be exported to foreign countries and drained away from the people."

"Did they have a way of adjusting the money supply?"

"Yes, this was, and still is, the key issue," I said slowly with added emphasis. "They understood the quantity of money in circulation had to match the productive demand for it. More or less could be issued allowing the quantity of money to be flexible or elastic, to increase or decrease with the current ebbs and flows of people's productivity."

"Too little money circulating in society seems worse than too much," Sam added.

"Especially for people working and contributing in society. Keeping the money supply too small, or out of reach of most people, is the way monopolies, or a few people, capture power and have dominated populations throughout history."

"How did the colonists adjust the amount of money circulating?"

"Money often had an 'expiry' date, so it would be retired after a certain amount of time. New money could be issued to match demand, and existing money could be drained out with a short-term tax, if needed, allowing the money supply to be monitored and controlled. The quantity of money in circulation was kept in balance with productivity."

"This means the colonial government used taxes to control how much money was circulating," Sam said as he slowly digested the concept.

"Right, taxes were a mechanism used to drain excess money when needed. Taxes were not originally created as a source of revenue. Remember how David Graeber explained that kings used taxes to motivate people to accept their money, and get them to take care of their standing armies, not to create revenue to run kingdoms. Used as a tool of manipulation—for better or worse, for specific means and ends."

"Ah, the money kings created or taxes levied had nothing to do with providing the rulers income. In fact, they created coins and levied taxes as bait, compelling people to act in ways they wanted."

"Yes, and effortlessly. Issuing a tax, payable only in the currency issued, makes people need and accept the currency. Interestingly, we did not have a permanent federal income tax until 1913, the same year that the Federal Reserve banking system was instituted."

"When the income tax was payable only in new Federal Reserve Note dollars, people instantly needed them," said Sam.

"The main point is that governments able to issue their own money supply do not need money *from* the people to operate. Just like the 'banker' in Monopoly doesn't need to create debt and take money out of players' pockets to get the game started, or to keep it going. He creates the money and deals it to each player. Originally, the government was meant to issue the money and make sure the *right* amount was in the economy."

"Like the colonists understood," Sam said, "the king issued a certain amount of coin, the right amount, to keep the people in business and armies fed. The right amount so people could participate, and that everything flowed. Likewise, the banker in Monopoly doles out the right amount to keep the game going, making sure there is $200 to collect every time we pass GO."

"The colonists created the money supply and spent it into circulation, attempting to equal the amount of money with the real productive capacity and needs of the colonists. The colonial governments didn't go into debt to issue money for the people to use."

"If the colonial governments created their own money, the governments didn't have to borrow the money from bankers. There was no interest to pay," Sam gathered. "No taxes to collect to pay interest because the government was the issuer of the money. They simply needed to balance the amount of money with the real productive capacity of the colonists."

"Right, the problem of inflation which is blindly linked to governments creating their own money supply is a red herring. Inflation doesn't arise from creating one's own money supply, it comes from maintaining too much money in circulation. And conversely, which doesn't get discussed enough—deflation comes from maintaining too little money in circulation."

Watching Sam's reaction reminded me of my own when I first learned this. The more time I spent thinking about it, the more obvious and simple it became. The original role of the government was to oversee that the right amount of money was in circulation, like the king of the kingdom or creator of the game, plain and simple. Money, itself, didn't mean anything more to the government than tickets its citizens used as a tool of exchange.

I shared this idea with others from time-to-time; drawing a lower-case "t," I explained the federal government issuing the currency was on the vertical line and everyone else was on the horizontal line. Sam, my neighbors, the fifty-state governments, corporations, and I were players playing in the game, where economic surpluses and deficits were real. We did not have the ability to create money by spending it without debt, and we quickly felt the consequences if we didn't have an income, take care of our budgets, and pay off our debt. Whereas the federal government was the intended banker, the moderator overseeing the economy of the players, not a player in the game. If the players did not have enough money, it was the federal government's job to create more money and spend it into circulation. If there was too much money relative to the people's capacity, its job was to create a temporary tax to take the excess out.

I took Sam back through colonial times to show him that Benjamin Franklin understood this. In fact, Franklin and the colonists knew their most important role was to be able to control the amount of money in circulation. It was not what backed the money, like gold or silver, that mattered. Instead, the true power of money was in controlling *how much* money circulated. Their job was to ensure the quantity of money equaled the productivity of the people, which determined whether freedom or enslavement prevailed. Just like keeping a set of scales balanced, keeping the money supply balanced with the productivity of the people was the most important task.

In *A Modest Enquiry into the Nature and Necessity of Paper Currency*, Franklin described the success Pennsylvania and Massachusetts experienced when the amount of paper money circulating was properly controlled to match the people's needs. Not all colonies were so diligent. Depending on how well they managed their money determined whether they thrived or struggled because balancing the quantity of Scrip with their productive capacity was critical. Dispersing too many Scrip, or withdrawing too few, depreciated their value as inflation ensued. Likewise, if the amount in circulation fell below what was needed, trade was obstructed and deflation rose. Nonetheless, they stumbled upon the greatest power of self-governance and self-determination: the self issuance of money.

Yet, the British considered the colonial Scrip system to be full of mischief and something they intended to control. The British

Parliament passed the Currency Acts of 1751 and1764, obstructing the colonies from issuing their own money. The colonists suffered, and by the end of 1765, Francis Fauquier, the Governor of Virginia, remarked, "circulating Currency [had] grown very scarce [as] people were distressed for Money of any kind." The British hurt their own local economies as the colonists no longer had money to purchase goods from them. Being able to control the quantity of the money supply is what allowed the colonies to become empowered and flourish. They were alarmed as they lost the right to regulate their own financial affairs, as Parliament took full control of their banking system. It was unacceptable, an appropriation of their natural right to govern themselves. Making matters worse the Stamp Act arrived next, which mandated that colonists pay sales tax on all paper goods such as newspapers, playing cards, marriage licenses and wills, affecting everyone regardless of status. Stamped paper was required to make these goods which could only be purchased in gold or silver, draining what little money was circulating as poverty continued to grow worse.

Sam was wide-eyed soaking in our history as he connected the dots.

"So, like Elizabeth Magie and people playing The Landlord's Game, the colonists were forced to stop playing prosperity, as they found themselves in the monopoly game."

"The British debt-based money system reasserted itself."

"What happened next?"

"As their debt-based money system took full control, the money supply was cut in half. This instigated tremendous anger and ultimately resulted in the American Revolution. It was too early in the world's history for the world's powers to simply accept and make way for empowered, far-away colonists to control their own money systems. These monarchal powers had been creating order and the sense of stability for centuries."

"Whoa," exclaimed Sam as the realization dawned on him, "This was the real cause of the American Revolution in 1776. It wasn't just tax on tea or the pursuit of religious freedom."

Indeed, many think that Franklin believed that Parliament's termination of the colonists' money freedom was the principal cause of the American Revolution more so than any other act the British took. In 1883, Peter Cooper, Vice-President of the New York Board of Currency, wrote in his book *Ideas for a Science of Good Government,* "After Franklin had explained...to the British Government...the real cause of [the colonies'] prosperity they immediately passed laws, forbidding the payment of taxes in that money. This produced such great inconvenience and misery to the people, that it was the principal cause of the Revolution. A far greater reason for a general uprising, than the Tea and Stamp Act, was the taking away of the paper money."

"What happened, did the colonists reinstate their money system?" Sam asked.

"Yes, when the colonists needed to pay for the Revolutionary War they created their own debt-free money called Continentals."

"Continentals?" Sam paused and looked at me. "They became worth almost nothing, right? They printed too many and destroyed them?"

I loved his questions. They were insightful, and direct. He asked the questions we all needed to ask if we had the opportunity. But, of course, that would only happen if we had the chance to learn how our money was really created. Sam's point that Continentals were ruined by printing too many is where much of the confusion about governments issuing their own money and inflation comes from. I wanted to clarify this issue with great care, breaking the information down into key points to remember.

First, it was important to understand that the colonists' Scrip money worked so well that it empowered the colonists to control their own destiny, and it allowed their communities to flourish. They were not dependent on getting loans from Great Britain or other foreign powers for their economies to grow, when there was real productive demand for money. They could issue and withdraw their own Scrip from circulation in the amount needed, as needed. If they were conscientious of how much money was required as

Pennsylvania was, they prospered. If they weren't they caused instability, as Rhode Island did. In 1781, Alexander Hamilton estimated that metal coins made up only twenty-five percent of the money supply, and that on average each person had just two dollars in coins, without the Colonial Scrip money they would never have survived, let alone thrived.

Second, the great European monarchal and lending powers were aware of how much freedom this power to control one's money supply held. The world wasn't quite ready for this flattening of power structures, and it wasn't in the interest for those keeping the order to yield to the colonies' ability to create their own debt-free money. They feared that it would be a matter of time before the people in Europe sought to set themselves free as well. Debt-free money was a danger that needed to be eradicated. They knew the quantity of money in circulation needed to match the real productive capacity of the people, so by inflating the money supply they sought to ruin America's economy and win the war. Like David and Goliath, without the technology of today, Great Britain had a phenomenal advantage over the ragtag colonial armies and people themselves. The British undertook an enormous counterfeiting campaign as they sent ships to America stocked with printing presses, producing as many fake Continentals as they could. They gave the new money to anyone and everyone for pennies on the dollar. They inflated the money supply massively and successfully disrupted the balance the colonists labored to create. It seemed to work. They destroyed the value of the money, but not the determination of the colonists.

Nonetheless, the battle to control the money supply continued to rage on even after the Revolutionary War. In fact, it has persisted throughout the history of the United States, and still presses on today, as the topic remains riddled with confusion. During short periods of time, the people secured the power to control the quantity of money and access to the supply. This idea—that it is the right of the people of the nation to be able to issue the nation's money debt-free—has been conflated with the idea of inflation. Instead, money was intended to be issued *debt-free* on the national level, and the critical matter was keeping the quantity issued balanced with the changing productive capacity of the economy. Power hungry people and their special interests have kept this idea shrouded in perplexity in order to siege the right to create nations' monies, indebt countries, and, ironically, keep the money supplies too small.

I took Sam through a deeper review of our monetary history, so he could see how *this*—the greatest power—of issuing and controlling the quantity of the money supply was the back story of all history, and what we needed to comprehend in order to truly find freedom and secure our liberties. Thomas Jefferson, Andrew Jackson, and Abraham Lincoln championed the people's cause. As did many other courageous and noble people, like the great congressman from Nebraska, William Jennings Bryan. But those looking to control and limit the money supply for their own interests did not give up.

In 1782 to 1791, the British bankers were able to establish a privately owned central bank in new America. Capitalized with $10 million, $8 million of which came from foreign private investors. It was surreptitiously named the Bank of North America, implying the bank was owned by the people. Instead, the bank created the nation's money and lent it back to the people—at interest. Thomas Jefferson opposed the bank, as he suspected that it created a monopoly for private financiers, merchants, and their creditor interests, subjugating farmers and the needs of the producing public. He wanted to terminate the bank during his presidency but his term ended in 1809 and the charter did not renew until 1811. The renewal drew a contentious debate as most Americans wanted to disband it.

It was rumored that the British bankers warned if the bank's charter was not renewed there would be war. It was not, and within five months the War of 1812 ignited. By 1814, the British had burned down the White House and the Capitol building. As I recounted this to Sam, I remarked that I often forgot about the War of 1812, as it had always seemed odd to me that young America went back to war with England so soon after the Revolutionary War. But within the context of the British wanting to control the American money system, it seemed more plausible.

In 1816, there was another attempt to install a privately owned central bank. James Madison who had long been against the idea of the Second National Bank reluctantly signed the act to establish it, as debt from the war soared. In January of 1817, the bank opened, capitalized with $35 million. Only 20% of it was government owned, while the remaining 80% was owned by private interests. There was widespread discontent against the bank as it extended credit too quickly, created bubbles and subsequent panics, and drove the economy into steep recessions. Public opinion mounted against the bank as it cut the number of circulating banknotes in half, called-in loans early, and did not have enough gold and silver to meet redemptions. Amidst worsening depressions, deflation and high unemployment, the people were unhappy.

By 1828, Andrew Jackson arrived and took the issue of the bank head on. In 1832, Jackson was reelected and vetoed the bank's charter renewal. The bank president, Nicholas Biddle, threatened to further contract lending, call in loans, and cause a deeper depression if the veto wasn't overturned. Biddle was hoping for a backlash against Jackson, but the lack of money caused the economic depression he threatened, and reinforced support for Jackson's case that the bank was created to serve the interests of wealthy financiers and not the American people. Jackson cursed the bankers as he said, "You are a den of vipers. I intend to rout you out and by the eternal God, I will rout you out."

Jackson was courageous. He paid the debt off that the nation had accumulated from borrowing money from the bank. He left an important warning for posterity. "The bold effort the present bank made to control the government, the distress it had wantonly produced, are but premonitions of the fate that awaits the American people should they be deluded into a perpetuation of this institution or the establishment of another like it." Attempts were made on Jackson's life. Would-be assassin Richard Lawrence, shot two loaded pistols directly at him and they both misfired, one after the other. It must have been Providence that kept Jackson alive. The bravery and courage of so many before us was an unending source of strength and encouragement, as they tirelessly held onto the noble ideas they knew to be true.

Twenty-five years later, Abraham Lincoln found himself in the midst of the money sovereignty battle. America was still the greatest threat to the hierarchical powers of the world—the European monarchies and their bankers. France and England hoped to divide and conquer America. Lincoln wanted to keep the country united and focus on its development. Yet, he didn't have the money to fight the war. France and England offered him money at sabotaging rates of 24% to 36% interest, a deal dead on arrival. His Treasury Secretary Salmon P. Chase introduced a solution: debt-free paper notes as "lawful money and a legal tender in payment of all debts, public and private, within the United States." It was a brilliant new idea, or more appropriately, the return of an old one. They created and issued debt-free national currency called greenbacks. As a child, I remembered hearing about "greenbacks."

"Is that where the dollar's nickname greenback comes from?" Sam asked.

"Yes," I explained, "Abraham Lincoln signed off on creating greenbacks to help pay for the war, dollars printed with green ink on the back. It was government debt-free money 'legal tender.' Almost one-hundred years later, Chase took a page out of the colonists' playbook. Lincoln was reluctant to do so at first, but without issuing greenbacks the war would have been lost and the country divided."

"That's incredible," Sam remarked.

"Not only was the union saved, but a great economic expansion boomed. The steel industry burgeoned, the Pacific Railway Act brought the East and West together, the Land-Grant Colleges Act provided opportunities for industrial classes, and funded new machinery for farming. The Homestead Act provided ownership of land to anyone willing to cultivate it. Lincoln was in favor of every man having a home."

"Being able to issue debt-free money and control the amount of it makes all the difference to the wellbeing of a country."

Despite this victory, the battle to regain private control of the money supply reemerged with new vigor after Lincoln's assassination in 1865. The British sent private bank lobbyists, armed with millions of dollars, to persuade Congress to eliminate Greenbacks, and to "oppose anything that would restore the government issue of debt-free money." They knew debt-free money would interfere with their ability to control the money supply, and that the future of their debt-based money system depended on eliminating it. In order to recoup control, bankers were encouraged to reduce credit in general by calling-in loans early, and refusing to make new loans. They foreclosed on farmers, forcing them to return as tenants to rent their own land, spurring one another on as they bragged they could take any farm at any price. American families and, particularly, farmers were bankrupted by reducing the quantity of money in circulation.

Greenbacks were not the only form of money targeted to be extinguished, silver money was also under attack as President Ulysses S. Grant signed the Coinage Act of 1873 which discontinued the minting of silver dollars. Nicknamed the "Crime of '73," it reduced the money supply further, produced financial panics, and a deep depression. The intensified suffering increased the demand for more Greenbacks, the return of silver money, and formed the National Greenback Party. Instead, in 1875, the Resumption Act passed which retired existing Greenbacks. This created so much contention that, by 1878, the Greenbackers won fourteen seats in Congress, but they failed to reinstate Greenback money. The Bland-Allison Act passed the same year, which restored the coinage of limited amounts of silver bringing some relief. But the campaign to end silver continued for the rest of the century, and finally succeeded with the passage of the Gold Standard Act in 1900.

As Sam and I looked at our money history, we discovered *why* history repeated itself, as the same game was used over and over. As long as money was created as a limited thing that was scarce, made easy to borrow for periods of time, driving up the prices of homes and farms—creating economic booms until the debt load was too big or the money supply was made too small, the bust ensued. Life wasn't complicated or hard to understand, the plot driving the events we witnessed was quite simple.

Sam shook his head.

"As the money supply was confined to gold, it was reduced by 84% and caused unprecedented suffering."

"That's unfathomable! Everything must have come to a standstill," Sam speculated.

It *was* unfathomable. The economy was paralyzed as the money was taken away. The private bankers who controlled nations for hundreds of years, had the United States firmly back under control. The American people could not break free as financial panics continued, and the people suffered more and more as money circulated less and less. The battle that birthed the nation carried on. From the beginning, America fought to maintain her right to create her own money.

Despite the unrelenting challenges, the people did not give up. William Jennings Bryan, one of history's brilliant forgotten heroes of the late 1800's and early 1900's, worked for the people's right to issue money. Bryan said, "Those who oppose us tell us that the issue of paper money is a function of the bank and that the government ought to go out of the banking business. I tell them that the issue of money is a function of the government and that the banks should go out of the governing business."

In 1913, when the Federal Reserve Act was proposed, bankers appeared as though they wanted to work with Bryan, and seemed willing to create a central bank that issued debt-free money by the government. The legislation was presented right before Christmas and it was cryptically written. As it turned out, the new central bank would create the money *as a debt of the government owed to the*

Federal Reserve Bank, which was, and still is, owned by a consortium of private commercial banks.

It seemed William Jennings Bryan was outmaneuvered. The government did not create the money. Instead, that power went to The Federal Reserve Bank, who created it, and then lent it to the government. So, not only was our money created by borrowing mortgages, and other debt from commercial banks, but the Federal Government, whose sovereign right it was to create the money supply, now, borrowed its money-as-debt too. Thomas Edison pointed out how the American people were used. He said, "If our nation can issue a bond, it can issue a dollar bill. The element that makes the bond good, makes the dollar good. It is absurd to say our country can issue $30 million in bonds, but not $30 million in currency. Both are promises to pay, but one fattens the usurers. And the other helps the people."

Sam looked at the *Monopoly* money still on the table and said, "The government creates treasury bonds, or debt, in exchange for Federal Reserve notes or dollars. We create debt so the Federal Reserve Bank can lend us *our* money. This doesn't make sense."

"This is the reason Henry Ford said if the people understood the banking and money system, there would be a revolution before the morning arrived."

"Money should be created by and for the people. If you stop to think of it, the credit that the money represents is the work and effort of the people," Sam affirmed.

"Right, without people's productive capacity money has *no* value —whether a lump of gold, a sheet of paper, or a digit on the screen."

"So, we are back to where the colonists started. We managed again to let go of our right to create debt-free money. Important social programs are on the chopping block—along with tax increases. Politicians tell us we don't have enough money, regardless of how productive we can be. But, it is our money to create—it comes from *our* output."

"During the financial crisis, Sam, our money supply was reduced by 40% in just one year. Compare that to the Great Depression where the money supply was reduced by 48%. The quantity of money fell dramatically and—disproportionately to our productive capacity. Today, we don't have enough money in circulation where real people are working."

"Money suddenly evaporated during the financial crisis, despite the fact that people were willing to work, and others needed their services. But everything collapsed because the amount of money in circulation evaporated. We are living the same scenario that Benjamin Franklin witnessed when the British bankers reduced their ability to self-issue money."

"To those who made the way before us, it seems we have lost our way, our history, and the recognition of what is going on. The government could create money to pay down the debt, yet people in their ignorance scream 'inflation!' before any other idea can be considered.

It all seemed a tragic irony to me. I recalled the many times I shared this perspective with others trying to allay their fears, as they worried about what they heard on TV about our unpayable debt. I would do my best trying to find an effective analogy to capture the inaneness of our created predicament. I shared that it was like being in a house that was on fire, and as we gathered water to put it out, someone took it away warning that we might cause a flood as we continued to watch it burn. I shared my frustration with Sam.

"The trouble is the thinking is ingrained," Sam considered.

"We are so used to thinking of government debt as our own debt, when it is really the opposite. We can't get out from under the mixed-up thinking."

"Kristen, the question is— how do we change people's thinking?"

"We have to relearn what those before us knew. Then, we could create debt-free money, and not borrow it at interest. Like Andrew Jackson, we could pay off the national debt if we wanted to. Technically and legally, it can be done today. If enough people understood this and let common sense prevail. We have to extract ourselves from the brainwashing of the fear of inflation, and see that how much we paid off and how quickly would be determined by keeping the amount of money balanced with our productive capacity."

"But, how will enough people learn this?" Sam asked, "Look at how our monetary history has been marginalized, edited, and changed. Buried in the shadows."

"Without our history, we've lost the plot and left the decision making to others."

"What would happen if someone with enough power created enough debt-free dollars, then paid off all or some portion of the debt?"

"More than likely there would be hysteria on the news. The hysteria would hammer the markets and the dollar in the short-run. But it would all calm down as the debt burden was released and the economy freed. Again—we have to extract ourselves from the stronghold the fear of inflation creates, and simply regulate how much debt we pay off and how quickly—by determining the quantity of new money we need relative to the volume of our productive capacity."

"Hmm..," Sam mused.

"We could fix this tomorrow, if we wanted, by executive order," I interjected, "The President could simply issue debt-free money in the public's interest, rather than bank borrowed money at compound interest. It would be the pace of how it was done that would matter, making sure it was in balance with our real productivity."

"Imagine that the government doesn't *have* to borrow? The right to create its own money is its single greatest power."

"It *is*," I said slowly. "Creating and issuing its own money is what makes a nation sovereign. A sovereign nation is a nation where the people rule themselves. When a nation loses its ability to create its own money it can no longer be ruled by its people."

"This truth has been lost in history. We don't need to have a national debt. We don't need to borrow money. Paying off the treasury debt would not necessarily lead to inflation, it's how it is done —we need to keep the quantity of money in balance."

"A nation properly issuing its own debt-free money is the single most significant ability it can maintain."

"Being able to issue and control the quantity of money in circulation is the real power in society."

"Yes, Sam, the more you look, the more you see it's the means by which our economy and our political systems are largely regulated. This is why when we blame the government for anything, we have to look behind the wizard's curtain to see who is at the levers of control. It's not that our Constitutional Republic doesn't work, it's that we can't have one without the power to create our money."

"It is our money after all," Sam emphasized.

"Yes," I agreed. "It's our money after all." I opened my bag and took out a DVD and a new book for Sam.

"What are these?" He asked as he eagerly reached for them.

"The movie is *The Secrets of Oz*, by Bill Still and *The Public Bank Solution* is a book written by Ellen H. Brown. Both Ellen and Bill have researched monetary history and offer a solution as how the public could influence the money supply."

Sam turned to read the back covers and flipped through the pages as the train pulled into Back Bay station. It was late and already dark, and yet we hadn't noticed the time pass. We were engrossed uncovering the truth lost in our forgotten history; lifted and encouraged by those who came before us. They lived with the same confusion and challenges we did, and remained committed, even, as they stumbled in the dark. They held onto the keys that led to freedom and prosperity; they were a beacon of truth. They shone the light so brightly, that their glimmer could still be seen by those to come long after they were gone, and with such passion that those distant future hearts could reignite with the knowing of all their possibilities.

9
SURRENDERING TO QUIET WARFARE

It was Patriot's Day in Massachusetts, the third Monday in April. Or as it was better known to locals, Marathon Monday, the day of the Boston Marathon. A holiday for most Bostonians, people flocked to the city to celebrate the race. Starting in Hopkinton, 26.2 miles west of the city, the course wound through hills and roads, and ended at the finish line on Boylston Street at the side of the Boston Public Library. The Back Bay was filled with spectators crowded on both sides of the street, congratulating runners as they reached the final stretch. Many also gathered at Heartbreak Hill near Boston College, between the 20th and 21st miles, cheering runners on where they usually ran out of steam.

Patriots Day wasn't named for the marathon. It was the national day commemorating the Battles of Lexington and Concord, the first battles of the American Revolutionary War. On April 19th, 1775, the first shots were fired at the North Bridge in Concord, and the battle ignited as the colonists set out to win their independence. They were the "shots heard round the world" as, poet, Ralph Waldo Emerson famously described. The Boston Marathon was on the same day as Patriots Day to honor the commitment and endurance freedom required from all of us. The word marathon originated from the Battle of Marathon in 490 BC, where the Greek people fought for their sovereignty and defeated the Persian Empire. Hundreds of years later, a young new America gave everything she had to claim the right to life, liberty, and happiness.

I saw Sam coming down the road in full stride. I was at the finish line where the clock read his running time. He never ceased to amaze me as he ran the race in two hours and fifty-nine minutes, averaging just under seven minutes a mile. It was becoming a beautiful day, and warming up as the sun began to break through the clouds.

"Sam! Congratulations! What a run." I greeted him with a big hug.

"It was a great run. Next year you're going to run with me!" He said giving my shoulder a small tug.

"Ha! No promises, Sam. Come on, let's get your stuff and something to eat."

We wove through the crowd on our way to the park. Sam picked up his well-deserved commemorative medal and put on his official Boston Marathon jacket. We headed a few blocks back to Sola's Pub at the Lenox Hotel. It was a prime location in the middle of the action. Sam ordered a Guinness beer, quite fittingly as we sat in one of Boston's most celebrated Irish pubs.

"I have been reading *The Public Bank Solution*," Sam said loudly. We squeezed in at the edge of the bar as people poured in through the doors. "Ellen Brown covers our financial history with humor!"

"What do you think of her solution?"

"States creating public banks, like the state of North Dakota? I do wonder how the power for states to create money would not be corrupted by political interests. But, I would like to learn more—there are thought provoking ideas in her book."

"I am impressed with the awareness she has created about who can control and issue the money supply. I'm heading to Switzerland at the end of next month to attend one of her lectures."

"Really?" Sam stopped for a moment, "At the end of next month? I'll be in Europe for a project we're working on. We start in Rome and end in London. I think I'm scheduled to come home right around the time you're heading in. Maybe I could stay a few extra days and head down and see Ellen with you."

"That's a great idea," I said with a big smile. "And of course, it will be worth your time. How about I fly to London? Then, we can head down to Switzerland together?"

"Sounds like we have a plan, Kristen. London, it is!" Sam said raising his glass to toast the next stop on our journey.

Spring was flying by as the warm heat of summer was rolling in. It was a beautiful time to be in New England, and the perfect time to embark on a trip to Europe. I packed a small bag and hailed a cab as I headed to Logan airport. I slept the whole way to London and finally woke when the lights came on as the flight attendants prepared the cabin for landing. Shaking off drowsiness, I made my way through customs at Heathrow airport and found Sam waiting just beyond the doors.

"Well, good day madam, welcome to London!"

"Thank you, sir. But, I think you might need to work on that accent." I laughed. "You still sound pretty American."

"In my defense," Sam said as he took my bag, "I've only been in the United Kingdom a week. Come on, let's get some lunch. It's gorgeous weather, and there's no rain in the forecast, but I have an umbrella—just in case."

Sam and I were off in a taxi heading toward Caviar House and Prunier on Piccadilly Street. It took well over an hour to get there, but I didn't mind as it turned out to be a beautiful drive through the city.

"How was your trip to Rome? Is your project going well?" I almost forgot Sam came to Europe for work and not just to see me.

"Fantastic, the project is moving along smoothly, and we

enjoyed some unscheduled time touring historic sites. In fact, I learned something just for you," he said proudly. "Did you know that at the height of Rome's greatness they used inexpensive metal coins? Government issued debt-free fiat money, made of cheap copper and bronze—widely distributed and easily accessible to the people."

"I love it, Sam. They figured out the key to prosperity was to make sure the quantity of money in circulation was in the right amount, and matched what the people needed?"

"Yes," Sam affirmed. "They weren't confused thinking gold, or something of value needed to back the money to make people accept it. Instead, the Roman Republic supplied the right amount of money and was able to support prosperity for everyone."

"They built magnificent temples and so much more."

"Using the right kind of money was key. It empowered Rome to its greatness, until Julius Caesar arrived on the scene."

"He changed the money, didn't he, Sam? He took the 'valueless' cheap money away, reduced the money supply, and created money only out of gold, right?"

"He minted gold coins and put his picture on them. He consolidated power into the hands of the rich."

"Ah, yes, he brought back Plutocracy, rule by the super-rich, by reducing the money supply."

"Perhaps this is the reason the senators killed Caesar," Sam hypothesized. "Who knows? Sadly, the gold money gained a firm foothold, so, it remained even after his death. They got rid of the inexpensive copper and bronze coins. Demonetized them as money. That was the end of the Roman Empire, everything spiraled down after that."

"So, thousands of years earlier, bankers took away the money that allowed freedom and prosperity to flourish. They understood how to control people and deliver power to themselves. Simply by changing the money into something 'valuable' and scarce, they reduced the money supply and limited the access to it."

"That's right," Sam agreed. "By using something scarce as

money they quickly cornered the market, or bought up all the supply, and immediately gained power over everyone else...by doing nothing, contributing nothing of value or service to anyone. Just by changing the rules."

"It's so simple and maniacal at the same time, isn't it?" I said feeling sad, "They controlled everyone else, as people were left to compete for crumbs of bread."

"It's amazing how the place and time changes, but the story stays the same, Kristen."

The taxi pulled up at the corner of a busy intersection. We got out and hurried across the street to the restaurant. It was located in a beautiful, gray swirled marble building. Enormous glass windows stretched from the floor to the ceiling with large double-pillar columns every five feet between them. We climbed a few steps to reach the entrance. Two tall urns filled with bright green, chiseled boxwood topiaries flanked the grand black enameled door. The building was an experience of the understated drama and sophistication that was iconic London. Sam held the door open as we stepped inside.

"Welcome to Caviar House and Prunier," Sam said pulling out my chair. "I think this will be a most proper place for a New Englander to enjoy some proper seafood."

"What a great suggestion, Sam. Have you eaten here before?"

"No, not yet," Sam answered as he scanned the menu.

"I think I'll try the Balik Salmon Tartar."

"We have to try the oysters," Sam excitedly urged. "Let's start with the Jersey oysters, then the Portland Princess and Kumamoto Rock next."

The service was impeccable. Our waiter was attentive and anticipated our every need. The food arrived displayed on large, bright white plates to showcase the beauty.

"Sam, you know England didn't always use debt-money. Actually, for a long time they had a system of successful government-issued money that was spent into society matching the people's demand for it."

"Really?" Sam said with most of his attention on the oysters. "Wait, really? Here in England? Where the gold-owning private bankers caused all the misery for colonial and early America?"

"Yes," I said with a smile. "Literally for over 700 years, they had a fabulously successful money system. They created money out of wooden sticks. A 'valueless' material that was plentiful. It made it easy to create and issue as much money they needed, and when they needed."

"Wood? Sticks?" Sam puzzled as he paused to look me in the eye. "Come on, how did they stop the money from being counterfeited?"

"With some simple creativity and insight. They took the pieces of wood and cut prescribed notches in them to denote different money values, and then split them down the center. The large 'half' was called the 'stock' and the smaller half or 'short end of the stick' was called the 'foil.'"

"Interesting." Sam considered the concept. "Each stick would split apart in a unique way, with a unique pattern of the wood grain, like a fingerprint. You couldn't 'make' a piece of wood match the other half. That is ingenious!"

"King Henry I started the system. Rather than borrowing gold from bankers, he had 'stockbrokers' cut and polish sticks of willow, pine, and hazel wood, carve notches to denominate values and then split them into stocks and foils. The king's treasury systematically introduced them into circulation, accepted them for taxes, and so they easily circulated as money. The king issued money without creating government debt. The treasury kept the stocks and the foils circulated. When the tax was paid, the two pieces of wood were matched up. If they didn't fit, it was clear there was something amiss. This method worked beautifully and was a successful, powerful form of money, known as 'tally sticks.'"

"Tally sticks... when did they start?"

"In the Middle Ages, in 1100. These sticks were money for over 700 years and they unleashed a period of creativity and prosperity for the common people. In fact, at the height of this system 95% of the money supply was made-up of tally sticks. That means 95% of the money was created and issued debt-free. There was no need to borrow money from bankers. The king issued more money, if it was needed to match the real productivity."

"Seven hundred years is a long time! Is this where the word 'stock' comes from? Like a stock or share of a company in the stock market?"

"Yes. The person holding the 'stock' has 'equity' or a portion of value in a company."

"And the foil?"

"The short end of the stick. It was a debt owed." I winked. "England flourished with tally sticks, and King Henry I was a progressive leader. He created a Charter of Liberties which limited some of his powers."

"That's interesting. Well, when I think about it, democratizing and liberating money in society is the basis of freedom."

"True, Sam. The middle class with social mobility sprung out of this movement. In 1215, the Magna Carta was drafted, the foundation of our own Constitution. Forty years later, the first parliamentary government took shape where the people began to rule themselves. Self-rule was, and is, rooted in the freedom of *being able* to control the money supply."

"King Henry I provided stability for the people. He supported them until they were secure and prosperous enough to take over the reins themselves."

"Like the eggshell and the baby chicks, we saw on the Jumbotron in Times Square. The shell provided stability for the chick to grow, until it prevented its progress. Safety becomes a prison. Tally sticks propelled prosperity far and wide. So much so, that the containment wasn't needed any longer, and serfdom came to its natural end as feudalism was banned in the 1600s."

"The bankers lending gold must not have liked this system of debt-free government-issued money."

"You are right, Sam! They worked hard to 'foil' the system. And, they made inroads in the late 1600s. They were even able to convince the government to create a privately owned central bank in 1694."

"Ah! They *were* foiled! Pun intended." Sam laughed. "That's terrible. England stopped creating its own money and started borrowing it from private bankers? That's probably when they started to squeeze the colonists."

"Right, and tally sticks were outlawed in 1826."

"What happened to all the tally sticks?"

"Funny you should ask. It's an amazing story, another sign from Providence. Are we far from the Parliament, the House of Lords and the House of Commons?"

"It's not far," Sam answered. "Why? Do you want to go there?"

"If we can. It will make the rest of the story much easier to picture."

We paid our bill, hailed a taxi, and headed to Westminster Hall. Big Ben, the great clock tower, stood in the distance as we approached the elaborate gothic complex, an inordinate expanse of marble. We made it to the British Parliament and walked to the visitor center just as a tour was starting. We snuck in at the back and quietly joined the group to listen in.

"Welcome, Ladies and Gentlemen. This is Westminster Hall where the old Palace of Westminster once stood, next to the River Thames. It used to be the home of kings and queens and was given to the people as a place for Parliament to meet. Parliament originally met in the old St. Stephens Chapel. It was a cramped and old chamber in need of renovations. As they began to clear it out, they found huge piles of old tally sticks left in the cellar below the House of Lords.

"On October 16th, 1834, the decision was made to burn the lot of the wretched tally sticks. Two workmen were given orders to feed them into the furnaces in the cellars of the House of Lords. The fire got out of control creating an astonishing blaze. The whole of the House of Lords caught on fire, and they could not put it out.

Then the House of Commons caught fire, and it suddenly seemed the whole of Parliament was burning. The old Palace of Westminster was almost completely destroyed with only the great Hall left standing. It had survived nearly 800 years yet, soon, the roof started to cave in. The people scrambled to save it. Finally, the fire was put out, and they were able to save one remaining part of Parliament.

"In the morning as the sun rose on the charred remains, there stood a single half buried and half burnt tally stick mocking them. It was time to rebuild, and a competition amongst architects was launched to design a new palace. They decided to build an enormous clock tower, so people could see their Parliament from miles away."

"That's Incredible!" Sam said, "Burning the tally sticks burned the Houses of Parliament down to the ground."

"And how symbolic? As they destroyed the remnants of the money that gave them freedom, and liberated them from serfdom and feudalism, they destroyed the Parliament, the house where they ruled themselves."

Sam and I turned as Big Ben started to chime. It was three o'clock.

"The bell tolls for us," Sam said quietly.

The clock tower could be seen for miles. Big Ben reminded us that government and law-making belonged to the people. The tower rose, out of the ruin caused by burning the tally sticks, out of the annihilation of the people's power to create money. The rule of the people belonged to the people, but only when the people claimed their power to create their own money.

It was time to head to Switzerland, and before we left I took a picture of the remaining tally stick on display in the museum. The photo became my prized souvenir from our time in London. And, of course, it was much more than that. It was a valiant symbol, evidence that money was done correctly for over 700 years, before it was finally destroyed.

We took a taxi to the airport and boarded a quick flight to Basel from London. It was only an hour and a half. As the plane began its descent, the majestic ice caps of the Alps broke through the clouds. The land below was an endless sea of green. A patchwork of rolling pastures and farms occasionally interrupted by lakes, that looked like dots of blue. The landscape was surreal. When we landed, we found Basel's airport was small, modern, and efficient. We got our bags without a problem and caught the train to our hotel.

As we stepped out of the train station, we saw our hotel to the left. It was the Hotel Euler, beautiful and quaint, a Bavarian-styled building painted in robin's egg blue. Basel was a medieval town situated on the Rhine. It was 2,000 years old and formerly part of the Roman Empire. Sam was impressed how the architecture spanned the course of history. Gothic cathedrals and antique row-houses stood in contrast to the modern, avant-garde museums and tech-savvy sustainable buildings.

After getting settled in, we went downstairs to the terrace to enjoy the sun and order something to eat. The patio was clean and cheerful with crisp white tablecloths and flower-boxes overflowing with bright red geraniums. As we chose our table, the waiter stopped to open the awning that hung overhead. We sat down under the canopy, dyed in a rich, vibrant blue, as it provided just the right amount of shade.

"This is your kind of place," I said as I noticed the look of contentment on Sam's face.

"It does seem like life is good here with nature that's easily accessible, history, architecture, and sustainability. And I have a feeling that it's not too hard to find plenty of good food around here," Sam said confirming my hunch.

"Ok. So, how's your German?" I asked. "Or, perhaps, your French?"

"What is that?" Sam interrupted as he pointed to an eighteen-story circular skyscraper in the distance.

I turned my head to see a striking work of architecture. "People call it the 'Tower of Basel.' It looks like a boot, don't you think?"

"It does," he agreed. "The lower side of the building looks like the foot, and the circular tower next to it makes it look like a big boot. That is ugly. Who would put that in a beautiful place like this?"

"It's the headquarters of the Bank of International Settlements or the BIS. The BIS is the private central bank —for the nations' central banks."

"There's a global central bank in charge of the national central banks?"

"Yes, there is. When the BIS formed in 1930, they preferred to remain unnoticed. They wanted to maintain their anonymity. So, they convened to work in an abandoned six-story hotel, the Grand et Savoy Hotel Universe near Frey's Chocolate Shop—right over there. There was no sign, so Frey's shop became the way people located it. Finally, in 1977, they came out from the shadows and built that monstrosity as their headquarters."

"Weird," Sam said, "and, spooky."

"Spooky is right. It has a nuclear-bomb shelter, fire department, and hospital inside. Underground, below that 'boot,' lies twenty miles of archives."

"What?" Sam paused. "What does the BIS do? And why do privately owned central banks need a central bank?"

"More or less, the BIS sets the rules for national central banks—its member banks. Largely, the BIS controls the entire Western world, and then some, by setting critical parameters which herd and corral our central banks. The BIS sets the capital requirements banks must follow. Remember that is the amount of cushion or capital banks must have to protect themselves from going bankrupt when loans fail."

"By setting the amount of cushion banks must have, they determine how many loans banks can make, and how much risk they can take." Sam did a double take up and down the building.

"Yes, the power is tremendous," I agreed, "Dr. Carroll Quigley, an influential thinker, and professor of history at Georgetown University, wrote a well-known book called, *Tragedy and Hope: A History of the World in Our Time* in 1966. He is better known for being President Bill Clinton's mentor. In the book, he explains the role the BIS plays behind the scenes."

Quigley was in favor of private, international bankers dominating the world's money systems. I was surprised how unabashedly he wrote of his vision for world control. He had no shame about his intentions, and it still shocked me as I explained it to Sam. In Quigley's own words he said he wanted "nothing less than to create a world system of financial control in private hands able to dominate the political system of each country, and the economy of the world as a whole. This system was controlled in a feudalist fashion by the central banks of the world acting in concert, by secret agreements arrived at in frequent private meetings and conferences. The apex of the system was the Bank for International Settlements in Basel, Switzerland, which was also a private bank owned by private corporations."

"This is why some people think the building was made in a shape of a boot, as a metaphor, of how the banking system controls humanity."

"You mean like stepping on someone? Putting *'a-boot-on-their-neck'*? Putting pressure on someone to make him do what you want?"

"Yes, Sam, just like that. Many suggest the powerful people that come to the BIS meetings stay right here—at this lovely hotel."

"Interesting."

"People suggest that creating state public banks is a way for the public to gain back some of these monetary decisions the BIS makes."

"How would that work?"

"If states create their own public banks, the assets and property states own would act as their capital keeping them solvent—these valuations far exceed the limitations the BIS sets."

"Hmm, I'm looking forward to Ellen Brown's lecture tonight."

"Me, too. Are you ready to order? I think the wiener-schnitzel is calling your name." I winked, as I knew he must have been starving.

We arrived just in time at the hall where Ellen Brown was giving her talk. Her presentation was ready to go with the title already on the screen, *Public Banks, and Why We Need Them*. Everyone quickly filled into their seats. She was promptly introduced, as the program started right on the dot with perfect Swiss punctuality.

"North Dakota was the only state in the United States to escape the credit crisis of 2008. It was the only state to avoid a budget deficit and have a surplus for two years after the financial crisis, and its surplus has continued to grow since. It recently reduced individual income taxes and property taxes. It maintains the lowest foreclosure rate and the lowest credit card default rate in the country. The bank was so successful that it returned 19% on equity last year. Compare that with the state of California pension fund that lost 25% and 30% consecutively for the last two years.

"Indeed, there's something very special happening in North Dakota. North Dakota is the only state in the country with a state-owned bank. This bank has a long and interesting history. It was created in 1919 by a movement of irate farmers struggling to gain access to money and obtain some measure of control over financial decisions. These farmers realized there was a plot to get their farms and diminish their power. They became outraged and decided to take control of their destiny. They formed the Nonpartisan League which took control of local legislatures and chartered the Bank of North Dakota (BND). North Dakota is a very conservative state; they came together, not out of socialist interests, but in the interest of their own sovereignty. They wanted to control their money and the wealth they created and worked for instead of giving it away to private bankers.

"The interest paid on loans by borrowers to commercial banks is paid back to the state bank, which in turn is paid back to the people! 'The BND returned over $350 million to North Dakota's general fund in the last decade, easing pressure on the state budget.' Other mineral-rich states don't have anything close to the results we find in North Dakota.

"The BND operates as a 'Banker's Bank' or a mini Federal

Reserve. As the Bank of International Settlements (the BIS) determines the capital cushion requirements for commercial banks in their system, those under the Federal Reserve System in the United States, the Bank of North Dakota operates freely outside of it. As regulators increase the size of the cushion, smaller local community banks get squeezed, having to raise more money, and lend fewer loans; they lose profits and are more likely to go out of business as they are bought up by larger commercial banks. The few Megaliths banks, known as the Too-Big-to-Fail Banks, only get bigger. Competition decreases, and people have less access to business investment. The BND is impervious to the tremendous pressure from the BIS, right here in Basel, Switzerland."

Everyone stood and clapped as Ellen smiled in a modest way. She was smart and savvy. She was responsible for bringing the idea of public banking out from the shadows where it had long laid dormant. Her Public Banking Institute grew every year, reaching more and more people.

"The state banking model," Sam said, "lets each state create loans people need, and invest in businesses and community projects. It is a Jeffersonian model."

"Yes, public banking is a way to empower our local communities and states. During downturns, state banks keep going because their capital is vast, and is tough to erode. They can help people to keep going so they are less likely to lose their homes."

Sam paused and his furrowed brow as he said, "But, we still need to incorporate rules like Professor Keen and Dr. Hudson pointed out, to make sure loans are created for investment, and not speculative bubbles or Ponzi schemes."

"This is the question, Sam, how exactly that would be done?" I added.

"State banks are certainly a step toward creating our money, if we are able to keep political interests at bay. States vary too—not all states are fiscally responsible like North Dakota."

Sam and I spent the rest of the evening talking with Ellen and she invited us to the Public Banking Institute Conference in Philadelphia in July. Sam assured her we would both be there, even before I could nod in agreement. We had a day left in Europe before we headed back to Boston. So, we decided to spend it in Paris and catch the train after breakfast.

It was another beautiful day. We checked out of the hotel and crossed the street to the train station. The trip to Paris took us up to Strasbourg and then west across the country. The route took us through endless farms and open countryside. I felt as though I could have spent the whole day on the train.

"It's peaceful here," Sam said. "I can see why people move to the French countryside."

As the beauty of the countryside rolled by our window, I thought about how many European nations had given up their sovereignty to join the European Union or EU. The idea for the EU started in the aftermath of World War II. It seemed to be a noble idea, one that was intended to foster peace. By engendering economic interdependence among previously warring nations, many believed future conflicts would be avoided. In 1958, the European Economic Community (EEC) was formed between six countries to increase trade and collaboration. It grew as more European nations came together. The EU was formally adopted when the Treaty for the European Union, or the Maastricht Treaty, was signed in Maastricht, Netherlands in February 1992. When the idea first circulated, I was naive. I thought it was an interesting idea and believed it would foster economic growth and better relations among European countries.

But, the Maastricht Treaty set the critical terms of how member countries would be *allowed* to run their economies. By joining the EU, the European countries gave up the right to direct their own economies. Most importantly the Euro was created, the new currency of the EU which replaced the existing national currencies. Countries joining the EU, adopting the Euro, in place of their own national money, gave up their *Sovereignty*. They lost their most prized power, the power that makes them free—the power and ability to create their own money.

There was so much propaganda that led up to the creation of the Euro, and such a sales campaign on how free-trade would improve their economies, that countries wanting a better standard of living were mesmerized. I also fell for the concept of the Euro when it was first proposed because I had not learned the truth about debt-money. Most people at the time had not learned it either, and still have not today.

The tragedy in Greece was a direct result of losing its power to control the amount of money in circulation. When Greece gave up its right to create Drachmas and began to use Euros, created by the European Central Bank or the ECB, it was no longer a nation. Instead, it degraded itself from a nation to a state controlled by the European Union. A change so drastic, it would be as if the United States gave up its nation status and became a state controlled by a hypothetical "North American Union." Moreover, the Maastricht Treaty spelled out severe restrictions that most countries struggled to meet. Mainly limits on inflation, but most importantly joining nations were no longer allowed to run deficits greater than 3%. If they ran out of money beyond that, they were unable to create more money or run further deficits to keep things going. But, deficits were going to happen, and at a much greater rate than 3%. Especially for the smaller nations as they were forced to play with bigger nations in the same game, with the same rules.

The rules were written as if the money was *not* debt. Yet, the money-as-debt system meant success was a sheer impossibility. When money is debt, the pressures are so great on people and their economies that national governments must backstop them when the money doesn't flow. Those in the EU can't do that anymore. The EU nations must run the debt-money race as the "seven imperatives" dictate the terms of their lives at super-speed, putting tremendous pressure on the smaller, less productive nations like Greece, Italy, Spain, and Portugal. When they can't keep up, the responsibility lands on the bigger nations' doorstep and their citizens have to forgo what they have as they pay the debts of others.

The EU was designed in such a way that failure *had to be* the outcome. Much like the reparations levied against Germany after World War I, the rules of the EU were written that destruction and implosion were inevitable. The rules were impossible to satisfy without creating desperation for the people of Greece and other smaller nations, and anger and frustration for those in Germany and other more productive nations. It was as if some form of magical growth was assumed, and assumed again and again, allowing the treaty specifications to be met. I had to wonder how the vastly different cultures of these countries, let alone the incompatibilities of the type and size of their economies, could have been ignored.

"It was set up for failure," Sam said somberly.

"Yes," I agreed, "the EU reduces the power of all individual member states. It squarely puts the power to control the quality of their lives in the hands of the European Central Bank, ECB, which is under the BIS system. None of these countries, if they needed to, could create their own money to pay off debt, like England, Japan or as we still can in the US."

"They gave up their power to a set of private bankers. Wait, did you say England? Wasn't England in the EU and then left with the 'Brexit'?"

"Yes," I nodded and smiled. "They joined the EU, but curiously opted out of taking on the Euro. They kept the right to their own currency or at least borrowing it from their central bank."

"Strange. Weren't they singing the praises for years that creating this united Eurozone for Europe was in everyone's best interests? Didn't they encourage the old Soviet bloc countries to strive to be included in the club?"

"True, Sam. But, the risk of Greece defaulting, leaving the Eurozone, and clearing the way for Italy, Spain, Portugal and who knows next...didn't give them a great feeling. They feared that they would be left holding the bag of worthless debt, that didn't get repaid. They preferred to leave that ugly reality on Germany's doorstep."

"How did Greece become such a problem? I thought a country couldn't have much debt before getting into the EU."

"The Maastricht Treaty didn't allow Greece in the EU with the debt it had, but Goldman Sachs figured out a way to 'get it off' their books by offering fancy financial products. In essence, they sold Greece a huge loan, almost five times more than what they owed before. Mind you, the people didn't create that debt. Politicians in sales meetings took their advice and created the debt. It was a failure from the get-go."

"Wow, did Goldman Sachs make a lot of money from doing this?"

"That deal made up 12% of their more than $6 billion of trading and investment revenue that year."

"That's a huge number!"

"Within three months," I added with a sigh, "shortly after the September 11th events, Greece couldn't pay, and Goldman Sachs swooped in again with an even bigger deal and Greece's national debt nearly doubled in size."

"They had a captive audience," Sam noted. "The Greek people couldn't create their own money to get out of debt, and the Greek government could no longer play that role for the people. The country was at the mercy of the ECB, no longer a nation—at the mercy of their private bankers."

"Exactly, Sam. Government officials continued this dance with Goldman Sachs, creating more and more debt for the people, who day-in-and-day-out were called lazy and entitled on TV. This debt was put on them. More or less like the corrupt dictators that indebted the people in Madagascar that David Graeber wrote about."

"Is this where the policy of 'Austerity' comes from? The idea that they have to tighten their belts and pay back these debts as their moral responsibility?"

"Through policies of austerity, pensions and social services have been drastically cut. Greece has become like a third-world country. There are stories of mothers and sons committing suicide, jumping from bridges as they lose hope for the future. We are led to believe they suffer because they are lazy and irresponsible. And look at how much 'better' their lives are after joining the EU?"

"Haven't the German people suffered too?"

"People in Germany had their pensions cut and many other pressures put on them, as well. See, this is really a form of debt-engineered imperialism. A 'bloodless' war, absent of army invasions, a way to take-over nations and colonize the people. It is a quieter way to do warfare. After all, it would look confusing to people at home watching TV to see Greece and Germany invaded, our allies."

"This is amazing."

"The people end up capitulating with the debt they 'owe,' as the wealth accumulated by the work of generations is sold off to meet the obligations put on them. Their homes and most-prized national treasures are all on the chopping block to make these debt payments. Let alone their pensions and social service programs. Their public resources, like their water systems and even access to their roads are ripe for the plucking, at bargain-basement prices, for international bankers, and other wealthy buyers."

"This is what happened to the American farmers in the late 1800s. It's the same method used time immemorial."

"Dr. Hudson describes it perfectly, when he said 'Finance is the new form of warfare, without the expense of a military overhead and an occupation against unwilling hosts. Issuing loans weaken people by putting them into debt they can't pay. Then the vulture capitalists swoop in to buy up natural resources, real estate, public infrastructure and even foreign companies on the cheap. Who needs an army when you can obtain the usual objective, monetary wealth, and asset appropriation, simply by financial means? Now if people start building the wealth they need without private bankers' money, then the private bankers' money becomes useless, and they will find a way out.' And Dr. Hudson is right, Sam—there is a way out."

"Greece could really go bankrupt, couldn't it? Unless they started issuing their own parallel currency again."

"And take much of the Eurozone down with it. You hear people screaming the United States is basically bankrupt and soon will turn into Greece. Or, worse, like Zimbabwe or post-WWI Weimar Republic of Germany, both of whom experienced hyper-inflation. As they became so indebted that they couldn't repay their debt and their currency plummeted."

"Yes, for sure." Sam nodded. "I hear that all the time. Their currency lost value so quickly that prices went up every day, if not every hour. Until it took a wheelbarrow of money to buy a loaf of bread."

"Yet, the debt they owed had to be paid back in *someone else's* currency, So, in Zimbabwe, all the loans they are literally dying to pay must be paid in dollars—our dollars, not in theirs. The same thing happened in the Weimar Republic in Germany, the unpayable debt engulfed the people, and they also couldn't print their own currency to pay off the debt. Borrowing vast amounts of money in other peoples' currencies creates hyper-inflation. A nation that owes debt in the money it creates can do what Andrew Jackson did—create the money and pay off the debt."

"Maybe that's what Greece will do," Sam pondered. "If their suffering gets bad enough, they will tell the ECB and their private bankers to go home. And use their own currency again."

The train pulled into Paris. The station was a grand hall, busy with people crossing left and right. There were endless bakery cases filled with cheese sandwiches and plates of cut fresh fruit. The buckets of fresh flowers seemed endless. I knew this had to be Paris, and we hadn't even left the station yet. Beauty abounded everywhere we looked.

"To *la boulangerie!*" Sam announced as he pointed ahead. "*S'il vous plait, Madame!*"

"*Oui, Monsieur!*" I laughed hoping my years studying French in high school would produce some return, "*Ooh la la, a la patisserie!*"

Sam and I headed out of the station to find a cab to take us to a cafe he promised I would love. He knew just where we were going. As we got in a car, he directed the driver to take us to Du Pain et des Idees at the corner of Rue Yves Touduc and Rue de Marseille. The breads and pastries were like pure gold beaming through the storefront window. As we opened the door, we were overwhelmed by the heavenly scent of sheer delight. We stepped into a French pastry wonderland as we were surrounded by trays of butter-filled airy croissants, chocolate cream eclairs, and Napoleons.

We ordered two pieces of opera cake. It was made of a delicate almond cake, soaked in espresso syrup, layered with a thick buttercream and a bittersweet chocolate ganache. We didn't stop there; the range of artistic macaron cookies was just too tempting. I wanted to try them all, and yet they were almost too beautiful to eat. But, they were simply too irresistible not to, and so I decided on the lime basil, salted caramel and, my most favorite of all, lily of the valley.

"I wonder if this is how Marie Antoinette lived," Sam reflected, looking at our decadent feast, "in the late 1700s as the French Revolution erupted, surrounded by the most lavish pastries and cakes, as the common people suffered extreme poverty. Maybe she took her sterling-silver fork and cut an ever so delicate bite of the cake as she gazed undaunted at the sight of the hungry peasants outside her palace window, and said to her servants, 'What? Don't they have any bread? Well, then, let them eat cake!'"

"How downright decadently evil! But, the best we can find in history, suggests she never said that. Philosopher Jean-Jacques Rousseau made the saying famous when he used it to characterize another noblewoman. At that time, Marie was only eleven-years-old. She was only nineteen when she became the queen, and her marriage was difficult. She was called Madame Veto by the press because she refused to reduce her extravagant lifestyle."

I took a bite of the cake and continued, "France had become involved in the American Revolutionary war and owed huge debts to its private bankers. The French people bore the brunt of the debt, suffering all the austerity put on them. Marie became the symbol of what stood between the people and their freedom. In their rage, they rallied for her execution when the French Revolution broke out. As she made her way to the guillotine, she was told to have courage. She said, 'Courage? I have shown it for years; think you I shall lose it at the moment when my sufferings are to end?' Raised in the legacy that strong monarchies were the way to best care for the common people, she tried to do her best for her country as a strong monarch. But, as today, the bankers stole the power from her to govern. Attempting to smash through the chains of the banker's debt was more than she could grasp."

"That's amazing," Sam said. "Kings and queens were captured in the web of debt as well, not just the common people. The ultimate power resided in controlling the quantity of the money supply. Everything else was and *is* secondary."

"You know Sam," I reflected, "all this scarcity and imposed suffering is really an illusion. Created by rules that are made up, with people simply following them. These rules become real, because people don't question them—where they came from and who made them."

"Interesting, just like Greece. Look at what JP Getty said about who had the problem when it came to paying money back...He was right, wasn't he? After all, the Greek people owe so much money that *They really don't have a problem* but, the banking system under the Bank of International Settlements does."

"It's true." I smiled. "We are living in scarcity because we buy into the illusion. We believe that people must suffer, at all costs, to repay debts they didn't necessarily take from bankers, who *never had the money* in the first place to lend! Creating money and debt out of thin air. What do you think we would find behind the curtain, if we had the courage to look? We would find abundance waiting for us to wake up and recreate the rules of how our money works."

"Abundance." Sam smiled. "That's what we find in everything nature does. We need courage, Kristen. The courage to see that abundance is the natural way of life."

"Funny, you know, maybe it is appropriate that this brave,

young, and misunderstood queen was marred with such derogatory and heartless words. When we see through the illusion of scarcity, we will no longer reduce ourselves to grovel for a piece of bread and fight for the crumbs. Instead, we will remember abundance is our natural state. We will let ourselves eat cake, and celebrate life!"

Sam and I finished our pastries, delighting in every decadent bite.

10

PEACE NOT WAR

I heard a faint ringing in the distance. As it grew louder, I began to realize I was in a deep sleep, and that the sound was my phone. My bedroom was pitch black with all the shades drawn tight as I fumbled and struggled to answer the call.

"Hello?" I eked out.

"Kristen," Sam said, "it's 8:30 in the morning. Are you still in bed?"

"Oh, Sam, I'm so tired," I said, still unable to imagine getting up, "I've been up late every night researching. Did you say it is 8:30 already? I wonder why my alarm didn't go off."

"You probably slept through it. Listen, do you want to come to Washington DC with me this weekend? I have two tickets for the Department of Peace conference. Marianne Williamson has been championing the movement to create a Department of Peace through the Peace Alliance. There is a great list of speakers lined up for the event."

"Oh, I love her. She is a powerful teacher and activist. I've read almost all her books over the years. Is it Memorial Day this weekend?"

"Yes, it is." Sam laughed. "Come out of your cave, sleepyhead, and out from under your piles of paper. Pack a bag. I will pick you up early Friday and we will go from there."

"How could I say no to that?" I yawned and chuckled. "You know me well. See you Friday. Thanks for being such a great friend."

We arrived in Washington DC mid-afternoon and the weather was beautiful. We were happy to be there, even though we were two months too late to find the magnificent cherry blossom trees in bloom. The streets were crowded with people, from all around the country, traveling to the Capitol for Memorial Day to pay respect to the fallen. We had two hours before the conference started, and we wanted to visit the commemorative parks as well. We headed across the Potomac River to find Arlington National Cemetery, one of the country's oldest and largest national cemeteries with more than 400,000 graves spanning over 624 acres of rolling hills. Sam and I looked for the burial site of President John F. Kennedy and First Lady Jackie Kennedy.

"When President Kennedy was buried," Sam shared, "Jackie Kennedy was the one to light this eternal flame burning here in front of their graves."

"It is a testimony to his vision."

"The cemetery is peaceful, and elegant," Sam added as he scanned the landscape. "But, the sheer size of it is overwhelming. What a statement it makes about our endless wars…"

We crossed back over the river to the National Mall and the Memorial Parks. The reflecting pool was long and large in front of us, as we walked up its perimeter toward the grand Lincoln memorial. It stood tall in the distance, and it was truly majestic. The Lincoln Memorial was a temple in its own right. It was modeled after the Greek Parthenon, an enduring symbol of ancient Greece, the temple built to honor the goddess Athena. Thirty-six fluted columns, each representing the states in the Union at the time of Lincoln's death, encircled the nineteen-foot marble statue of Abraham Lincoln sitting in a grand chair. His Second Inaugural

Speech and his Gettysburg Address were immortalized, etched on the walls next to him.

"I remember memorizing the *Gettysburg Address* as a child," Sam said as he touched the letters on the wall, "It means more to me now."

"It has to be one of the most powerful two-minute speeches ever given." I reflected. "What a man he was."

"Especially this part," Sam said as he read from the wall, "'It is for us, the living, rather, to be dedicated to the unfinished work which they who fought here have thus so nobly advanced. It is rather for us to be here dedicated to the great task remaining before us—that we here highly resolve that these dead shall not have died in vain—that this nation, under God, shall have a new birth of freedom—and that government of the people, by the people, for the people shall not perish from the earth.' I think we let them down by not guarding the main tenant of our sovereignty —what they fought for—the power to create our money."

We walked along the Constitutional Gardens and found the District of Columbia War Memorial for World War I. Over five million Americans fought in the First World War from 1914 to 1918. It was almost inconceivable to appreciate the magnitude of how many fought, and how broadly American families were affected. As we continued to walk, we came to two pavilions which honored the more than 400,000 Americans who lost their lives in the war. Next, we arrived at the Korean War memorial. Made of bronze statues of soldiers with anxious faces and heavy, protective gear, the memorial conveyed the intense battles they faced from 1950 to1953. It was a gripping sight to see. Finally, we descended a long pathway, carved in the shape of a V from polished granite. We were at the Vietnam War Memorial. It was 247 feet long and displayed the names of 58,245 soldiers who lost their lives in the extended conflict.

"What a daunting display," I said. "Look at how much war we have engaged in. I don't think it's ever really ended. Such suffering."

I was feeling slightly dazed and decided to sit down. As I scanned all that surrounded me, I reflected on how I studied the

American presidents a few years earlier while working on a master's degree. One of my favorite professors had a special fondness for President Adams, the second one, the son, John Quincy Adams. Adams warned America to mind her own business and to not get involved in wars that were not hers to fight. The professor lamented that Adams advice was long forgotten and wished that every military boardroom have Adams words inscribed on the walls.

On the Fourth of July, in 1821, he delivered an eloquent speech before Congress warning America. He said, "America has, in nearly half a century, without a single exception, respected the independence of other nations while asserting and maintaining her own. She has abstained from interference in the concerns of others, even when conflict has been for principles to which she clings."

President Adams continued with, "America goes not abroad, in search of monsters to destroy. She is the well-wisher to the freedom and independence of all. She is the champion and vindicator only of her own. She well knows that...(if) she would involve herself... in all the wars of interest and intrigue, of individual avarice, envy, and ambition...The fundamental maxims of her policy would insensibly change from *liberty* to *force*...She might become the dictatress of the world. She would be no longer the ruler of her own spirit..." He feared that if we strayed off this path and became entangled in other's wars that we, as a people, would be enslaved by the wars we waged, and all the havoc they brought. He ended his speech with, "(America's) glory is not *dominion,* but *liberty.* Her march is the march of the mind. She has a spear and a shield: but the motto upon her shield is, *Freedom, Independence, Peace."*

We long forgot his wise words and America had engaged in ever-increasing wars that were less about her own interests. In 1961, President Eisenhower left us with a similar warning, as he witnessed a frightening rise in the military industrial complex, and the growing hunger for war. Concerned that the people's interests and freedom were already displaced, and soon to be completely disregarded, he urged the nation to limit the military's power. By the end of the Eisenhower administration, military expenditures exceeded the net-income of all United States corporations. Sam and I were surrounded by the evidence of war's terrible fruits, and, sadly, it was clear that his advice was ignored, as well.

"War has never stopped, Sam," I reflected.

"True, isn't it?" Sam agreed. "War is the only industry thriving in America. Fighting ubiquitous enemies, without defined national borders. Look at the escalation in the last fifteen years—from Iraq, Afghanistan, Lebanon, Yemen, Libya, and Syria."

"When we use money-as-debt," I said, taking a breath, "the seven-imperatives push for this madness. Money-as-debt demands that we create more debt—more and more, faster, and faster—at the speed *only* war can produce. Creating and sustaining conflict with ghost-like enemies, and trying to fight these ever-present terror events, produces a never-ending cycle of debt. *This debt is the inexhaustible fuel the system needs.* We could not have a debt-money system without having war."

"It is frightening." Sam paused. "And, think about it—the confusion of who our enemies are, where they lurk, and the devastation and terror these conflicts create captures our attention. It is all we see. We don't see using money-as-debt is the actual menace."

"If you are going to create money," I added, "by the means of creating debt and taking on loans, there is no way business or investment will ever create debt fast enough, as the massive war machine, ravaging humanity and the planet, will."

"Marianne Williamson is right," Sam said as he looked me in the eye. "It is time we had a Department of Peace, and put our energy into developing institutions that represent our highest values."

"Instead of fostering and baiting our lowest expression," I added as I stood up. "The registration desk must be open at the conference. Should we head over there now?"

The sun began to set as we looked over and saw the Jefferson Memorial, shining like a beacon of hope. Thomas Jefferson was the main author of the Declaration of Independence, which set forward the principles for our government. The Constitution, a product of centuries of careful thought and painstaking analysis, outlined how our government would function. Jefferson and the founders passionately dissected and debated the best ideas from those who came before and produced a masterful framework of self-governance, one that safeguarded freedom and the right to liberty when enforced. Yet, using money-as-debt undermined and threatened the Constitution, as it stole the power the Constitution prescribed to the people. Worse, money-as-debt lusted for war, with its voracious appetite driven by the imperatives for perpetual debt and growth. It yearned and longed-for debt, unable to quench its hunger for the massive, endless debt that only war could produce. Using money-as-debt brewed beneath the foundation of our lives, bringing death and destruction where ever it went. It ripped up the seeds of peace we tried to sow, and cast out any hope of lasting prosperity.

Marianne Williamson promoted the creation of a Department of Peace in the United States Government through the work of the Peace Alliance. I thought it was an important movement on many levels though I knew that no lasting peace could be achieved until money-as-debt was no longer the means by which we created our money. To create a world that lived in peace we had to find another way to do money. Nonetheless, establishing a Department of Peace was a powerful idea. As a nation, we had yet to institutionalize a power equal to the Department of Defense dedicated to developing and sustaining peace. I wanted to support it as a tangible means of peace building. Establishing a Department of Peace would signify that we believed in peace, and perhaps, even valued it more than war.

Marianne took the podium, dressed in her iconic understated elegance. After a long applause, she graciously thanked everyone for coming and began her comments. She spoke with uncompromising power and poise.

"Our politics often don't seem to express the better angles of our nature. American politics in particular often seem to be the handmaiden to an economic order rather than to a humanitarian order. When we started the Peace Alliance, we created an opportunity to have a different conversation, a heartfelt conversation, not only as individuals, but as a country and as a planet.

"The reason we chose this particular piece of legislation to campaign for is because it establishes a cabinet level Department of Peace. It provides an institutional platform for the peace-building community. It creates a voice that will be heard by the President. The role is to facilitate, research, and articulate the best peace-building practices taken from around the country. You don't just wait until violence erupts and throw people in jail, or bomb a country. Rather, you proactively seek to cultivate conditions of peace. Any time you have large groups of desperate people you have an inevitable trajectory in the direction of eruptions of violence.

"The Department of Peace will put equal attention on domestic issues as well as international issues. Just as we have a military academy, we will have a peace academy. Therefore, we can have a much more sophisticated approach to analysis of what it would take to create a peaceful world. Today there is no place in our government where that is the primary function.

"What is important in this inquiry in which we are involved is that we are asking fundamental questions: What does it truly mean to be human? What does it mean to be a country that is centered in its heart? There is some in-depth rethinking going on.

"Sometimes in life you do not need to know what you can do, but you show up for whatever needs to be done... and because you showed up, what you do then appears. I think that people think we are naive when we say let's start by empowering the people, feeding the women and the children. Well, I think that people who think we can continue on this planet the way it is with the large forums of suffering people that exist.... I think they're naive.

"We need to be courageous and powerful enough to not apologize for that when people patronize us and are condescending toward us. We must say to them, 'No. No, you've had your way and the way it's going is putting us precariously close to an unsustainable future, whether it is nuclear, environmental, or social and economic.' We are not angry, but we are serious and here to stay. It is time to turn this ship around."

It was a beautiful speech, pragmatic and deeply moving. Everyone was inspired. It was clear that, as we left what no longer worked behind us, we moved forward and created a new way to live with a new future. Our problems were the demand from the world that we rise and evolve. Perhaps, all that was required was a shift in our perception, a powerful and profound shift. One that allowed us to see what was not working was *not* actually broken, but the wrong way to perceive things. As the paradigm of lack, disempowerment, and suffering disintegrated, our unquestioned, conditioned ways frayed at the edges. Our job was simple. We needed to take our attention off our old ways of living and imagine new ways to come, to give life to the new paradigm as we birthed the unspoken truth that stirred in our hearts.

"For humanity to not only survive but thrive, the next evolution of our species is required," Sam said.

"One that embraces the understanding that we are fundamentally connected, spiritually and materially," I agreed. "We are surrounded by nature displaying this blueprint of life, holding the map waiting for us to recognize this greater reality. To see the encompassing web of connectedness that pervades everything. Nature continues to embody this wisdom as she whispers in the corner of our ear, waiting for us to listen until we are able to hear."

"Luckily for us, nature is patient and slow to react," Sam responded. "But, you have to wonder when our time will run out."

Deepak Chopra, a well-known doctor, and author, took the podium next. A legend in his own right, I had read many of his books over the last twenty years and traveled to hear him speak. It was a treat to see him at the conference, and I was sure we wouldn't be disappointed.

"As humans, we are a quantum leap of creativity. We might be poised for the next quantum leap. As Nietzsche said, 'Where you have chaos within you, you have the possibility of a dancing star.' And, so, we need to embrace the uncertainty before us to take the next leap in our creativity and transformation. A shift in our perception transforms our consciousness, and when consciousness transforms, everything else transforms because everything finally is consciousness. This creates a metamorphosis. What is metamorphosis? Metamorphosis is a transformation so great that it is beyond a radical change in form.

"Look at how the caterpillar becomes a butterfly. It is not just a new worm with wings. It becomes an entirely new creature. At a certain point in its life, a caterpillar begins to consume more food than it requires for its metabolic needs. It begins to over consume, taking more from the environment, more than it needs to survive. Consumption becomes its primary activity."

"Can you see this happening in us?" Sam whispered in my ear. "Consumers. As we said before we refer to each other as consumers."

"Divine beings degraded by consumption consuming our lives," I agreed. "And the lack of gratitude we have—for all we have. We've become vacant, empty beings, possessed by the crude state of wanting more and more. Angry at what is not enough."

"We consume more of earth's resources now than any time in history."

"It's scary, Sam, the hunger to consume never ends. Look at the staggering obesity we suffer with and piles of throw-away junk that are everywhere."

Deepak continued, "The caterpillar begins to die as it over consumes. Its body actually starts to die off and decay. Its body becomes less solid and malleable, losing its structure."

"Our collective mythos is dying," Sam said looking at me. "Everything we believed in, the American Dream, faith in our governments and trust in corporations, is dying. We have watched our financial institutions turn to dust in front of our eyes, watched our health implode as cancer, Alzheimer's, and autism skyrocket."

"Our identity is disintegrating too, Sam. The idea of what a good life is, and who we think we are, is coming apart at the seams."

We were coming apart at the seams in so many ways, losing our structures and questioning their meaning.

Deepak continued as he changed the slide and shared that the very same decaying body of the caterpillar became food that the caterpillar fed upon and that within the depths of decay scientists found something truly amazing. They found new cells, entirely different from the existing cells, which they have named imaginal cells. He pointed to the slide as he captivated our attention, "They vibrate at a different frequency, and they look and act very differently from the existing cells. So much so that they are seen as foreign entities and the immune system attacks them, trying to kill them off. But, the imaginal cells keep growing. They don't give up. Finally, the immune system cells stop fighting them."

"I love the name," I whispered. "The cells imagine a new reality, a new essence, and a new being. Robert Frost described how the founding fathers created the country. He said, 'The founding fathers did not believe in America, they *BELIEVED* it in.'"

"They were the new cells," Sam added, "the visionaries who not only proclaimed there was another way, but maintained the new, higher frequency. They became what they wanted to create, and by embodying it, it took shape through them."

Deepak continued to take us through the scientific process of metamorphosis. Sharing that as the imaginal cells start to find one another, they connect, and then cluster. The connections continue to form in more and more clusters, until one day they reach a critical threshold. Then all of a sudden something seemingly magical happens: a dormant gene, that has always been there, switches on and springs into life. This gene has information coded on it for an entirely new creature as it begins to build what we know as the butterfly. He slowed down to emphasize the mystery of this metamorphosis, underscoring that the butterfly is not *just* a worm with wings. Instead, what is created is an entirely new creature, one with a new skeleton, new eyes, new heart, new antennae and of course, wings!

His words flowed with his melodic eloquence and wisdom as he emphasized that this magnificent process was indeed, "*a radical quantum leap of creativity.*" As he looked at us, he said, "When we dream, and take action, we get these radical leaps in *our* creativity, and that's what we are doing here dreaming the Department of Peace."

"That's what we're doing, Sam," I said feeling alive. "All those willing to follow their hearts call in this higher future. We hold the frequency of things unseen, new ways of being and living, and anchor the signal until we make it real."

"The power of coming together in groups, no matter how big or small, is what strengthens us," Sam added. "We remind each other what is true. There is a power in this clustering, an exponential power. It strengthens our intention, vision, and power to create."

As Deepak finished his talk, he a left us with the most inspiring curiosity, "Adding to the mystery and beauty of metamorphosis is the gene carrying the code that creates the wings of the butterfly. It is the same code that makes your heart beat right now. Three hundred million years ago the intelligence of the universe put this code into the human heart. In the same heart that we find the longing for compassion. As we move to the next stage of our evolution, we will find awakening in our hearts the longing and yearning for compassion and love. And the impulse to live as Sat Chit Ananda, or joy itself."

"Fascinating," Sam said. "It is pretty incredible that there is a gene that switches on and transforms the caterpillar in the midst of its doom, radically transforming it from an earth-bound creature to one that can fly and soar. And that, that same gene lies dormant in our hearts."

"It is beyond words, Sam," I said, searching to express how I felt. "It is hard to imagine that our suffering is not about activating a higher way of living. Moving us from living with a mind centered in the cold and calculating brain to a mind centered in the awakened and compassionate heart."

The last speaker took the podium. It was Dr. Michael Bernard Beckwith, author, teacher, and founder of the Agape Church in

Centerville, California. I had been a long-time fan of his as well. He was passionate and endlessly motivated, seeing the miraculous potential ever present in the human spirit. He took the podium and began to share his magic.

"With the arrival of the internet, endless technology, and ubiquitous access to Wi-Fi, we can get information about anything from anyone almost anywhere in the world whenever we want. In essence, we have manifested the global brain. The world is now a small place. We have advanced rapidly with technology and our intellect, but we have left wisdom behind. We need to evolve spiritually. We are at the point where we will destroy ourselves if we do not manifest the Global Heart. As we awaken from this dream of separateness, we activate a great shift in mankind."

"Sam, I've never thought of the internet this way. It is true, what we see is limited. We have lots of knowledge, but no wisdom."

"We only see a sliver of perception," he agreed. "Though our point of view seems rational, our view is incomplete."

"Yes, and when we feel compassion for others, as we suffer ourselves, we start to feel genuine love for each other. This activates the reality of our connectedness that we can't see."

Dr. Beckwith continued as he spoke of the need to awaken the Global Heart. He shared the Bible story of Jesus feeding the thousands with five loaves of bread and two fish. "When Jesus stood before the crowds of thousands who came to hear him, they were hungry and looking to be fed. They were hungry for the truth of love, and to see life in that light. Jesus created that field. He was the harbinger of the state of consciousness of love igniting their hearts. They felt empowered as he stirred the truth of abundance within them. As the basket moved from person to person, they were moved to dig into their pockets and put food into the basket, not to take out of it. Soon the basket overflowed feeding the many. Jesus created the field of love that moved the crowds into the ever-present state of abundance, the state that was dormant within them, waiting to be activated. We must do this today. It is time for us to step into a greater reality, activating that which lies dormant within us."

"Kristen, as we step into this new state of what is possible, we become imaginal cells. We move beyond the belief in suffering, in defense, and war. Beyond lack, persecution and dying to make ends meet."

"When we step out of the 'web of debt and war,' and into the 'web of interconnectedness and love,' the idea of plenty becomes obvious instead of impossible to imagine."

"We are the caterpillar becoming the butterfly," Sam affirmed. "We are being reworked on every level. Birthing new understanding, integrating it, and emerging with a new mind and heart, and as new people with a new way of living."

"We are leaving scarcity behind," I added, "and our exchanges are no longer mere transactions. Instead, we are beginning to value and respect each other for our collective contributions and creations."

"And we are recognizing how much we need and depend on each other."

"Leaping forward, Sam, creating a world founded on what Nature knows—that she is pure abundance. The world of plenty is knocking at our door, even though it may be hard for many to imagine."

I felt inspired. The conference fed my deepest hope that life had not abandoned us, to self-destruct in our misery. Instead, life worked on us, preparing us to evolve and live in a higher way. A new paradigm was dawning, as the old one slipped away. The anxiety we experienced, and the fear of change was the birthing process of the new paradigm. The escalating anger and violence we witnessed was the shedding of the old, as its remnants fell away.

The increasing instability in our world forced us to experience the pain that came with it. The loss of certainty in our world and fracturing of our belief systems brought us face-to-face with our old stories of victimhood. There was nowhere to hide, and we could no longer run from our discomfort. We saw our resentments, and other injustices, sprang from failures in our perception, created from our limited view. As we were no longer stuck in fear and anger, or wanting to blame others, and even ourselves, we grew. We took responsibility for the world we lived in, and, even, embraced the adventure and mystery of creating the new one to come. The more we grew, our anxiety and isolation faded, and our sense of security and connectedness increased. And, our old systems of scarcity disintegrated, as they were no longer compatible with who we were and the world we envisioned. It was inevitable.

The suggestion that the scarcity and suffering we experienced, with all the misery, contention, and confusion we found in the world, was *the process of our metamorphosis* seemed naive, and a mere beautiful thought, to most. Yet, I could see that it was not only possible but more likely, that it was part of the process. And yet, there were many days that I questioned how we would all come to express the beauty and majesty lying dormant within us. Even if there were imaginal cells already among us, I wondered if there would ever be enough to trigger our collective transformation.

It was in these moments I remembered Margaret Mead, the renowned anthropologist. I first learned about her when I was in college as I studied anthropology as my second major. I respected her courage and determination, but it was her famous words that left an indelible impression on me. They echoed in my head throughout the years, especially when I needed to see how the impossible was possible. She said, "Never doubt that a small group of thoughtful, committed people can change the world. Indeed, it is the only thing that ever has."

Mead's words reminded me, that to initiate this sweeping change in humanity, only the few who had eyes to see, ears to hear, and hearts to feel were required. They were the brave, inspired first adopters who anchored the new vibrations of creation into our reality. They forged the way ahead as they made contact with what was possible, and made the path ready for it to express, while it remained undetected and invisible to the rest.

It was Sam's nature to be cautious in his optimism, carefully considering all the evidence in front of him. For me, it was more of an indescribable knowing that continued to grow in certainty. Nonetheless, after listening to these impassioned visionaries, he started to see it might be happening after all, and, even, how the transformation could spread to everyone.

"Kristen, do you think this is where the 100th monkey principle comes in?" Sam continued, "The phenomenon discovered while observing monkeys on an island. Where one monkey got the idea to use a stick to fish out ants in a tree hole. While nearby monkeys watched, they learned from him and began to use sticks as well. Soon, this idea passed from monkey to monkey—until it reached the 100th monkey."

"Then the magic took over."

"Just as the imaginal cells hit a critical mass in the caterpillar creating the butterfly," Sam continued to explain, "a key threshold in the monkeys' collective-consciousness was reached, and, suddenly, monkeys everywhere knew how to fish out ants with sticks, even those on different continents separated by oceans."

I nodded and added, "The unseen collective-consciousness of monkeys received the knowledge at once, and they all changed. This shift in the whole was precipitated by the shift that took place in just a small percentage, and, yet, all monkeys everywhere were transformed."

"This could happen to us," Sam proposed. "When humanity is pushed to the brink, we can experience a quantum leap forward in our consciousness. Even if only a few of us are able to see and believe it in."

"Sam, I bet you are willing to believe this new reality *in* with me?"

"Yes, you got that right," Sam said firmly with a beautiful, radiant smile. "I am ready to *believe it in* with you."

11
MONEY AND WEALTH ARE NOT THE SAME

It was Friday before the Fourth of July. Sam and I headed to Philadelphia for the Public Banking Institute conference. Sam sent me messages during the week about the speakers, and we looked forward to seeing Ellen Brown again. The meeting took place at the Friends Center on Chestnut Street, just two blocks from City Hall in Philadelphia. The Friends Center was built by the Quakers with the intention to support those working for peace and justice. It was a beautiful old brick house with rows of seemingly endless windows.

The conference was in full motion with hundreds of people buzzing around. Seeing so many like-minded people in one room reassured me that we were growing in numbers and change was possible. Ellen thanked everyone for coming as she was introduced. She opened the conference with a report on the headway select states and cities made toward establishing their own public banks as they navigated the labyrinths of their local legislatures. Next she turned to something we had not thought much about, the United States Post Office.

Ellen explained, "The US Postal Service (USPS) is the nation's second largest civilian employer after Walmart. Although success-

access to loans, and other basic banking services, people need, but can't get where they live."

I looked out into the audience and noticed Paul Glover sitting in the back. He was an icon in the community currency world. He started the well-known, successful "Ithaca Hours," a local complementary currency system in Ithaca, New York. After, he moved to Philadelphia to start another community currency. As well, he decided to create a new model to provide healthcare services to low-income individuals. He organized a network of community contributed medical services, where they delivered free healthcare to their members. He was an inspiration and a living legend. His work and accomplishments proved that with a vision, intention, and a whole lot of commitment, the impossible could be achieved.

The day had flown. People congregated in the hotel lobby downstairs, relaxing and networking. As Sam and I walked in, I spotted Paul Glover sitting on the sofa chatting with others. There was a small crowd around him, and I tugged on Sam's arm as I steered him toward the group. Paul was an energetic and friendly looking man. Rugged and strong, his life experiences served to reinforce his dynamic and tireless spirit. As we approached, we heard him talking about Ithaca Hours.

"Maybe you need more money, you work hard or you'd like to, but you find bills piling up. You may have skills or time available but cannot find a way to be paid. Perhaps your community needs more control over jobs, money, housing, fuel, food prices and bank loans. Maybe you'd like the economy to be fairer, and more fun; rather than waiting for these things to happen, we can print our own money now and trade it for goods and services and even lend it interest-free. We can stimulate new businesses, strengthening our sense of community. Our local currencies connect people while the national money just controls people. Community currencies are legal. They don't replace dollars, they just replace the lack of dollars. Some cities even accept them for taxes and fees. My book, *Hometown Money*, explains how to design, print, issue, promote, and grow a local currency. I have done it in Ithaca, New York where millions of dollars of Ithaca Hours have traded since 1991. And you can do it too."

I looked at Sam and shared, "You know they got started when a local grocery took them for payment, and, then, a bank accepted them! They have a complementary currency bank that issues loans in Ithaca dollars. Merchants saw how many people had Ithaca dollars, and they decided to accept them, and, of course, then sold more goods and services."

"What an easy way to increase business, and the wealth of people. By their own determination, by coming together, and believing in each other."

"Think of crowdfunding, Sam. It is another way communities support one another, whether by empowering local entrepreneurs or through virtual communities online."

"Crowdfunding lets us directly invest in innovations we want. This is how lending in capitalism is meant to work. Crowdfunding gets around gatekeepers and other traditional barriers. This type of lending would never create asset bubbles or Ponzi lending like what happens in housing or tuition prices."

"Great point," I said as I reflected on the idea. "It is a democratic way of raising money. People go online to see what projects others are dreaming up, putting their hearts and souls into, and then they vote with their dollars by funding them. And say 'Yes!' to the things they want to see created."

"Through large or small crowds, people fund projects with as little as a dollar up to $1,000 or more... all done by securing pledges of money, in return for the promise to deliver the goods when the production is complete."

"Yes, and no bank to be beholden to with loan payment schedules. No sales numbers to desperately hit to pay loans back. Instead, people put their full attention on their projects and their creativity."

"People who want to share their innovations now have the opportunity, Kristen. It fosters a human approach to producing things in a material world."

"It's not just about making money," I agreed. "It's so much more."

"People who fund projects are usually inspired by the projects they support. I like how developers post their progress, insights, or the challenges and delays they run into. It creates a connection between people, like community currencies do. Not the separation that trying to make money does."

"It supports a deeper sense of community, and reputation matters, like it did in colonial times. Trust is the basis of these exchanges and the ability to raise money. If someone wants to create something, and doesn't make good on their promises, then they won't be able to get on the crowdfunding platforms again."

"Kristen, when I think of it, it fosters a natural sense of stewardship, that sense of pride we have, when we create something others will value and appreciate."

"I agree."

"What bothers me, is these great ideas, from public banking to community currencies, and crowdfunding is that they still use money-as-debt. Even these useful Ithaca dollars are still based on the value of debt-dollars."

"It is a problem, Sam. Public banks can issue loans with low or no interest, if their communities decide to fund projects interest-free, but they still use debt-dollars. So, the seven imperatives still ravage our lives. It is also critical that communities make sure they maintain control over their state bank initiatives and lending projects, or they could be manipulated for special interests and even intensify the growth imperative. Community currencies inject money into circulation without debt, but they are equal to debt-dollars. One community currency dollar equals one debt-dollar. Its purchasing-power falls as the purchasing-power falls of the debt-dollar. You might not put your life-savings into community currencies, in case the community disintegrates."

"If only there were a way to create money without debt, to disconnect us from the destructive mechanisms of the debt-machine."

"What about Bitcoin, Sam?"

"Yeah, I'm not sure I understand it even though I am hearing more and more about it?"

"The best way to describe it is to think of it as digital money. Like a digital token of exchange used to facilitate buying and selling things between people who have Bitcoin and people who accept it as payment."

"Are there really many people willing to use it as money? Is it really a viable alternative as a currency?"

"It is significant," I said. "Millions of people own and use Bitcoin around the world every day. It is issued without debt, so Bitcoin is a form of debt-free money. People's willingness to use it as money, without a government and central bank regulating it, is a major step forward, in the liberation of our money system. Liberating our money from the monopolies of the debt-money treadmill."

"It is really interesting," Sam remarked. "Bitcoin has nothing to do with banks or governments? It is simply digital token; money created by computer geniuses? What gives Bitcoin its value?"

"Bitcoin was created by Satoshi Nakamoto. But that is a pseudonym, and more than likely, it was a team of advanced developers who created it. It is a mystery and probably safer for Bitcoin's evolution and ability to take root for no one to know. That way no one can be threatened or even smeared as it continues to function in our society. The developers planned that there would only be 21 million Bitcoin ever created. So, it is valued for its scarcity and the complicated way it comes into existence. The Bitcoin community has a tremendous self interest to keep the accounting system it runs on in good order. So, there is more veracity to it than it might seem at first glance."

"Hmm, I see that Bitcoin represents significant progress, in breaking free from the debt-money predicament. But, it sounds like it embodies the essence of scarcity principles, the opposite of where we want to go. It sounds like it could be similar to 'digital' gold."

"Right on the money, Sam!" I said impressed.

"Interesting, we've seen how keeping money limited, and scarce, was used to successfully control people throughout history...and still is today."

"This is the unseen danger with creating a money token out of something kept scarce. The more it is accepted, and becomes the dominant form of money, the more the power increases for those who own it, and the more it increases the competition for others to get it. That isn't the role money is supposed to play; it becomes a speculative commodity, not a tool to help the economy function."

"Doesn't the price of Bitcoin swing wildly? On a weekly or even daily basis?"

"Yes, it is volatile," I answered. "But, hundreds of mainstream merchants announced they will accept it for payment, even Starbucks and AT&T. Even though people use it as money, the price has yet to remain stable enough like money as we know it. But the lows have been getting higher and the highs, also, have been getting higher. No one knows completely whether it will survive or how much people will continue to trust it as competition grows, but chances are very good. Even Ecuador, quite profoundly, recently declared Bitcoin to be 'legal tender' the first country to legitimize it so substantially, and Brazil is rumored to be next."

"Interesting, wow, but in many respects," Sam added, "it is the opposite of a form of money that can liberate us, from the clutches of our debt-money system."

"No, I wouldn't say that," I clarified, "Bitcoin is very important—it proves that people can take their power back by creating money tokens, used in a community, and protected by that community. And there is the accounting ledger—the Blockchain—which has tremendous value of its own. It is a continuous list or ledger of all the transactions that have ever been done anywhere in the world with all the Bitcoin that exist. It is simply an online, unchangeable, or what is called immutable ledger, like a database of record keeping of who spends what amount of Bitcoin and when. Though it doesn't name people, it names the coin's unique public key, like the serial number on a dollar. This allows anyone to access the record and verify that a coin transferred to them is legitimate and a valid token of value."

"Who controls this accounting record?"

"The community does. It is big business now. The technological professionals called miners verify the transactions between people and transfer the coins. They do the job normal banks do when we spend and receive money. The fundamental difference is there is no centralization, no middleman or regulator in between to verify the transactions."

"So, it is a peer-to-peer system of exchange without banks or governments regulating or verifying anything between the transfers of money?" asked Sam curiously, "How does this remain safe?"

"There is no middleman. This is good because 'money' tokens can be exchanged without creating debt. Since there is no regulator to prove your money is your money, as banks do, the developers solved this issue with some very high-tech math. I do believe governments will regulate and look for some oversight in time as Bitcoin is more accepted in society. Each time a transaction is made using a Bitcoin, the miner's computers must do a very difficult mathematical problem called 'proof of work' which is verified on both ends of the transaction, the one sending the coin and the one receiving it. This allows the network to verify that the coin can be trusted. Since the ledger cannot be changed—the 'block' of transactions is 'chained' to all those preceding it and all those following it—the blockchain is an amazing technology that produces a time-stamped record of activity that is immutable."

"This is fascinating. So, beyond Bitcoin is this very interesting piece of technology called the Blockchain ledger."

"Indeed," I shared. "Blockchain technology is as revolutionary as the internet itself. The idea that there is a running time-stamped ledger that anyone in the world can access with the internet has implications to change record-keeping and our processes of documentation. For example, using the Blockchain we could record and prove events in history, track the genetics of real seeds, claims made against titles of property we own or want to buy, use it to copyright original works and eliminate censorship. There is so much more."

I continued, "In fact, there are many blockchains besides the one Bitcoin runs on. Ethereum is the other major blockchain where new projects and utilities are exploding. Peer-to-peer lending, money transfers—all kinds of financial services— which are efficient and accessible and maybe even, more accessible than people hope post office banks could be. Everyday new financial infrastructure grows on blockchains and eventually their services could prove to be safer than commercial banks and even, public banks."

"So, even though Bitcoin gets a lot of attention—the big news is that there is a whole new ecosystem being built under the surface— that most people outside of the 'FinTech' world, as this new financial technology space is called, would not know about."

"Regardless of what happens to Bitcoin, the blockchain will change our lives more than the internet has. Blockchain networks flatten our world, empower our ability to connect directly with one another, verify information and bring transparency to our exchanges. The success of Bitcoin is testimony to the fact that a few developers created a digital token to act as money on this exceptional network and it is so widely accepted. It's a profound step forward in the money revolution. But, properly engineered money should be valueless, and the quantity should easily, increase or decrease, in relation to how much actual productive capacity there is or supply and demand."

Before we knew it the two and a half days were over, and I wanted to tour the Liberty Bell before we left. It was the Fourth of July, after all. Sam went downstairs to pull the car around. He was waiting in the front circle when I walked out of the hotel. We loaded the car and drove downtown. Everywhere we looked, we saw red, white, and blue banners hanging from building tops and the American Flag waved proudly on every pole. The historic district was packed, as people gathered to celebrate freedom in the City of Brotherly Love.

"Have you ever heard of the Bangla-pesa?" Sam asked.

"Yes, I have. Have you?" I laughed, amazed that Sam was bringing up a local community currency created in a remote part of Kenya, "How do you know about this?"

"While I was waiting for you I was listening to NPR." Sam winked. "The program focused on this special new community currency called the Bangla-pesa."

"How about that Sam! It is another positive development in money freedom. The local people found themselves with more goods and services that they wanted to trade, and not enough money to do so."

"Not enough Kenyan Shillings," Sam added. "There were too few bank created government dollars to go around. So, the real economy was artificially suppressed, and it resulted in creating pent-up demand, as the people's capacity to buy and sell what they really wanted was limited."

"Will Ruddick, a Peace Corp volunteer working in the community, understood what was happening. He organized a local business network with more than two-hundred small business owners called the Bangladesh Business Network (BNN). Together, they decided to create a local currency called Bangla-pesa, which was backed by their goods and services."

"When they created this new money," Sam added, "the prosperity, that was suppressed, started to flow. They reported a trade increase of 22%, within the first three weeks."

"It's only grown. The key to their success was making sure the amount of money, in supply, was equal to the actual capacity, ready to flow, — to keep that 'all-sacred' balance."

"They understood what we're learning, Kristen. That the money token, itself, has no value. The money used is valid, if the quantity of it is equal to the business ready to be done."

"What I find particularly interesting about the Bangla-pesa system is that they incorporated something called a 'baseline survey study' to help them figure out how much money they needed to create."

"Can you explain it further?"

"Their business network, the BBN, surveyed its members to find out how much business they each felt they could legitimately do, and then they used the data to determine the right amount of Bangla-pesa needed in circulation. This is an advancement in community currencies. It's active management, allowing the community to determine the quantity of money they need in the economy."

"Talk about empowerment," Sam remarked.

"The Kenyan Government felt threatened at first. They thought the people were trying to overthrow the national currency, when they were simply trying to add more money to the economy, and legitimately increase the supply of money. Will Ruddick and other leaders were thrown in jail. Luckily sanity prevailed, as they were vindicated and set free."

"That's frightening, glad that got cleared up. The Kenyan government now permits people to open bank accounts and save in the Bangla-pesa currency, right?"

"Yes, the government realized how productive the Bangla-pesa was for the people, and ultimately the country too."

"They interviewed Will Ruddick," Sam added. "He said, 'Allowing hundreds of micro-businesses to trade without depending on scarce money is a revolution in how we think about sustainable development and poverty reduction. People have a huge, untapped capacity for trade and that they only need a means of exchange to unlock their economy.'"

"I think the idea of asking its network members to come together to analyze and define how much money is needed, is a major step in empowering people. It puts the power in the hands of the people themselves."

"What struck me listening to this," Sam shared, "is that people are wealthy! The idea of being poor relates to not having money, not wealth. People just need the right tool of exchange to let goods and services, innovations, and ideas ...the stuff that is real wealth...

flow. This idea that people are poor because they don't have money is part of the illusion that keeps them trapped."

"Sam, you hit the nail on the head! That's exactly it. We are wealthy already. When we see that our poverty and lack come from agreeing to use a form of money that is kept scarce and controlled by those in power, we see that we are indoctrinated to believe and live in nonsense— it is fake scarcity."

"What about micro-lending? Didn't someone win a peace prize for developing it?"

"Mohammed Yunus, an economics professor at Chittagong University, won the prize. He created the Grameen Bank to make loans to poor women in the India. He shattered the myth that 'people in poverty are not creditworthy.' In fact, statistically, they are very creditworthy, and they pay back an extraordinary percentage of their loans. Yunus suggested that the main issue was they were simply unbanked, without access to loans and other financial services. Today the World Bank estimates that nearly 160 million people in developing countries use micro-finance loans."

"It's a compelling idea, don't you think, Kristen? It attracts a lot of people who want to help and do some good, but don't know how they can make a difference."

"On the surface, it looks like a good idea, but when you pull back a few layers a different picture emerges."

"What do you mean?" Sam looked at me curiously.

"Many borrowers are illiterate," I explained. "They can't read the loan documents, so they don't know what they are really getting into and frankly, they desperately need the loans. The interest they pay is *very high*. Most loans are made through intermediaries called Microfinance Institutions or MFIs. Due to the fact small amounts of money are lent, like twenty-five dollars to a few hundred dollars, the costs of administering these loans can be up to 30% of the loan, per loan. These costs need to be recouped by the MFIs, so despite the fact that borrowers are very likely to repay, they are charged anywhere between 10% to 35% to borrow and sometimes more."

"I thought that when I lent my money to a microlender, I lent my money for free?"

"You do, Sam, but the MFI charges borrowers high rates, similar to those the loan shark type payday lenders charge in low-income neighborhoods. What's worse is that MFIs lend to the entire community, and that puts tremendous peer-pressure on each borrower to meet the payment schedules."

"Because when one person fails," Sam gathered, "the whole community fails?"

"The whole community gets a negative mark from the MFI which makes it harder and more expensive for the community to get loans in the future. Many people commit suicide, as they face losing everything and are ostracized when they fail. It results in total devastation. People suggest this is why impossible amounts of money are repaid on-time. The penalties are the difference between life and death."

"Wow, that paints a different picture than a newly empowered businessperson, trying to 'bootstrap' herself out of poverty, thanks to a micro-loan."

"The loans help, and they have done good," I shared. "Yet, it is a sobering look at debt and lending, and the utter lack of choice people have when it comes to money."

"Micro-lending is supposed to be a savior for people who don't have money. They want the micro-loans because they don't have access to other loans. But, why are they borrowing debt-money? Why don't they just do what the local people in Kenya did?"

"That is the question, Sam! There is no need to borrow money when they can create their own. People are wealthy, already. They have resources, talents, and great creativity inside them."

"Why should people in Africa, India, inner-city Philadelphia or some fancy suburb, buy into the idea that they are 'poor' just because they don't have the national currency, or bank created debt-money, in their hands?"

"We are indoctrinated that money is wealth," I shared, "that we need loans or debt to create money to materialize our own wealth.

This indoctrination brainwashes us to believe we are separate from our wealth, and that we need people with debt-dollars to give us a chance to get where we want to be."

"Well, we need to stop and take a new route. We must see that people are not poor, that instead a new technology of exchange—a new money is needed."

"I agree, Sam. Micro-lending is based on this old negative premise. I have long believed it is a backdoor-entry, used to get more people into the debt-money system. Convincing them they are poor, and that they need the debt-money system to get out of poverty. Instead, micro-lending furthers the mission of the debt-machine—to indebt people. Intending to or not, micro-lending extends the tentacles of the debt-machine around the world, as it injects the seven imperatives into people's lives holding them hostage, wherever they live."

"How unnecessary. Money is a social idea, something we design for ourselves. We need to see through this old mindset. We need to understand what money is and how it is supposed to work."

"The only thing communities lack is enough money tickets to use for exchanges. Not too many, and, certainly, not too few. In equal balance with our productive capacity. Then, there will no longer be a need to indebt ourselves to a system, that lives and dies on creating debt."

"We need to do what the people of Kenya did, Kristen. We need to create our own money based on how wealthy we are. We have all the power we need, but we need a shift in perception."

"Now, if only there were a way to take what the Kenyans did one-step further, and create our money without its value being tied to the national debt-currencies," I said as something fell from my bag.

"What's that?

"I don't know," I responded as I took a closer look at it, "Someone gave it to me at the conference. It is a movie about the money system and debt, made by a Canadian money reformer whose name is Paul Grignon. I think he's proposing a new solution."

"Interesting," Sam said, "Hey, I think that is Independence Hall. We are here."

We entered the hall, and filed in line with others waiting to tour the great bell. It was impressive, twelve-feet in circumference and over 2,000 pounds. It was made mainly of copper and tin, and inscribed with the Biblical verse from Leviticus 25:10: "Proclaim Liberty throughout all the land unto all the inhabitants thereof." The tour guide signaled she was ready to begin and we gathered around her like little children, all wanting to hear the story of the bell.

"Tradition tells of a chime that changed the world on July 8, 1776, with the Liberty Bell ringing out from the tower of Independence Hall summoning the citizens of Philadelphia to hear the first public reading of the Declaration of Independence by Colonel John Nixon. The bell became an icon of freedom when abolitionists selected it as their symbol. They named it the 'Liberty Bell,' in reference to its inscription. After the Civil War, Americans sought unity. To help heal the wounds of the war, the Liberty Bell traveled across the country. On every Fourth of July, children who are descendants of Declaration signers symbolically tap the Liberty Bell thirteen times, while bells across the nation ring thirteen times in honor of the patriots from the original thirteen states."

I was surprised to learn the Liberty Bell was not only a symbol of freedom, but also one of unity. It was a profound message for us today. Without reestablishing unity, coming together in our shared values of liberty and respect for individuality, we could not find the healing our country needed. As we celebrated our precious freedom, I knew that monetary freedom was the basis upon which all freedom rested. We were reclaiming our lost knowledge, and finding common ground with one another, as we restored our deeper wisdom. We were coming closer every day.

Sam held my hand as we walked outside. As we looked up at the night sky, it began to explode with the awe-inspiring power of fireworks. Big bursts of red, white, and blue boomed, one fading into the next, as the crowd cheered filled with delight. Indeed, it was the Fourth of July, the celebration of our unending spirit searching for freedom, in love with liberty without which there could be no life.

12
THREE FUNCTIONS OF MONEY

It was late Thursday night by the time I got home from work, and there was still so much to do. The list of chores was long, with groceries to take in, trash to take out, and laundry to do. First, I stopped at the building's mailbox room to get my mail. As I turned the key and opened the small brass door, a stash of crammed-in mail cascaded out, spilling into my hands and onto the floor. Amidst the usual catalogs, flyers, and mundane looking bills was a brightly colored red envelope that immediately caught my eye. I was curious and put the letter on top of the pile as I gathered the mail, and walked back inside wanting to open it. As I unsealed the envelope, I found a beautiful card with a magical, multicolored elephant painted on it. Regal and proud, standing in all its glory, the elephant was ornately drawn as the artist spared no detail. The word IMAGINE shimmered with gold and silver glitter above the elephant. I looked inside at the card and found a hand-written message:

> *There is a treasure buried in your consciousness. If you will dig it up from the debris of superstition and fear that covers*

it, you will gain a freedom and self-mastery that will lift your life to a higher plane.

This is the money power in you.

The power to create money with which to purchase wealth, health, and happiness actually lies dormant within you. You have thought of the power as something remote from you and beyond your grasp. You have dreamed of the good you could and would do if you had the money power. You have blamed others for not accomplishing this good, you have blamed them for evil economic and political conditions; for unemployment, for poverty, for crime, for war...

You, in cooperation with other intelligent persons, can drive economic and political evils further and further from the area of your life and ultimately, they may be driven from the face of the earth. You can do this by the money power in you, expressed first in your own prosperity and happiness, and then radiating to others. You can do it and you Must do it.

There is No power outside of you that can bring these blessings to you.

E.C. Riegel, Private Enterprise Money, 1944

At the very bottom, I found one more line:

Nothing can stop an idea whose time has come.

It was from Sam. I smiled. He had watched Paul Grignon's movie which I loaned him the week before. I felt supported by my dear friend. His card served as a powerful reminder of the truth I held close to my heart, the truth I returned to, time and time again, when doubt or hopelessness would attempt to take me down. The message gave me a potent dose of encouragement. I found my eyes welling up with tears as I picked up the phone to call him.

"Hi," I greeted him. "Thank you for the card. It means more to me than you know."

"The least I can do ma'am," Sam said in a kind voice as his smile came through the phone. "You have changed my whole worldview; I owe you a lot. And, about this Paul Grignon... all I can say is wow."

"You liked his solution, huh? It is really interesting, isn't it? It is simple, but revolutionary. I think it is something people in communities can easily put together without having to convince anyone, change anything, or fight against anything. I think he has found the answer we are looking for Sam. He's gone far beyond what the people in Kenya have done with their Bangla-pesa."

"I agree. It's elegant and solves all the problems we've faced with creating money-as-debt. I think he brings home E.C. Riegel's message. Paul Grignon's solution shows us that we have the power to create our own money. Like Riegel said, no one ever really had the power to separate us from our wealth. I'm pretty excited."

"Me, too, Sam. I think others will be as well, especially if they learn what we have learned about money, and our history. The power to materialize our own abundance is within us. Paul developed a blueprint for us to follow."

"Don't you think we should go see him?"

"I meant to tell you, that I reached out to Paul last week to thank him for his work and let him know that it has made an impact on me. I asked him if he might have a weekend available to meet him and talk more about this idea."

"You know I want to come too."

"Of course! You think I would leave you at home?" I laughed. "Besides we will learn more with both of us there. The best news is that Paul and his wife Tsiporah live near Vancouver. What could be lovelier than a late September trip to the Northwest?"

"I've never been to Vancouver and I've always wanted to go. When are we leaving?" Sam asked already in full reservation-making mode.

"Sam, why don't you come over in the morning? Let's get some coffee and make our plans then."

"It's a deal," he confirmed. "Get some rest and I'll see you in the morning."

The encouragement and conversation gave me new energy. I finished my chores easily and drifted off to sleep. I woke up early as the morning sun made its way through the blinds. Knowing Sam would be along shortly, I got out of bed and got ready. All I needed next was my morning coffee, good coffee. Before I had another thought, the door-bell rang. Sam had arrived as punctual as ever. I grabbed my bag and met him at the front door.

"Good morning, Sunshine," he said, giving me a kiss on the cheek.

"Good morning! Ready for some excellent Italian coffee? Let's walk up to Hanover Street and get coffee or an espresso at Modern Pastry," I said as I led the way.

The North End was one of my favorite neighborhoods in Boston. It was brimming with activity, crowded with locals doing business and tourists sampling an endless selection of fine Italian cuisine and delicacies, not to be found anywhere else in the city. It was known as Boston's Little Italy, with compact streets lined with small shops, one after the other, selling the best Italian goods from select cheeses, freshly made breads, to homemade pastas and specialty oils. Heavenly scents filled the streets; it was endless delight. We headed up to Hanover Street, the North End's main street. As we got close to Modern Pastry, the line was already out the door. Sam and I found our place at the end of the line, a half a block down the street, taking heart that it would move faster than it appeared.

"Look at how alive this neighborhood is? I should move to this end of town," Sam said.

"The North End feels like an old medieval village, don't you think? With the sheer abundance of their traditional, homemade goods in every store. This place is brimming with creativity."

"Yeah, it has the look and feel of an old romantic village," Sam said while looking up and down the street. "There have to be over a hundred restaurants and small eateries right here...let alone, all the shops with pastries, gelato, and espresso."

"Mmm, I am ready for an espresso!" I smiled as we moved up in line. Glancing down Green Street, I pointed to a trio of shops. "Look at that, there is a cobbler next to a tailor, who is next to a barber! In only one square mile this place is packed with endless goods and services."

"It is a bewildering amount of creativity, talent, and productivity. Look at all the food here. Despite all of this, if there suddenly wasn't enough money, all this activity would just stop in its tracks."

"It is amazing when you think of it," I agreed. "If you got rid of the money, all this buzz would come to a standstill. Yet, at the same time, if all the money disappeared the actual wealth wouldn't change or go away, instead, it would be here all the same. You would just need something else to act as money to get the wealth flowing again."

"Kristen, have you ever really thought about what money is supposed to do?"

"What do you mean?" I answered. "Like how money as a tool is supposed to function?"

"Yes, I thought about how Ithaca Hours and Bangla-Pesa were created by people empowering themselves from their wealth. It made me wonder about money's technical role. Money is just a token, that is supposed to help us exchange our goods and services with each other. How do we define what money, as an instrument or a tool of exchange, is supposed to do?"

"I'm not sure I've really studied that. What about you Sam, did you research what money is supposed to do to function properly as money?"

"Guilty as charged," Sam said, "I did, and I think it's interesting. Understanding what money has to do, to do *the job of Money* well, is very useful as we find a way to free ourselves from the mess we are in."

I felt Sam was on to something very interesting. In examining the specific ways money was meant to work, we uncovered a simple set of rules we could use to analyze how well different forms of money worked. Not only that, we defined guidelines to follow as we attempted to design money properly. The concept of money, meant to be something simple, was mired in the power struggles of the world, and now, the understanding of its basic duties eluded us.

"I'll give you a hint," he started, "there are THREE specific jobs money must perform to be successful 'money,' and accomplish its job for us."

"This is great, Sam, please tell me what they are." I lit up and put my full attention on him as we both forgot about our place at the end of the line.

"Well, to begin with," Sam explained, "money is the unit *in which we measure* the value of something."

"You mean the value OF something?" I clarified.

"No," Sam replied. "Think of an inch, a pound, or a degree, you know, units of measurement...the prescribed quantities we measure things in. Measurements are easy to understand because they are a fundamental part of our lives. We use them almost unconsciously, as we gather information that we need about our world. We use them to calculate one thing *in relation to* something else."

"You mean, that we can tell how far something is or how cold something is? That it means something because that data or value I receive, is relative to some other data or value?"

"Yes, just like if I say one restaurant is forty miles away and the other is four blocks away. Or, when you tell me it is 32 degrees Fahrenheit outside, I can get an idea of how much colder you are than I am, while I enjoy a Pina Colada on the beach in 82 degrees Fahrenheit weather."

"So, money is a tool or a unit of measurement. We use it to compare the relative values of what we want to buy and sell?" I asked.

"Right. Let's look at an example. When I buy a coffee, I measure the value I receive now *relative to* the value I gave someone else, at an earlier time stored in money. I may decide that spending five dollars for the coffee is too much of the relative value I gave someone else. Or, I may feel this particular coffee with all its attributes—location, ease, quality, ambiance, is worth it to me. I measure the comparative values I am exchanging *in units of money*, like miles or degrees."

"So, money performs the same role a scale, ruler, or meter performs. It helps us gauge the relative value of what we are trading with each other. Instead of trying to barter actual goods and services, money makes our lives easier by helping us compare, measure and understand the values we want to exchange."

"Right, Kristen. Even though one party comes to the transaction with cash—be it dollars, checks, or credit cards, none of that matters, they are all tokens acting as money—and the other comes with goods or services, *both parties bring the value of their goods or services rendered now or earlier.*"

"So, every time we buy something or sell something, both the buyer and seller are exchanging a good for a good. Using this framework, you can see how buyers and sellers cannot exist without each other. I think we've lost touch with this idea, as we focus on how much things cost under the pressure our debt-money system creates."

"The primary function of money is to act as a unit of measurement to help the buyer and seller meet on common ground, assessing the values they exchange. It's not meant to make us try to get a better deal, or the most for the dollar. It is a technology of exchange, meant to help us equate one positive with another."

"When you think of money doing its job like this, Sam, it is easier to appreciate and recognize buyer and seller as equals, as partners. In our culture, the person with the money has the upper hand, and the person with real goods or services has the lower hand, trying to prove they are worthy of having some of these dollars thrown their way. The person selling something is encouraged to capture as many of those dollars as possible. It twists our perception into one of trying to get more from the other. We become adversaries with one another, at best."

"Yes, our perspective becomes contorted; this is what happens. Instead of seeing each other as equal participants, offering contributions to serve the community, both needing each other to produce and consume, in alignment with the give and take nature of life."

"Wow. What's the second function, Sam?"

"Money acts as a receipt for goods or services rendered. The person who provides goods or services to another receives money as proof, or as a receipt, that he contributed a certain amount of value to others. The money received is the receipt showing that goods or services were delivered."

"So that brings us to the third function, right?" I asked. "Money's third role must be to store value, the value we contributed earlier, ready to use when we want to use it."

Sam smiled. "Yes, that is the third function. Money acts as a storehouse, to keep the credit we receive for doing good things for others safe. Letting us 'cash' in our credit whenever we want or need to use it."

"So... putting it all together?"

"Money is the unit 'in which' we measure the relative value of goods and services we want to exchange, the receipt we receive as the result of our contributions, and—it is the container in which we store credit."

"Nice. Understanding this helps me see money is just a tally or a scorecard that we use as we keep tabs of who's contributed and consumed what. Maybe one day, we will evolve beyond keeping score, and get rid of money altogether. Until then, a proper form of money will protect our freedom and help us live happy lives."

"One more thing is needed, to make sure whatever we use as our money, or our scorecards can successfully perform these three functions."

"What is that?"

"Stable value," Sam answered. "Just like an inch or a pound remains constant regarding size and weight, the quantity of money circulating in the economy must be equal, or maintain stable value, to the real productive capacity of society."

"I love it!" I blurted out. "Yes, indeed. The heart of a healthy economy is money that functions properly. You need to make sure the amount of money flowing represents the amount of wealth that is ready to exchange: Not too little, and not too much. The real supply and demand for our productive capacity. When we use money-as-debt, or a scarce metal, like gold, stable value cannot be maintained."

"Well 'money' as a concept does not have an independent existence of its own. It is a symbol used to measure the value of the goods and services we exchange. Without our real-world contributions, money is meaningless. Just like other tools of measurement."

"Let's test it out," I suggested. "Picture an inch. What are you seeing?"

"I see a ruler with short lines running up the wooden stick to the number one."

"Ok, picture a mile. What are you seeing now?"

"I'm seeing the road along the Rose Kennedy Greenway to South Station and everything on it."

"So, it's true, Sam. You didn't see an inch or a mile. You saw a wooden ruler and a road. You saw the specific length that we agree is the measurement unit we call an inch and a mile. But, the thing called inch or mile does not exist by itself. We can't grow, harvest, or mine inches or miles!" I said as we laughed.

"When we want to measure things, we have all the inches and miles we need," Sam added, "and if we have more to measure we keep counting. Our ability to measure is limited only by the physical things we want to measure, not by the units we use to measure them in."

"These units of measurement, to compare the value or size of things, is something we have made up and agreed to use. As a society, we create the units, and if they work and make life better, we keep them."

"Otherwise, just like any other rules we create, we can decide to redesign them."

"So, money isn't a thing at all." I said as I paused for a moment. "When you stop to think of it, money is really a verb. Money is *a happening*."

"As two people decide to buy and sell," Sam added, "they gauge the value they exchange, in terms of units of money, and as a result of the wealth changing hands, the proper amount of money is 'doled out as a receipt.' Money is the by-product of the cycle of giving and taking. It happens. It comes into existence when we contribute to one another naturally, not when we take a debt out from the bank, and then we store it for the receiver to use in the opposite role later."

"What creates money is contribution," I said. "If we used a proper form of money, money would represent what we did for each other. It's kind of beautiful."

"Not only is it clear that money isn't a Law of the Universe that we have to deal with, like gravity—but it is our invention, our creation. Money is something we *get* to design, and we need to design, in such a way, that it performs the three roles properly, and maintains stable value—so the quantity of money in circulation matches our real-time productivity and demand."

"Yes, and not only that, Sam, money has no meaning without society. If we got lost in New Hampshire, somewhere deep in the White Mountains, and while we tried to survive we stumbled on a cache of dollars or gold, we would quickly figure out that the 'money' had no meaning to us. The money would lose its value because there would be no one to use it with, no one to measure values with anymore."

"Well, it wouldn't have any value other than being able to burn the paper or use the rock to reflect some light and signal help. I've watched *Survivor* many times you know," Sam joked.

"Oh brother," I laughed, "good for you. True enough. There is only one thing backing money, and that's what creates everything we have. Trust, our trust in each other."

"Look at the North End," Sam said. "When these merchants opened their stores, they trusted that people wanted what they had to contribute. That goes both ways. The circle of contribution and acceptance is the basis of community. We trust that life is richer and fuller together."

"It's so true," I added, "we can't survive without each other. In the end, who would want to? What would be the point?"

"And yet, if there was a crisis and all the money dried up as debt imploded, all this wealth would completely still exist. Nothing would change in terms of wealth and this abundantly rich society. People would still be as talented and creative as they are today. All this beauty, inspiration, and real stuff would still be overflowing."

"I think this is the heart of it, Sam," I suggested. "Money is made-up. Wealth is completely independent of money. Wealth is real, and it comes first, existing whether money is floating around or not. Wealth comes from life. It's more than that. It is part of our being, part of being alive."

"Wealth exists, whether money exists at all," agreed Sam. "It seems so obvious, and, yet, so strange at the same time. Many people wouldn't know what wealth is without money, because we are so conditioned to think wealth is about the money. But wealth is everything that we use money for. At a deeper level, it is our endless creativity, ideas, and capacity to do physical work."

"And all the resources from nature," I chimed in. "It is truly amazing how we've all been brainwashed to think that the source of our abundance is separate from us, that money can limit how much wealth we put out into the world and experience."

"Right, money is not wealth. Instead, it's just the unit of measurement, the ticket of exchange and the receipt we use to maintain our accounts of what we give and take. It is a way we seek to store the value of what we contribute, in order to use that value when we want."

I felt the heat of sudden anger flush across my face. It was stunning to me how wealthy we were. The creativity in each one of us was inseparable from who we were and how we moved through the world, and, yet, we had come to believe we were dependent on money and that money is what made us wealthy. The misperception was a damning one, disempowering us and our ability to realize our desires to create throughout communities across the globe. We lived as paupers, pressured by our perception of poverty, and steeped in insecurity, without remembering how powerful we were. We had been misled by this perspective and our world was set up in such a way that our attention was focused on *getting money*. When in reality, money was just the by-product, the after-effect that culminated when we exchanged our contributions with one another.

Before we knew it, we were standing at the counter and placing our order. The cafe was still full as all the tables were taken, and the line had grown as long as when we arrived. We took our coffee and Italian cookies, and headed down North Street to the Greenway Park. We were in luck as we found an empty bench under the veranda by the waterfront, an-undisturbed place for us to sit and talk. The harbor was serene as sailboats drifted about, as a single ferry slowly shuttled back and forth. The sun danced on the water and seagulls swooped and circled high as they scanned in search of some breakfast.

As I watched the splendor unfold around me, I saw nature was the most magnificent teacher of all. She was inherently wealthy, and took everything and everyone into her fold, without a single thought of how much she might have to give. Everything in her unending kaleidoscope of beauty depended on everything else, giving and taking of itself in a perfect, divine order. Her unfathomable power supported and sustained our lives. As she did her part she asked nothing in return, trusting that we would do ours.

Nature knew we were part of her, and that we were profound, creative beings. We recognized this too, even if only on a deeper, unconscious level. The creativity that pulsed through our veins was the love of being alive. When we appreciated and fell in love with what we created, we were grateful for the life that was ours. Giving, contributing, and connecting with others was the natural impulse of life flowing through us. Aligned in this truth, there was no time, and our work was effortless. The idea of money simply no longer mattered because in these moments we knew, like Nature, we were *wealth* itself.

Sam and I started to walk back to my place. We still needed to make our travel arrangements to see the Grignons in Canada. As we walked up to Commercial Street, we stopped, taken by the sight of young children learning basic math skills in a daycare center. Through the large windows, we saw the teacher in front of a big board and the children gathered around her in a semi-circle. On one side of the board, she had brightly colored equations such as, 1+1 and 2+3. On the other side, she had brightly colored single numbers, like 2 and 5, and so on. One-by-one she called out an equation, and asked the children to point to the appropriate number to solve it. Two or three children jumped up at once, and ran to the board. We could hear their gleeful screams through the glass. Each time they made a match the teacher drew a line connecting the sides of the board, and each child took turns making a big equal sign between them.

"This reminds me of our discussion," Sam said while looking at the children. "Every time they match an equation with the number representing equal value, they are doing what buyers and sellers do when they exchange. Each time equations match, an equal sign is automatically produced. They would never be unable to solve an equation because they ran out of equal signs."

"Interesting," I said with a pause. "Since money is an instrument gauging equal values, it is just like the equal sign the children draw when they find a match. We could never be prevented from creating money when wealth was ready to trade between two parties. First, comes wealth, then comes money, not the other way around."

"Saying the amount of money limits the amount of wealth we have, is like saying we only have five equal signs so we can only solve five equations—even though there are ten matching math problems on the board. Money is dependent on the flow of wealth, a tool of measurement or technology of exchange, here to facilitate the abundant flow of wealth that already exists in us and all around us."

"When we begin to understand this, Sam, we will unleash our freedom. We will be able to picture and even, accept the possibility of a plentiful world."

"I think the people in Kenya using the Bangla-pesa have begun to grasp the concept," he added, "and the colonists certainly did."

"Did you ever study what happened in the Great Depression and the late 1800s, when the money supply was severely suppressed by private banks artificially?"

"Not more than what we've talked about."

"In the late 1800s and during the 1930s," I explained, "there were plenty of able-bodied men wanting to work. They were hungry, hungry for work and for food. The fields were ripe for harvest. The only shortage around was the shortage in the money supply. There was not enough money in the economy to hire them."

"Did they let the food rot and go hungry?"

"They let the food rot, and the people stood hungry in lines for soup-kitchens. The harvests were lost, and the people were starved of their dignity. Just like these equations, there was plenty of work to do and plenty wanting to do it. Actual wealth, ripe and ready, was waiting to be exchanged. Yet, there were no equal signs—no money in sight. The problem was, of course, that they believed in money *as a thing*. They imagined they needed money before they could access their wealth, instead of the obvious opposite."

"So, the people, amidst all this wealth, waited for someone else to provide them with the money power? Rather than taking it upon themselves as E.C. Riegel wrote about in the 1940s?"

"That's right, Sam. They did not recognize they had the power, the money power within them. The power to create our own money is within us, because the source of wealth—all the abundance of life, is within us."

"Can you imagine," Sam proposed, "if the colonists, Andrew Jackson or Abraham Lincoln witnessed the Depression Era. What they would have said? Can you imagine how they would wonder what happened to these people, why they waited for someone else, some kind of authority figure outside of themselves, to get things going? They had food and were ready to work. All they needed was a token to measure the relative good exchanged. They only needed a receipt for the good given to act as a credit to cash in later."

"And today too," I agreed, "if they watched our plight, using money created from debt issued. We've lost what they knew. We've forgotten that money was created to serve us and empower abundance."

"They would be disappointed, Kristen, to see that we have made money our master and become its servant."

"Money alone holds no power or value other than what we ascribe to it. We are held captive by a misguided ideology, allowing debt-money to unleash its seven imperatives, and in the process, destroy our lives, and nature."

"The good news is that money has no power of its own," Sam gathered, "just like the equal sign or the inch has no power of its own. It is created when we transact our wealth with one another. So, we need a way to create money that shows up in the perfect quantity when wealth is produced and exchanged. Just as the proper number of equal signs appear as these children match their equations."

"That's what Paul Grignon has discovered, hasn't he, Sam?" I said, touching his sleeve.

"I think so, Kristen," he said as he smiled at me. "It seems that he might have developed something that we have been looking for all this time, a way people can create their own money in the perfect quantity, always in balance with supply and demand."

"I think this is how it was truly meant to be as society matured and evolved. The people creating the real wealth in the world were meant to be the ones who actually issued the money, not the governments. To think of how difficult it would be to get the government to create money properly again, and to maintain that control is daunting. And, all of this becomes unnecessary with Grignon's model because people creating real things create the right amount of money with their customers now."

"Especially with the technology we have today, Kristen. I think we may have finally found the way to unleash the Money Power within us that E.C. Riegel spoke so valiantly about, pointing to the truth waiting for us throughout the decades of time."

"Well, Sam. Let's go book our tickets and find out for sure."

13
THE MONEY REVOLUTION IS COMING

Our trip to Vancouver had arrived. The days passed quickly that led up to our departure, and the flight was smooth and pleasant. As our plane descended, I looked out the window to see the landscape emerge. It was breathtaking, with endless coniferous forests and rocky cliffs jutting out into the Georgia Strait.

We moved easily through customs and found our hotel. Vancouver was more beautiful than we imagined. I called Paul to let him know that we arrived, and how much we looked forward to meeting him. He chuckled as he explained that we were still a short seaplane ride away. Paul and his wife, Tsiporah, lived on an island off the coast of Vancouver, not in the city itself. Sam and I had somehow missed this detail, so we quickly gathered our things, and headed down to the docks where we found a puddle-jumper to take us to the island. The flight was one of the most scenic flights I had ever taken. The Grignons lived somewhere near heaven.

The water splashed against the window as the plane landed in the bay a short distance from the harbor. As we motored to the dock, I looked out the window and saw a man waving. It was Paul, pleased that we arrived. I was excited to meet him, and I felt fortunate for the opportunity to spend time with such a perceptive and intelligent man. We introduced ourselves, loaded our luggage in the car, and we were off. We drove through the towering evergreen forests and within fifteen minutes we arrived at their home.

Tsiporah was standing outside to welcome us as we drove up the driveway. The Grignons were radiant and fit, and lovely people. They came to the island in their twenties, almost forty years earlier, and set up camp. They built their own house, much of it with recycled lumber, and as the years passed their family grew larger and so did their home. They cultivated extensive gardens on their property which they maintained with care. The Grignons were reflective, thoughtful people who lived their lives according to their values and ideals. Paul was not only a brilliant money reformer, but he was also a talented artist. He had a studio-gallery adjacent to their main house filled with his paintings.

"Welcome to our beautiful island," Tsiporah said with a gracious smile.

"Thank you for inviting us," Sam said, "It's our pleasure to be here."

We settled in and gathered on the porch overlooking the gardens. It was a lively scene as the chickadees darted about, and the bees, butterflies, and hummingbirds entertained us.

"Do you two recall the remarks Robert H. Hemphill, Federal Reserve Bank insider, made in 1935 about the Depression?" Paul asked. "He said the cause of the breakdown was that there was no permanent money. That money appeared as debt was issued, and disappeared when it was paid. He encouraged people to investigate how our money system worked. He knew that the stability of society depended on changing the system."

"It is amazing to me, Paul," I responded, "that we do not have money—that we *only have debt masquerading as money*. What we use —as money— is a loan someone agrees to repay to a bank. Repayment must be in cash. Banks don't accept real goods or services as payment."

Sam said, "New money only comes when someone takes a loan.

We are limited to the amount of money we have circulating by the amount of total debt we can handle... and that gets less every day!"

"What is worse is we are given a different impression," Paul added. "Do you remember seeing the endless footage of government printing presses on television as children? Leading us to believe that governments create our money?"

Paul continued, "But the truth is that ALL of our money is created by someone's willingness to go into debt to a bank. Cash and bank reserves, about 3% of the total normally, are usually created as taxpayer debt to the central bank. The other 97% of our money supply is created as debt to commercial banks, most of it as mortgages."

"I think the biggest shock for me was learning that repaying loans, not only gets rid of the debt, but also the money! Since both are created by the promise to repay debt, both are erased when debt is repaid. If people pay their debts, society has less money circulating and needs new debt to replace what was repaid."

"That is the major problem, Kristen, isn't it?" Paul asserted. "It is what Robert H. Hemphill pointed out when he warned us there was no permanent money system. No debt means no money!"

"People are so talented, capable, and have so many resources," I questioned, "why are we dependent on bankers to create debt for us to access all our wealth?"

"It is astounding," Paul exclaimed, "despite the incredible resources, innovation, and productivity that surrounds us, almost all of us—governments, companies, individuals, are heavily in debt! If only people would stop and think—How can it be? How can it be that the people, who actually produce all the real wealth in the world, are in debt to those who merely lend out the money—the money that represents *this wealth*?

"Our money is debt, once we realize that if there was no debt, we would have no money. Of course, if this was news to both of you when you first learned it, I assure you, you are not alone. Most people have no idea the money system works this way."

"Using debt to produce our money means we can never pay the

debt off," Sam added. "We must increase the amount of debt we have exponentially year-after-year, and so we must increase our growth exponentially too."

"In this system," Paul explained, "growth is not a soft line that trends up at a slow-grade, it is an exponential curve, growing steeper and steeper—straight up, until it explodes and takes everything down with it."

"The growth imperative," I said, "requires that we endlessly use the world's resources, and our energy, to produce stuff to get people to buy things. These resources are taken from all this natural beauty, and processed, as fast as possible, into things that we need to buy, as they ultimately become junk, and garbage."

"When we create money-as-debt," Paul said looking out into the woods, "we need to push as hard as we can to avoid an inevitable collapse. It doesn't make any sense, does it?"

"When governments can create all the interest free-money needed," Sam asked, "why would we choose to borrow money from private banks at interest?"

"I knew I liked you, Sam," Paul smiled. "Why not create money that doesn't have to be perpetually re-borrowed at interest to exist? Why not create a money system that does not require perpetual accelerating growth to build a sustainable economy? Isn't it logical that perpetually accelerating growth and sustainability are incompatible?"

"Can we do it, Paul?" I asked, "can we get rid of all this debt?"

"We can," Paul said with conviction. "First, we have to unhook ourselves from many, many years of indoctrination and misperception." He took a sip of his lemonade and continued, "We've been taught to believe our democracy and freedom is dependent on this ingenious and invisible form of economic dictatorship. As long as our entire society remains utterly dependent on bank credit, or money created from borrowing at banks, for its money supply, bankers are in the position to make the decisions on who gets the money and who does not."

"Kristen and I have spent this past year learning about the

history of our money. It seems that there has been, and still is, an unending battle going on for the people to gain more control over creating and allocating the money supply we need to live our lives."

"Don't give up hope, Sam," Paul encouraged. "What you have learned is the most important education you can find anywhere. It will show you the way forward. The good news is we can take our freedom back by working together in our communities. And this will make way for everything to change on a national—even global scale."

We decided to take a walk and explore the town before the sun went down. Several of the homes, like Paul and Tsiporah's, were also home businesses - a bakery, a sign shop and a builder of wooden boats.

As we walked up the road, the edge of a small rustic-looking building stuck out from the woods. Smoke billowed from the chimney. Then we were hit with the heavenly scent of freshly baked bread. As we got closer, we could see the log building where the island's commercial baker was making bread. The cob oven was open, its orange glow revealing hand-rounded loaves neatly lined up awaiting removal with a long wooden paddle.

"I don't think any of these loaves are still for sale," Paul announced. "Sorry to say they are already pre-sold to the baker's afternoon customers. Made fresh to order."

"Oh man, I can't believe it. That's sheer torture," Sam said, not hiding his disappointment.

"Don't worry." Paul laughed. "Tsiporah brought plenty home this morning. We will have some with dinner.

"Paul," I asked, "the key point you make in your third movie, *Debt as Money III*, struck me. You say there are two ways society can create money. One is by using the scarcity-model and the other by using the abundance-model. Can you explain this more?"

"Sure," said Paul. "Let's start with the Scarcity-Model. This is when we use something that we consider valuable, something in limited supply, as money. In other words, it is considered valuable because it is in limited supply and, now, that we use it as money—

there is tremendous demand for it. Like gold or Bitcoin. This puts those who have it in control, giving them more power than everybody else, thus, creating competition for it. Money-as-debt falls into this model."

"I think we all know that one a little too well," Sam laughed, shaking his head.

"Then there is the Abundance-Model," Paul continued. "This is where money is created from a promise to deliver *something specific —from someone specific—within a specific period of time*. This money's value is created by *our* demand for the *real* things it promises, keeping money in perfect balance with real demand. I call this the Producer Credit system."

Sam asked, "You use Anton-the-baker in your movie to demonstrate how abundance-money worked in medieval villages. Is this him? The famous baker from your movie?"

Paul laughed. "Oddly enough I made the movie and shortly after, McEwen moved to this neighborhood and built his organic stone ground wood-fired bakery, in part by borrowing against long-term promises of bread. We earned a whole years' worth of bread from him in exchange for renting a room. We can certainly use him as an example to explain how abundance-model money works."

"Please, yes. That sounds like a great idea," Sam agreed.

Paul began, "Let's travel back to the medieval village filled where merchants and tradespeople gathered to sell their goods. From time to time they experienced a shortage of metal coins, and still all the wealth of real things persisted. There were plenty of goods and services and plenty of demand for those goods and services."

"But there was an economic downturn," Sam interjected, "and there wasn't enough money to get their business done."

"That's when Anton-the-baker had a moment of revelation. Rather than remaining stuck, without enough money, he had a bright idea. He knew his bread was in-demand, as he had a steady stream of customers who bought it every day. He easily calculated how many loaves he produced and sold on an average day. Typically, he sold about twenty silver pennies worth of bread or eighty loaves."

McEwan winked, handing us each a slice of warm bread slathered with freshly creamed butter as Sam was overjoyed.

Paul continued, "Anton realized that he could offer to pay for other market goods and services with handwritten promises for his bread, up to a limit of twenty silver pennies. By doing this, it would create reliable 'money' that could be used by third parties in other transactions, before coming back to him for bread."

"The townspeople readily took them as payment," Sam added. "His product was in demand. And, after tasting this, I can see why. He was trustworthy, and they knew he would deliver. He was an all-around good guy!"

"That's right! And hard working like me." McEwen chimed in, removing a loaf from the oven with his medieval style paddle.

Paul explained, "Anton-the-baker self-issued his own credit by creating bread vouchers, redeemable within a certain period of time for a certain amount of his freshly-made bread. Because Anton knew on average how much bread he would sell, he knew the right amount of vouchers to issue, each worth a quarter of a silver penny or one loaf of bread. He created Abundance-Model money, produced from his future production—and the demand for it."

Sam added, "Merchants also used Anton's vouchers to buy goods and services from one another, buying things that had nothing to do with Anton, or his bread. Because the goods and the vouchers were both priced in silver pennies, it was as if everyone were spending actual silver pennies.

"Anton paid the dairy farmer for milk with his bread vouchers, the dairy farmer bought new clothes from the tailor with the bread vouchers, and the tailor purchased new shoes from the cobbler with the bread vouchers."

"That's right," Paul elaborated, "and if the cobbler wanted bread he returned the vouchers to Anton—the promise to deliver bread Anton originally made to the dairy farmer. These self-issued vouchers traveled a winding, circuitous route, throughout the community as money or took a short, straight forward route back to Anton. If the cobbler redeemed a voucher later that afternoon for freshly baked bread, the voucher was extinguished.

"Soon, many of the merchants were spending their own merchandise credits. There was now as much money as there was demand for things to buy."

"You know, Paul," I said, "what I find so simple and miraculous, about creating money this way, is the townspeople created the money they needed out of their capacity to produce goods and services. There was no waiting for the king or the goldsmith to create or lend them money first. They recognized that they had the power to create all the money they needed."

Sam added, "This form of 'barter' created money flowed through society, giving everyone money to use—without debt owed in scarce silver-penny-money. Instead, it was fulfilled in real products and services, the wealth that there was plenty of."

"The people broke through the illusion of artificial scarcity," I said, "by self-issuing their credit in the amount of their legitimate production. With their ability to produce, and trust in their society, the people broke free of the bounds of Scarcity-money."

"This system was very successful, wasn't it, Paul?" asked Sam.

"Yes," answered Paul, "because it fulfilled the essential purposes of money."

"Right," affirmed Sam, "it guaranteed the existence of enough purchasing power to buy all goods and services in demand."

"It's important to bear in mind," Paul pointed out, "that customers voluntarily accepted these self-issued credits as payment. No one forced anyone to take them. This put the power to create money, and fund products people wanted, into their hands. This principle gave the power to change society to the people—in an unprecedented way. It provided a simple and direct channel to empower people as they funded what they wanted and rejected what they didn't."

"Paul," clarified Sam, "let me make sure I understand. If we had a system based on these principles today, and if the local farmer, using organic, earth-friendly practices, wants to pay me for my services with his credit, I could choose to accept it or not. If I accept it, I support him and his efforts. Now, on the other hand, if the chemical company, Monsanto self-issued credit and someone wants to pay me with Monsanto credits, I could refuse them. I fund the world I want to see, rather than having no choice as when I use debt-money or Federal Reserve notes—I have no way of knowing if these dollars came from debt Monsanto borrowed in the capital markets on Wall Street."

"You're right on track, Sam," answered Paul. "Let's say you question some of the products a company produces or the way they do business. In our current debt-money system, when you are paid in dollars you have no way of knowing whose debt created those dollars. By accepting payment, you fund and perpetuate practices you feel are unethical or irresponsible. You, unwittingly, are part of your own demise. Debt-money is anonymous money, providing no information as to whose debt created it. None of us have any way of knowing who is supported or what is funded when we use debt-money. Using self-issued credits changes this by creating transparency that lets consumers choose whose efforts are funded as they accept credits."

"Wow, this is revolutionary," I said. "This would change our whole paradigm. Even the smallest consumer is empowered."

Paul continued, "The credits issued by sellers in my animated medieval market example were redeemed by the end of that market. However, in our modern context, credits could be specifically timed to production schedules with one year being a reasonable maximum. People have to redeem them for product or exchange them for new credits before the expiration date. Otherwise the Producer has spent them for free. Either way, the Producer's promise ceases to exist once its expiration date arrives.

"The Perpetual Debt that is the *source* of our current money, cannot even arise in a Producer Credit system. That is how different the two systems are."

"Imagine doing something like this today?" I suggested. "No

debt and no seven destructive imperatives. Freeing us from the unending pressure for growth, and the rigid, unforgiving game of musical chairs that runs our society—creating winners and losers, ultimately making losers of us all, as we are drained of our humanity."

"And we would level the playing field," Sam added with a nod.

"Creating money properly," Paul shared, "is the most powerful thing we can do to change the world. The money we currently use requires Perpetual Principal Debt to banks. In turn, this requires either the endless growth of the economy (on a finite planet!) or the endless devaluation of the money or, in reality, both. We can change everything, not just the economy.

"With the abundance-model, the money supply can expand or shrink without causing defaults or changing the value of the money, making a sustainable economy at least *mathematically possible.*"

"Since debt-money is based on scarcity," Sam said, "kept scarce, it becomes a tool of tyranny—at worst, or it allows a few to have more power than everyone else—at best. Scarcity consolidates its power, and facilitates control over the economy. This produces hidden, and sometimes not so hidden, oligarchies and plutocracies to reign."

"Paul," I said, "we endlessly hear that sound money is gold money which is supposed to be money that can't be inflated by governments. It has been repeated so often people believe it. Yet, we know history has shown gold money has always been inflated to fund wars. If a government were to limit money to the amount of gold, there would never be enough money for anything to thrive and most people would be shut out of the equation. It would create a depression of unprecedented magnitude. The people of the late 1800s knew this well."

"Yes," agreed Paul. "The people with the gold or scarcity-money decide *who and what gets funded, and when.* They *can easily crash the system*, Kristen. We have seen that gold and metal coins are easy to manipulate and money-as-debt destroys the foundation of our lives. Sound money is not metal money or limited money. Sound money is money in circulation equal to the real productive capacity."

"It happens automatically," said Sam, "when you create money from the real goods and services being produced. With producer-credit money, no one could starve the economy and suppress it artificially, and no one could flood the economy with vouchers that didn't represent real productive goods and services. It puts an end to the way free societies have been destroyed for generations and centuries."

"Millennia, Sam," Paul underscored. "With digital technology, it is easy to make it run smoothly and to eliminate counterfeiting. When our actual productive capacity creates our money supply, we create money in its purest form."

"But how would this work today?" I asked. "I can't imagine people issuing their credit. Most people aren't tradespeople. Are you suggesting we, individually, issue credit backed by something? Or, even, that a small jeweler turn her promise to deliver jewelry into self-issued credit?"

"Great question, Kristen, I used the medieval village to explain the key principles of abundance-model money." Paul continued, "Now, I am saying, that theoretically, anyone can create his or her own money, but does that mean people will accept it? Today, most of us work for companies that may have dozens, hundreds, thousands or tens of thousands of employees. Company Producer Credits are simply the individual employees' individual rights to create money based on productivity - *combined together*.

"In small communities, local producers may be able to spend their own credits based on personal trust. But logically, the credit of the large and long- lived organizations that currently provide us with most of what we need and want is going to be what most Producer Credits will be."

Sam added, "Understanding what abundance-money is and how to create it properly I can see how communities large or small, coming together could create money based on this model without debt. Without having to change laws, fight against anyone or any ideology."

Paul added, "That is what E.C. Riegel declared almost seventy years ago. He saw the suppression of people. He tried to help us see wealth is always ours, and that the power to create money stems from that. Nothing can stop us but our lack of vision, misperception, and acquiescence to our fears. Along the way, we have created some very good, very useful alternative currency systems. From barter exchanges, traditional community currencies to even time-banking where people trade an hour of their services with one another. These are all forms of self-issued credit. They serve communities in an important way. Now creating systems based on the producer-credit abundance-model, we can take the concept of self-issued credit *further than ever before*. Come on, let's head into town and go visit the community center."

We thanked McEwan for the tasty bread and got into the car to drive a few miles to the center of town. The country road curved along the winding edge of the forests, as majestic firs and cedars towered overhead. The sky was a brilliant cobalt blue. The sun was bright, interrupted only by an occasional passing cloud bringing some sudden moments of shade.

It was a pleasant afternoon and the town was alive with many people on-the-go. We drove up to a handsome A-framed wood-paneled building and parked the car. Outside the entrance, we were greeted by the local band who were in their mid-sixties. They were singing and strumming on their guitars without a care. Dropping in and out of the music as they stopped to chat with friends who passed by.

Inside the community center, there was a great hall that showcased local artists work. Paul took us upstairs to the gelato cafe where we found a full selection of homemade ice cream.

"Maple walnut... this is so good," Sam said with a spoonful still in his mouth. "The community center is an engaging building. The design not only highlights the islands' talent but encourages people to mingle and connect with each other. Nicely done."

"Kristen says you're a talented architect, Sam. I guess you would know about these things." Paul smiled.

"When designing building layouts," said Sam, "I try to create spaces that not only function well but also foster a sense of community. I incorporate as much contact with nature as possible to help people connect to their environment."

"That's a gift, Sam," Paul extended. "Your creativity is a service to people. Nature is the greatest teacher. She has the answers. We need to catch a hint of her boundless wisdom." Paul smiled and patted Sam on the back.

"I appreciate that about abundance-model money," Sam added, "our creativity is what empowers us. The system is built on our ability to express the genius that lies within us, in our creative ability, as nothing is forced and nothing is falsely demanded."

Sam scraped the last bit of ice cream from the bottom of his bowl and continued, "Do you think your money system could be created on a grand scale? Beyond the reach of communities? Used by regions, nations or maybe even globally?"

"Yes," Paul replied. "These systems can operate as far and wide as people want to use them. They can be created wherever, and in whatever networks, people choose to engage. Governments, after all, are service providers. Governments have a captive customer base called the taxpayers. The taxpayers have to buy the government services. It's the law. What else could create a more reliable demand? The whole Producer Credit system could start at the top of the scale with governments and Tax Credits or at the bottom with Producer Credits from small local enterprise. ... or anywhere in between."

"I see how easily credits can be created. If the particular issuer, for example, is a highly regarded farmer, I see how these credits can be used as money to circulate in communities. But, will these promises-to-deliver ever have significant scope in today's world?"

"Sure, Sam," Paul plainly answered. "I know it's hard to picture, especially since we never question our money, instead we simply try to get more of it. To picture creating money in a new way requires new muscles. We know the money we use is debt, and we realize how destructive and unsustainable, and frankly, how unsafe it is. We can wake up any morning and find the wealth we 'Store In' our debt-dollars has evaporated because the debt finally failed at such a level that it overwhelmed the system. People, in almost every culture, have lost all they've had, at one point or another, when the seeming fortress of their money collapsed."

Sam agreed. "I want to see the world create abundance-model money."

"Well," Paul shared, "we can achieve scale and scope—as never achieved before—by other alternative systems. Abundance-money can do this because this money is 1. a legal promise to repay something specific—secured by the enforcement governments provide; 2. backed by the demand for real things that people need to live, survive, or sustain life on this planet and; 3. redeemable by someone specific after a certain period of time, allowing the credit to be traded widely or stored as savings. Producer Credits, especially if held in a diversified portfolio, would be a much safer way to store wealth than in precarious debt-money or speculative metals."

"Like Bitcoin?" Sam added. "I didn't even know much about it before Kristen shared more with me. Now, I see it everywhere. One of my favorite restaurants in Cambridge takes it, and my bike repair shop. Hundreds of mainstream stores accept it and the list is only growing. And—it is just a digital token you purchase with your debt-money. By exchanging your dollars into Bitcoin, like exchanging your dollars into Euros or any other foreign currency. Depending on who takes them as payment, the number of buyers and sellers using Bitcoin, instead of national currencies, is multiplying every day."

"That's right, Sam," Paul said. "You know, in fact, after I finished my first movie on money-as-debt, the folks from Bitcoin called me and asked me to do some promotional videos for Bitcoin. I turned them down because I knew it was another form of scarcity-money. The promise was that there would only be 21 million of them, and again whoever owns them will control them. Even if it grows, those who own the majority of them will have the power. We want money to be elastic and liberate people."

"But Bitcoin's acceptance is growing leaps and bounds. This is testimony that shows there is a hunger to do money another way."

"There are many lessons to learn by examining Bitcoin, Sam. On the positive side, we learn that a network of people, who trust the token as money, can use it as money. That's a bit of a mental breakthrough." Paul said as he paused for a spoonful of ice cream and continued, "On the downside, if it fails, or is made illegal, everything stored in it vanishes. Just as others experienced, when their national currencies were attacked or sabotaged, they were left with nothing, just useless paper or tokens."

Sam started, "when we consider money backed by a legal promise of specific goods, like a specific amount of food, or other necessities, there is nothing to lose because we have an enforceable claim to receive a certain amount of goods from someone specific."

"Right," Paul explained, "abundance-model money does not have the risk scarcity-money has. And, even better, it removes the tactics used to make the money supply 'too small' or 'too big,' that commercial banking systems employ—as they steal our purchasing power and devalue our money. When scarcity-money systems fail, producer-credit systems are still up and running because the actual goods and services they promise-to-deliver still exist, and the tokens still circulate and keep the financial accounting going."

"But how would we build these systems today?" Sam asked.

Paul answered, "Communities can build these systems with a few participants who act as the key issuers to create the money for others to use, and jump-start prosperity. These communities can be large or small, virtual, or physical, local, regional, or global. Creating a network of exchange like Bitcoin is easy with honest money."

"What about corporations, Paul? Could companies self-issue credit and begin to circulate abundance-money?"

"Well, Sam, believe it or not, something very similar to this abundance-model is *already* used between companies today," Paul answered as Sam and I both leaned in.

Paul proceeded to explain that many large companies use "capacity credits" to get business done when they run out of money, and have done so since 1950. They use their excess capacity, such as a surplus of rubber or steel, to create credits or vouchers redeemable for a certain amount of product. Then, they use the voucher-credits to buy or acquire resources they need. The company accepting the voucher as payment either uses the voucher as money with another partner or saves it to redeem it for the specified goods later. These companies complete the business they want to do by establishing these credits, replacing the need for debt when scarce debt-dollars run out. Sure enough, just like Anton-the-baker's credit, one producer's "capacity credit" can be used among unrelated third parties as money.

Sam and I were especially surprised to learn that 20% of world trade was conducted with these 'capacity credits' today. In fact, the City of London, England's Wall Street, published a report, not only to examine these credits but, to encourage financial institutions to build infrastructure to allow for more of these credits to form and trade in a wider scope.

Paul pointed out that, "If individuals in the general society were able to use these already existing 'capacity credits' as well as the familiar customer reward points as money, that would be a rudimentary Producer Credit system."

Sam was encouraged, he proposed that as more of these credits were established and more people used them, they would take root in society, just as other forms of money grew after they were introduced.

"You know, maybe it isn't difficult to imagine," Sam ruminated. "Considering also how credit cards acceptance grew, or even how Bitcoin has taken root. The more people have producer-credits as money to buy things, the more sellers and society, in general, will accept them as money."

"That's right," Paul continued. "We have plenty of wealth: talent, ideas, and inspiration, desire to work and buy goods or services, but our money is controlled by private banking systems."

"Companies using 'capacity credits,'" I said, "figured out how to access their wealth, amongst themselves and without interference. Crowdfunding uses this principle to raise money, without gatekeepers. Bitcoin is growing as more users accept it as money. The people using the Bangla-pesa are closer to liberating themselves, even more so than with traditional community currencies. Taking the best of what these systems offer, communities, real or virtual, big or small, can create money in terms of actual product and services, and do something that has never been done before. We can create money correctly, without the debt imperatives, and liberate money to come into being as needed when needed, everywhere in the world."

Sam asked, "Paul, can you give an example of how a company would issue producer-credits?"

"Sure, let's take Toyota as an example," Paul offered.

"Ok, great," Sam and I said simultaneously.

Paul began, "Toyota credits would be worth some portion of a legal promise to deliver Toyota product. Toyota would spend Toyota credits to build Toyota products, Toyota's employees and suppliers would be paid in Toyota credits and spend them as money in general circulation. Between the time that Toyota spends its Producer-Credits on wages, plants, and supplies, and the time the customers redeem them for Toyota products—maybe a year—these credits can be used as money by third parties not related to either Toyota or the final customer."

"The money is trusted," added Sam, "because its value is defined in Toyota product and redeemable as a legal promise to deliver product in a set period of time. Could Toyota offer a discount on its products if customers bought cars using Toyota credits?"

Paul answered, "That would create an incentive for Toyota's customers to seek and obtain Toyota credits when they wanted to buy a car to get the best price."

"There is still one thing bothering me," Sam interrupted, "producer-credits are denominated in national currencies. If the US dollar loses significant value, wouldn't producer-credit money be affected too?"

"Very astute, Sam," remarked Paul. "The question is how do we separate the underlying value of the credits from the rapidly decreasing purchasing power our national currencies experience? The dollar has lost at least 90% of its purchasing power in 100 years because it is made out of debt. We want to distance ourselves from these debt-currencies as much as possible, and it is pretty easy to do."

"Really?" Sam was incredulous. "I am having a hard time picturing how to do that."

"Ok," Paul started, "This can be accomplished quite simply by using a set basket of globally significant commodities. We could use the Rogers International Commodity Index, (RICI). Are you familiar with the RICI index?"

"Sure," Sam responded. "well-known and highly successful investor Jim Rogers created the index. It is composed of the average price of the thirty-eight most used commodities in the world. Taking the daily price of each of these commodities, like cotton, wheat, metals, pork, oil, and such, the index produces an average price of what makes our world run. It gauges real inflation, based on the materials we use every day."

Paul explained, "Now remember in medieval villages they used the 'value' of a silver penny to value things in. We know we use dollars (created as mortgage debt) as a unit of value we can understand. We think of cost in dollars and we know what that means relative to other costs." Paul put his empty bowl on the table and continued, "Producer-credits can be priced in dollars too, where one dollar equals one producer-credit. But the best way to be independent of monetary inflation, the loss of purchasing power these national debt currencies create, is to price them in a unit of this basket of basic materials the world needs to operate, simply by using the RICI index.

"We could define our value unit as 1/1000th of the RICI index. If the index is at $3000 USD, then our value unit would be equal to $3 USD. If the Index is at $4000 then our value unit would be defined as equal to $4 USD. In every case, whatever the RICI index number might be, higher or lower, the Producer Credit would still buy the exact same basket of goods."

"This is good news for everyone," I said feeling optimistic.

"It is good news, Kristen," Paul said as he smiled. "We are looking at a solid blueprint for doing money the right way. Producer-credits come into being with demand and are completed when that demand is supplied. Order filled! They don't operate on the principle of scarcity, producer-credits operate on the principle of parity."

"I wanted to ask you about this Parity Principle," Sam chimed in. "Companies run themselves with the mindset of scarcity. Trying to grow, dominate markets, and see how much money they can make, no matter what the cost."

"In the abundance-model," Paul explained, "companies focus on something different. Companies issuing self-credits receive direct investment from customers. They must be good managers and focus on what they are doing. They can achieve success and be profitable— and wildly so, *but the race-to-the-bottom, corrupting their values and ethics is removed.*"

Paul began to explain this idea he called the Parity Principle. It was an important concept, and from the moment I first read his work, I knew it was a game-changer. With the money-as-debt system running our lives, companies were enslaved by the seven imperatives just as we were. The unceasing need for debt creation and growth led companies to seek profits endlessly, as they gave less and less in return for demanding more and more. Even if management wanted to do business another way, they were trapped like everyone else.

But in the producer-credit model of abundance-money, Paul developed a self-regulating mechanism that turned profits into a win-win for everyone: the company, shareholders, and the communities at large. Companies focused on delivering the right amount of product people wanted, instead of trying to sell as much as they could, as cheaply as they could. This changed everything—especially companies' behavior. They became good citizens in the world because their profitability and success depended on it.

Paul explained further, "Eventually, an online automated marketplace would be developed as the producer-credit system matured. It would monitor the real time offers to buy and sell the issuer's credit. Like the stock market today, the system would provide immediate feedback on the ratio of total buy orders to total offers to sell. Issuers would need to keep that ratio close to 1:1 parity at all times.

"If the buy order total exceeded the sell offer total, the credits would rise in value, requiring more goods to redeem them than was the plan. This would put the Producer at risk of defaulting on its promises.

"If total sell offers exceeded total buyers for them, the credit would be worth less, creating unhappy credit-holders. If the credit-holders started spending them in hot potato fashion the ratio would worsen even further.

"The 'compass' directing business decisions, would be the need to take immediate action to to adjust to real demand. Issuers and their employees would be kept in-line by customer demand for their credit, not driven by the race-to-the-bottom.

"What would that action be? From our current thinking, if a Producer's credit had increased in value, it would seem that the Producer had made a profit and increased its own buying power. But that would not automatically be the case. The credits, now worth more, would claim more of the Producer's product than was planned.

"The solution is, however, quite simple and *good for everyone*. The Producer would need to spend *more* Producer Credits, to bring the value back to par. The Producer could give company employees a bonus, donate to charities, or put people to work cleaning up the environment. The profits could also be spent selfishly. The point being that profits in the fully automated Producer Credit system *have to be spent to be realized*. The increase in the price of the Producer's credit would be a genuine increase in the Producer's purchasing power... but it would have to be spent immediately for the Producer to get the benefit. Otherwise, the profit would go to those redeeming their credits for real production at above par value. This spend it or lose it imperative for Producers guarantees that Producer profits continue flowing as money in the economy.

"Likewise, if there were more sellers than buyers, lowering the value of the credits, the Producer Credit Issuer would have to buy some of their own credits back to return their value to parity. The prudent Producer would have used some of its previous profits to buy other Producers' Credits or conventional money as savings to be spent in such a situation. Those familiar with the current system will recognize that national central banks keep reserves of foreign currencies with which to buy back their own national currency to counter unwanted devaluation. Each Producer Credit issuer would need to act as its own central bank preserving the stable value of its credit creating an online marketplace would be developed as the producer-credit system matured. It would monitor the average number of offers to buy and sell the issuer's credits.

"Otherwise, the credit holders would find their purchasing power reduced and their view of the Producer somewhat soured. However, were devaluing credits automatically spent first in "hot potato" fashion, the loss of value could be spread amongst many transactions, with no one's loss being significant. There could be no threat of instability to the system as a whole," Paul concluded.

"Hoarding of profits would be eliminated by design in the Producer Credit system," concluded Sam. "The scarcity of debt-money makes everyone focus intensely on having money in hand which deprives others of the use of it in trade. Hoarding stifles abundance-for-all."

"Producer-credits," I agreed, "make money less powerful. Money becomes a technology of exchange and accounting, what it was meant to be. It takes a backseat to our creativity, resources, and inspiration."

Sam agreed, "No one in a community is shut out suffering the consequences of the scarcity model. Instead, producer-credits lead to a broad distribution of purchasing power. Just as Henry Ford understood when he paid his employees three times the going wage or enough money to buy the model-T they built, producers make sure there is enough credit available to buy their products. And not too much to inflate the money supply."

"Yes, and profits still exist with producer-credits!" I said. "Created the same way as in our debt-money system—made by earning more than the total cost of production. Common sense and good management are required but the self-defeating cannibalistic race-to-the-bottom is gone."

"Well," Paul acknowledged, "I think you two have a good understanding of the basics of self-issued money. There may be a few more principles worth looking at today. You should continue to study the information I put together on my website. So far, no one has found a way to cheat the system or destroy a company when money is issued in the products and services it is redeemed with. That was the point with barter—everyone involved got something they wanted—in the value they wanted."

We left the community center and walked down the road to look at a couple of new houses under construction. We passed the post office and a community bank where most of the locals did their banking. The construction crew was still busy at work, and giant piles of wood were stacked, all harvested from the island's large supply.

"What about mortgages, Paul?" I asked, "What about building and selling houses? How does that work in the producer-credit model?"

Paul replied "Now, here's an opportunity to change the world. Rather than allowing our homes to be exploited by the debt-money system with ever-rising prices exploding into booms and busts, we can change the way we build, sell, and resell houses," Paul said with a twinkling in his eye. "Like any investment, it involves a long-term commitment. Builders would spend producer credits to build houses and their customers would need to earn those credits in order to buy those houses."

"Oh, this is going to get interesting!" Sam said as he leaned in.

Paul explained, "When we get a mortgage from the bank, we don't get money; we get 'bank credit.' We get validated by the bank that the bank believes we will earn enough money to pay off the debt, both principal and interest. The bank is at risk if we default, and if we do, it receives our home, our down payment, and all monthly payments we made before the foreclosure. This doesn't seem fair since it didn't have the money to lend us, just the legal ability to grant us 'bank credit.' We get a mortgage from the bank we don't get money; we get bank credit.

"With producer-credits, repayment is on a partnership model. The builder remains a silent partner until bought out by the first buyer and the first buyer remains a silent partner until bought out by the 2nd buyer and so on.

"Payback arrangements can very be flexible as there is no interest clock or rigid banker's schedule to adhere to, leaving builders and homeowners to mutually decide how best to arrange them. If the terms of repayment are not met the silent partner(s) can take control and evict the failing buyer but they cannot take away the equity already paid for. The defaulting buyer becomes another 'silent partner' until bought out. Builders' have to operate under the parity principle as well."

"Builders use the parity principle while building homes for people? Please tell me more about this." Sam prodded Paul to continue.

Paul said, "During periods where the demand for housing rises, builders' credit appreciates above the par value. In this case, spending more credits to build more houses or just raising prices would achieve the desired correction in the Producer Credit's value. However, assuming that demand is largely based on the existing prices, the obvious choice is to spend more credits to build more houses.

"If there is a downturn in demand for housing, the builder has to reduce the spending of its credits on house construction. But, since this is very long term, the builder is still receiving lots of income from previous sales."

"Right," I surmised, "because mortgages with producer credits are long-term partnerships, payments in the builders' credit continue to flow in to the builder at the previous rate regardless of the downturn in housing demand. The total supply of the builders' credits available would shrink and their value would rise until the builder would be forced to take action to keep their value down to par." I paused for a moment and then shared, "This means builders must spend more credit. They could even choose to pay laid-off workers or invest in community projects to keep the balance of perfect trade humming along."

"That's amazing," said Sam. "Can you picture the world where there is a downturn in housing, building slows, and yet laid-off workers are still paid? What a way to keep employees happy and committed to this joint-venture. This means no inflated booms or busts, and no devastation with foreclosures as people try to stay above water while their houses sink. Unlike today, where our debt-money system engenders Ponzi lending."

"You two are quick studies." Paul was impressed. "When families lose their homes, the whole community is affected. Neighborhoods are degraded as city tax revenue is lost. Schools and other community projects supported by taxes go unfunded. Families are left homeless, while houses stand vacant and vandalized, stripped of their parts. Most importantly families are ruined, relationships, and lives destroyed by a system meant to serve people. Now with producer-credits, the possibility of widespread foreclosure is eradicated. The principal paid as a down-payment does not evaporate, as it does with debt-money. Perhaps best of all, there is no new pressure demanding new loans be swiftly taken out to stabilize the shrinking money supply as the system reels toward collapse."

Sam and I listened as we imagined the many ways producer-credits strengthened our communities and transformed the way we lived. Paul continued, "Producer-credit partnerships will not prevent someone from losing a home or having to move to a smaller one. It serves as a responsible platform for people to work together. When someone sells a home, the housing share is sold to someone else taking over the payments, without losing the initial down payment. Buyers and sellers determine the amount of equity and the ongoing payments to the builder. All parties agree among themselves, no banks or brokers required."

"Could someone still use a broker or a bank if they wanted?" I asked.

"Sure," Paul said, "Brokers act as matchmakers. Banks could act as brokers with producer-credits, selling them to savers for conventional money. Banks would have to perform due diligence as to which credits could be trusted, thus acting as honest credit rating agencies in their own best interests."

"Paul, this money system uses the best principles of nature," Sam said, grinning widely. "Producer-credit money is a technology which promotes personal responsibility, and encourages people to do their jobs well. Without creating excessive risks and the constant peril of jeopardy."

"Communities can fund the common good," I added.

Sam suddenly got a spark in his eye. "I've wanted to start a green building company with some friends who are builders. I would do the designing but, I've been too conflicted to move forward. Looking at how the housing market is used to do the dirty work of the debt-money system, I was discouraged. However, this is giving me new hope. I would be interested in creating homes with the producer-credit model. I bet my buddies would too."

"Well," Paul said as he put his hand on Sam's shoulder, "it's in your hands to build the system and make improvements as needed. My work was to put the inspiration I received into a prototype for people to follow. I am counting on people like you and Kristen, to make this happen in the world. Begin with a humble framework, without technology if you have to, create producer-credits based on the dollar, and, even, ignore the parity principle. But as it grows, build and use the technology to make it fully automated and incorporate all its finer traits."

It was getting dark and time for dinner. Tsiporah chopped herbs and vegetables at home, as she prepared for Paul to cook dinner. They both were talented in the kitchen. Paul was known for his particularly good Indian food and promised to make his favorite Masala that night. Of course, Paul promised there was to be plenty of bread from McEwan's kitchen. Sam had not forgotten, as he mentioned it on the way home.

Our visit was filled with laughs, insight, and connection. During our weekend, the Grignons made sure we sampled all the island had to offer. Together we hiked through the forests, climbed the rocky paths of the beaches, paddled along in canoes as we explored the bay and delighted in the locals' creations at the island's weekend market. We enjoyed ourselves thoroughly, occupying our days and nights with talk of producer-credit money.

Sam and I knew Paul crafted his ingenious idea into a functional prototype. He outlined producer-credit money as a roadmap that we could use to create correct money. It was a realistic way to change the money we used for once and all, especially when we combined it with modern technology. The idea was a game-changer. EC Riegel spoke of the time when a money revolution would come. The Technology Age ushered in new possibilities faster every day while the debt-money system grew more unsustainable as risk increased in every way.

The adage 'don't fix what ain't broke' simply did not apply anymore. Most everyone knew something, if not everything, was quite 'broke.'

Our heads were full of ideas, and our hearts full of desire, to bring the right way to do money into our world. Knowing undeniably that the scarcity-model of money was 'the money-enslaver' destroying all of our lives, there was no going back. We wanted people to see what we could see, to learn what we now knew, and to come together and empower each other. Sam and I still struggled to fully picture how we could start the abundance-model in our world, but we were determined to find a way.

14
WE ALREADY HAVE THE KEY TO UNLOCK ABUNDANCE

It was barely dawn as we said our goodbyes to the Grignons. Having little time to spare, we hurried down to the docks to catch the first seaplane to the mainland. The flight back was as beautiful as when we arrived. The pilot landed on the water and we returned to the dock in Vancouver. As we gathered our bags, we looked toward the street hoping to spot a cab. Luckily there was one lone taxi idling at the curb.

We headed to the airport and straight to our gate. We just made the flight, boarding the plane as the crew prepared to close the door. I sank into my seat with a sigh of relief and drifted off to sleep. I woke as I heard the clanking of bottles and a loud, cheerful voice asking for drink orders. Still groggy, I glanced out the window and saw we were high above the clouds. Sam tapped my arm to place my order. I looked over at him and saw he was wide awake, and busy with papers scattered all over his tray-table.

"One club soda. No ice, and a piece of lemon," Sam said as he passed the glass to me.

"Thanks," I said as I sat up. "Aren't you tired? Have you been awake this whole time?"

"No, I'm not tired. We've only been flying for about an hour."

"What are you working on?"

"Reviewing the idea that there are two ways to design money: the scarcity-model and the abundance-model. It reinforces the simple truth about our money that you shared with me the first day, when we had lunch at Stephanie's in the Back Bay—that the money we use *is* the cause of all our problems. We truly waste our energy fighting with each other, lost in our politics, economics, and social views where the cause of scarcity can never be found, let alone the solution."

"It's bittersweet, isn't it?" I said, "The problem is clear, it is our money. Yet, we cannot discover this where we invest our precious energy looking, spinning our wheels, creating endless division and hatred amongst ourselves. And, yet, the good news is that the solution is simple. We only need to change the way we do money."

Sam agreed, "I knew you uncovered something important, but now I have a much better understanding. Change the money, change the world, literally."

"Debt-money as it is currently practiced is our obstacle, not just to happiness but our survival as well. Dependent on continuous debt, continuous growth, and continuous consumption—if we try to take a break form the treadmill, the weakest borrowers will fail, and it will spiral throughout society."

"That is it," Sam said. "There is no way to slow down or stop the pressure we are under."

"It's reckless, Sam, eventually the earth will run out of patience with the looting and pillaging we do to keep the debt-machine humming, and evict us from the planet. Look at how we have poisoned our water and destroyed the oceans."

"It all depends on how we create our money, whether it becomes our jailor or our liberator," Sam concluded. "Whether it is constructed as scarcity-money or as abundance-money."

"True."

"Paul defines scarcity-money as something limited in supply. The money has value to us because it is scarce and hard to get. Like gold or our Federal Reserve note money, created as mortgage debt..."

"Look at the history of the United States. The type of money we've used has changed over and over since the beginning. Did you know the nation's money has gone back and forth, between scarcity and abundance-money, eight times?"

"No, I didn't realize that...that's amazing," Sam responded. "Well, we've largely been living with not enough money throughout our history."

"Yet, there were significant periods of time when abundance-money ruled the day. With the colonists, Andrew Jackson, and Abraham Lincoln, abundance-money prevailed. In the Middle Ages, for almost 700 years, King Henry I used it with tally sticks in England. Today, in communities all over the world, alternative currencies edge closer to the abundance-model."

"Abundance money is older than scarcity money and has always been with us in one form or another. It's the back history of all history—what is being used as money and who is able to control it," added Sam.

"The battle between abundance-money and scarcity-money has literally gone on for the last 5,000 years. The worst part of the scarcity-model is that it gets us to work to keep the system in place, in hopes of having a more liberated, abundant life."

"It is sad, Kristen. Money is meant to be a mere technology of exchange, and when used properly, a liberating technology."

"I think abundance-model money can help us develop higher levels of consciousness, and even lead to a place where we will no longer need money or want to use it."

"I could see that over time," reflected Sam. "But, first, we have to redesign our money. There is no time to waste because the quality of our lives depends on it."

"The way to create abundance-money is to create money 'as a promise for something specific, from someone specific, redeemable only in that something.' It is our credit, just as Anton-the-baker issued in his own credit redeemable for his bread."

WE ALREADY HAVE THE KEY TO UNLOCK ABUNDANCE

"Understanding that 'money' is our credit is the key," Sam stated. "It is our PROMISE to deliver some kind of contribution to others, either by ourselves or working together in a group. Money is a delivery contract, *the promise to give others something of value*."

"When Anton-the-baker issued his credit for his productivity, he created money."

"Whereas our banks," concluded Sam, " use their keyboards to *issue our own credit to us*, in the form of their bank credit for a fee and at interest."

"This is key," I underscored. "When you think about it, we issue our own credit *already*, just like Anton-the-baker, when banks create the money they loan us. We just don't realize it because we are told the bank is lending us money when in reality we as the borrower are creating brand new money by signing a loan document."

"All the money they give us is *the promise we make to contribute to others*. We have to see this bank money is just our own credit, that the bank makes universally acceptable by agreeing that our credit is reliable to be paid back and extinguished."

"Yes," I agreed, and continued with a new sense of clarity, "They aren't lending *any money*! They are simply stamping their approval on our credit as creditworthy. It is as if they are saying to Anton-the- baker, 'You make good bread people want to eat and we think you will make good on your promise to deliver it. Therefore, we've decided you're worthy of us creating money by giving you a loan.' Then they type 'the debt-money' into existence for Anton-the-baker to earn and repay them, but there is no money being lent. His promise to repay the bank, by selling enough bread to others, is what creates the money on- the-spot."

"This is the point Paul works so hard to explain to people: *there really is no such thing out there as money itself*," Sam declared. "Money is simply the PROMISE to create, produce and contribute something of value. Whether through the scarcity-model or the abundance-model, people self-issue their credit, and what makes the 'money' valuable is our ability to make good on our promises. All 'money' is just the promise to create and produce something of value within a circle of exchange."

"But, if an authority can get us to believe there is a limited thing called money, separate from us, which is maintained and regulated, then the more scarce it becomes, the less power we have… regardless of what we produce."

"Instead, Kristen, if we see through this and see 'money' is the good we contribute to each other, no one can control or limit us."

"We can laugh and start credit-exchange systems of our own," I said as I began to smile.

"You know, I think the confusion begins when we go to the bank to get a loan," Sam started. "We don't realize that we create the money right there on-the-spot."

"We are the ones actually self-issuing our credit," I said. "Banks simply agree that we can make good on our promises. The bank gives a stamp of approval and takes on the responsibility to extinguish the money created if we fail to do so."

"It's true, Kristen, and our ability to pay this loan is dependent on that overall availability of money to us. If we can't capture money, we can't settle our debts."

"Using abundance-money is not debt-money since it comes into existence by promising to deliver goods and services, the real things we produce," I continued. "So, our money is no longer a scarce commodity. It is a delivery contract. It's a redeemable promise to deliver the vast array of stuff we make. It cannot be artificially limited and made impossible for us to deliver. In fact, we can always settle our debts by delivering real things and services, instead of aggressively, desperately competing and trying to pay in scarce debt-dollars."

"Interesting!" Sam underscored. "Debt-money is scarce just by the way it is created as debt. Regardless of how talented and capable we are, we may not be able to compete well enough to pay the bank back. With the abundance-model, money is a delivery contract of real goods and services promised. The system cannot work against people wanting to contribute. Too little money can't suppress real growth, and too much can't be issued diminishing our purchasing power."

"We must get this one point, Sam. We must understand that there is no such thing as money, after all. That, there truly is NO MONEY. We think money exists because we see dollars in our wallets, receive paychecks, or get cash from the ATM. But, in reality, we use our credit as banks permit. It circulates as something that seems like money, but it is just our promise to contribute."

"When we move past the illusion that there is something as money out there, we see there is only our credit, and banks are lending it back to us," Sam added.

"At interest!" I said. "Moreover, because we can only repay the bank in the scarce debt-dollars, federal reserve notes—we live in a system where there is never enough, through this framework...exasperating the fear of survival to drive us. *In the scarcity-model, our promise to repay is our debt, but in the abundance-model, our promise to deliver is our credit.*"

I paused, sat back in my seat, and let the idea sink in, that as we promised to deliver our good in the world, we already self-issued our credit as banks created our money for us on-the-spot. The idea of community members or companies self-issuing credit as producer-credits was not radical, at all. What we needed was to find a way *to make our credit creditworthy*. We needed to discover a way we could do what banks were supposed to do, in the by-gone eras when they served the good of the people, and extended legitimate credit to businesses and people who served the good of others.

If not, we left ourselves at the mercy of the money-as-debt system. A system that perpetuated speculation that bet and worked against all of our contributions, hopes, and dreams. The system that pushed loans to borrowers who could not pay, designed derivatives to bet against them to secure profits as loans failed, and furthered opportunists to swoop in to buy homes and other valuable property at bargain-basement prices, as borrowers sold at any price to escape bankruptcy. We remained victims because we had not seen that we were not meant to fix our current system. We were meant to master it, and claim the power to determine the creditworthiness of our credit ourselves.

The only reason this charade of creating money-as-debt prevailed was that we had not figured out: 1. There was no money, 2. There was only debt circulating which we thought was money and 3. Debt-money was really our credit, made legitimate by our own promise to contribute and be productive in society.

"So, all we need to do," I continued, "is *to find an alternative way to issue our own legitimate credit.* Without waiting for anyone's permission or mercy."

"This is it." Sam nodded

"But, where do we start, Sam? It seems like an impossible feat."

"Paul said there are two ways to start abundance-model producer-credit money systems. First to begin by governments issuing their own credit."

"If the federal government took back its sovereign power of creating its money supply, reviving what Benjamin Franklin and others did, the government would issue its own money redeemable for services it provides by creating and spending its credit."

"Pay federal employees with them," Sam continued, "fund infrastructure projects and issue social security checks in them. They could be called 'US Treasury credits,' circulating just like the money we use now. People paid with these credits would pay others with them. Nothing would change, except there would be no debt."

"I can see this in theory," I shared. "But it sounds like an uphill battle to change government money—to issue credit without debt again. It doesn't seem like the place to begin."

"I know," agreed Sam, "Let alone the corruption ingrained in our government. So many politicians, blue or red, seem to be owned by special interest money."

I sat for a moment and thought about what our money represents and shared, "In its purest form, the nation's ability to issue money comes from the productivity that the people create. Each one of us brings wealth to the whole community just by living together. We come to this earth with unique, divinely inspired gifts and talents. And when we keep money scarce, through these immobilizing debt-money systems, we starve our inherent creativity that is dying to reveal and express itself."

"Isn't that why many cities around the world, and even Hawaii, started initiatives to study Universal Basic Income programs or UBIs? Where everyone receives a check to cover basic expenses every month."

"Interest in these programs has cropped up suddenly. The argument for them is that many people don't get to contribute their gifts at all, sacrificing their creativity just to get a job to make money, to survive."

"Remember what David Graeber said when we were in New York?" Sam prompted. "Plato considered the lowest form of civilization as having to sell itself into slavery just to survive, which is our nine-to-five plus workday week."

"It's true—in theory—with basic survival needs taken care of—we should have the opportunity to unleash innovation and artistic expression we can't imagine today—but the idea discounts what adversity and the inherent challenges of life play in birthing our genius."

"I agree, but there is still a prevalent mindset in our culture that believes you have to beat people with a stick to get them to work," said Sam.

"This mindset is a residue of our history," I agreed, "Humanity has suffered so much and for so long that we have disconnected from the idea that life is meant to be lived, to be enjoyed, and to express our creativity. In fact, it is our *wanting to contribute* that comes from this love of being alive, not the opposite. Conditioned by the fear of survival, we reluctantly take jobs that rob us of our connection to our realer selves, bringing on desperate ideas to escape our predicament. Nothing can stop us from continuing to hover near what we love, what our hearts call us to create. Even in the system, we have today, draining so much from our lives, the passion to create is brewing inside, seeping through every and any crack it finds, to come through and express itself."

Sam said, "People are used to the idea that life is hard and meant to be full of suffering. We may wish to give this story up but it's the only reality most know."

"I am wary of Universal Basic Income schemes. In the end, these programs are more social engineered control where a few powerful people decide what everyone else gets, and when. Not only that, they inadvertently end-up solidifying the neo-feudalist state where the few wealthy own all the property and everyone else rents. Because as these payments are issued, the few with capital to invest will run out and buy up all the property. They will raise the rent and the value of the properties will double or quadruple."

"Because everyone was issued enough money to pay rent, the people, with capital to buy the property, would in essence be paid by the government to leverage it, speculate in the property market and be secured a win, as taxpayer money paid the rents due."

"That's right Sam, assured they win, a formal 'rentier' economy or neo-feudalist society arises because no one else can afford to buy property that is in high-demand. These checks could be the small crumbs the ultra-rich throw out to pacify the people as they try to keep the hierarchical systems in place, and their power intact."

"These scarcity-money systems cannot be maintained indefinitely. They always break down. In Biblical times they were sustained only through debt forgiveness. The impossibility of sustaining the debt-money system ultimately brings change."

I agreed, "Like the impending implosion of the $1.5 trillion of student-loan debt, of which 40% of student borrowers are behind in payments or have simply stopped making them altogether."

"The system, desperate for new loans to create more money, reaches a point where no one can or will borrow what is required and less money circulates causing sales to fall off a cliff, salaries to get slashed and job losses to skyrocket, resulting in inescapable and ever-worsening economic depressions."

"Well, Sam, as politicians try to fix this mess, everyone will eventually find that nothing can be fixed without changing the money. This poison is ultimately the medicine we need to find our cure. The destruction of scarcity-money brings about abundance-money, and, ultimately, liberation for all. And abundance-money comes from the people creating money from their wealth. And as E.C. Riegel underscored, not from being 'rescued' by some seemingly benevolent source that ultimately becomes our master again."

"It's such a painful process though, and heartbreaking," Sam said. "A debt-money system sets us up to blame and hate each other while the system itself destroys us, no matter where we fall in the spectrum of haves and have-nots."

"It will wake us up from all we've been incorrectly taught and programmed to believe," I said. "Yes, just like the beautiful elephant card you sent me, Imagine! When we see what is going on, that we are living with a poorly designed money system, mechanistically operating at odds with our collective and individual goals, we will see there is no power limiting us because we created the money system. We have the power to change it. In fact, the money power is in us."

Sam added, "The power lying dormant in us is waiting for us to wake up—we've had it all along."

"We have been lost waiting for experts, people in power, or the government to *save us*. This is it, you know," I said as I paused hitting a point of profound clarity for myself, "Those that argue for the government to take over, public banking or anything on the perceived 'socialist' spectrum, to those that diametrically oppose them, supporting private banks or corporations to run our systems, are really arguing for the same solution, the same way to organize society."

"What do you mean?" Sam asked curiously.

"They appear to be opposites. But really we find the same old paradigm—looking for some form of pyramidical, hierarchical structure to set the rules and control the power in an established order. This order created a measure of stability over the course of history; it has done its service to humanity, and brought us now to the pinnacle of where we are; in the midst of crisis—and opportunity. Indeed, the gift these old systems bring us now is that a new paradigm is begging to be born, one that unleashes freedom—not through central planning or someone deciding who should get resources, or skewing and dominating the market so resources flow 'in certain' ways. Instead, one which allows abundance to flow based on our own volition, creations, and contributions."

"Starting abundance-money at the producer level is the right way to begin," Sam said.

"And we can start now in our communities. When people use it and benefit from it, they will easily understand everything we've talked about, without even having to know it. It will simply empower us."

"Where do we start?"

"With farmers, or any good-sized food producer or food distributor. If we create credits valued in food, the credits will have value everyone understands and trusts because the credits are legally redeemable for food—not some hope or undefined promise."

"The most important thing is to find a town or a region with a strong sense of community."

"All we need is one prominent farmer to offer food credits or money denominated in a specific amount of food, redeemable in a set timeframe. We only need one, to issue credits as payment, and people to accept them. To get it started."

"One farmer or company issuing credit is enough," agreed Sam. "Anton-the-baker got the system started in his medieval village by himself with his bread credits."

"As people start to encounter them and use them, it will catch on."

"A grocery store, like Whole Foods or Costco, can issue credits, like gift certificates or product vouchers, and they can be used as money," Sam brainstormed.

"I can exchange some of my regular debt-dollars," I added, "for debt-free Whole Food dollars, redeemable for a certain amount of food, and pay my dry cleaner with them. My dry cleaner can pay her plumber with them, who, can in turn, pay his mechanic with them who can then return to Whole Foods and redeem them for groceries."

"As other people in the community accept them as payment, the circle grows wider and wider," Sam said. "All it takes is one farmer, or grocer, to create abundance-money to model the genius and self-empowerment possible for everyone."

"It's enough to get it started," I agreed. "Like planting a seed in the ground. Something so simple as this, so seemingly insignificant can take root, develop and have a massive impact."

"This is how all alternative currency systems begin," Sam recounted. "Someone makes a new form of money available. One merchant, then a few more, accept it as payment. As more people use them, more merchants do more business if they accept them too."

"And the more merchants accept them, the more people want to use them. It is a self-propelling, self-reinforcing dynamic that creates its own acceptance, growth, and success."

Sam added, "Food credits are infinitely usable especially to me, and easy to trust as money because they are redeemable for something we need to live —food!"

"The entire population rests on the production of farmers. Farmers make up only 1% of the population. Without them, especially our local farmers, our lives and our money would come to an end pretty quickly."

"Whoa, Kristen, that puts into perspective how much we depend on farmers and what they do for us. I imagined that farmers were a bigger portion of the population."

"Sam, think of how we already engage in farm shares or CSAs," I contemplated. "We prepay the farmer for food they harvest from late spring to late fall. Farmers get upfront investment money they need to develop and manage their farms better, and people get food at great value, grown to standards they want. It is a win-win for everyone."

"What matters is the money can be trusted. Good for something people want, issued in the right amount," asserted Sam.

I nodded as I thought about all the possibilities. "The goal is to find a way to introduce abundance-money into society and seed it like a positive, powerful tool that will grow and grow. Designed with the blueprint for abundance."

"Creating a simple food-backed currency is like sending an unassuming Trojan horse into the seminal of the debt-money machine. As it grows and is accepted, the debt-monster's grip will disintegrate." Sam laughed with a mischievous chuckle.

"Debt-money will be increasingly irrelevant—simply unselected, as it becomes less attractive," I grinned. "And frankly uncompetitive and, of age now passed, as people find this new collaborative abundance-money facilitates innovation and contribution. Like unpacking a present with untold blessings."

"Once we have one solid producer issuing food credits, next maybe solar producers or renewable energy producers could enter the scene," Sam proposed. "Or wellness-care centers, or even senior-care services."

"I was talking to a client last week who put solar panels on his house," I recalled. "In the winter, the panels didn't produce all the energy he needed, so he still had to buy electricity from the power company. But throughout the summer, the panels produced more energy than he used all of last year. He thinks he will have extra credit left over this year even as winter arrives."

"Can he sell his extra credits back to the power company?" asked Sam. "Or does he receive credit in his account to offset any power he needs in the winter? He is self-producing credit from the solar panels on this house!"

"All of the above, Sam," I answered. "He is producing credit he can use or sell from the energy collected. It would be very interesting to see how these credits can be built into an exchangeable, transferable network for other things."

"I find that very interesting," Sam shared. "Solar credits are being used as money only between the power company and the customer now. Yet, it already establishes an operational loop, transferring credits defined in energy."

Hock, emerged to turn things around. And indeed, he did. He almost single-handedly made credit cards the wild success they are today.

Dee Hock changed money as we know it. He was up against a world that didn't believe in him or his ideas. His potential customers did not see the value credit cards offered. But, Hock's passion, insight, and effective collaboration with others ignited the demand for them. He revolutionized the way we use money, and even what money was. He did not intend for credit cards to become the ubiquitous 'in-debtor' of all.

Instead, he was pragmatic, and focused on developing new markets and innovative payment systems. He gained a powerful reputation and significant status in the banking industry with his success. As time passed, he walked away from several lucrative promotions as he sensed the corporate structure, with its command-control rigidity, suffocated enthusiasm and inspiration. He said that most corporate institutions had become "not only archaic and increasingly irrelevant... [but also a] public menace, antithetical to the human spirit..." Surely, the money-as-debt system that drove profit models worked to ossify human creativity and stifle its great imaginative power.

As I learned about him over the years, I was taken by the depth of his insight and eloquence. He became an inspiration to me, and even a hero, who was ahead of his time. It was Hock's conviction in his vision of what we together were capable of creating when we believed it was possible and made the commitment to make it happen. It was the secret of his Herculean success. Inspired by his greater vision and hope for humanity, I read many of his writings as I studied the workings of the money system.

I turned to Sam to relay one of my favorite quotes of the many wise words Hock shared, "Money motivates neither the best people nor the best in people. It can move the body and influence the mind. But it cannot touch the heart or move the spirit; that is reserved for belief, principle, and morality."

"Beautiful, huh?" I asked. "What could motivate us more than creating a new money system to empower our greatest expressions? To create the opportunity to live in an abundant world filled with the ability to express ourselves and our dreams?"

"I can't think of anything," Sam said looking at me with a soft smile.

He glanced down as he reached into his bag and took out two gorgeous sandwiches stuffed with turkey, cheese, and avocado. He handed me one and said, "Freshly made with Anton's, I mean, McEwan's bread. Can't beat it!"

I took the sandwich and wondered what else he had in his bag. Amused and puzzled, I pondered how he managed to fill it without me noticing.

"Thanks, Sam," I said taking a bite. "Mmm, you're right this is pretty darn good. What do you say? Let's go to the farmer's market this weekend in Copley Square. It may be the last one of the season."

He nodded yes with a wink and then set his attention on his glorious sandwich. Soon I drifted back to sleep and woke as the wheels bumped along the runway. We landed in Boston, filled with enthusiasm, and wonder as to how it would all unfold.

15

CREATING THE GREAT SOCIETY

October had arrived, and the beauty of fall surrounded us. The leaves were alive in vibrant orange, golden yellow, and bright red. Pumpkins and oddly shaped gourds were everywhere, and flower boxes were filled with mums and purple-green cabbages. Sam and I took the train to get to the farmer's market at Copley Square.

"It looks like there are several local farmers here," Sam said as we walked toward the white tents on the green.

"What's this?" I asked, holding up a brochure with '*Slow Money*' printed on it.

"*Slow Money?*" Sam read aloud. "Maybe it's something about investing money in a patient way—to produce good things? Maybe it's the opposite of making fast money by trying to turn a quick profit with some risky investing?"

I perused the brochure and discovered he was right on target. It was a non-profit organization dedicated to socially responsible investing in farmers and local food producers.

"Looks like they are having a meeting tonight," I said as Sam picked up a brochure for himself.

"Interesting. Where is it?"

"In Cambridge. Just across the bridge on Garden Street, right outside Harvard Square," I answered. "It starts tonight at 5:30. What do you say, are you game?"

"With you?" Sam asked. "Absolutely. Let's check it out!"

"I recently read that hedge funds are buying up farmland in droves," I shared as I sighed. "Farmland and crops can often yield a 12% annual return. These growth hungry funds have their eye on farmers as the next best speculative bet to get their returns."

"First, they target our homes, then our education, and now our food supply?"

"One report I read," I continued, "said in the last decade hedge funds and university endowment funds poured almost $25 billion into US farmland. Even pension funds are involved. These funds race to buy up land to make returns, as high as possible and as fast as possible."

"Really?" Sam asked. "Wall Street players are the new buyers of prime farmland? They're just trying to make a fast buck and some serious profits. They push up the price of farmland and make it harder for farmers to purchase land to produce our food."

"It is incredible to think that the Teacher Insurance and Annuity Association—College Retirement Equities Fund, one of the world's largest pension funds, is a buyer."

"Talk about self-sabotage!" remarked Sam. "It has always been a challenge for farmers to own land, especially for those using organic and regenerative practices. Most farmers end up leasing their land."

"Now, they need to get there before Wall Street does," I added. "The Oakland Institute, a think-tank focused on socio-economic issues affecting the environment, points out this trend 'can lead to the worst kind of absentee-landlordism. Resulting in badly managed farms, poor labor practices, disempowerment of farmers, and increased speculation in land prices. Investors could even choose to frack the land, or sell it to a golf course developer—if that's more profitable than leasing to a local farmer.' How do you like that?"

"Ominous," said Sam solemnly. "All for a profit. The need to win returns for shareholders destroys farmers' ability to farm. We have entered the full-blown race-to-the-bottom as the 'last bastion of sanctity'—the land where our food is produced is under attack."

"Older farmers looking to retire have a dilemma too," I added. "With farmland bid up by large institutional funds, younger farmers can't afford to buy the land, and they can't get loans. So, many older farmers won't retire, even when they are ready. They keep farming to have money to survive, and it is labor! The whole thing is an opportunistic nightmare."

"What do younger farmers do?"

"They lease their land," I answered. "And leasing doesn't guarantee they can grow what they want, or even stay on the land and keep farming. If farmers don't stay on their land, there won't be any sustainable agriculture. These funds could buy $1 trillion worth of land worldwide with the money they have."

"I think we need to ask what they intend to do with this land," Sam asserted. "Wall Street fund managers know nothing about agriculture or which foods sustain communities. You know what they are good at…"

"Producing speculative returns," I answered, "and something yielding 12% today is too hot for the debt-money machine to ignore."

"What can be done to counter this?"

"There is a glimmer of hope," I shared. "There are socially conscious funds gathering pools of money to invest in farmers committed to taking care of the land and producing real food, as opposed to growing highly-profitable GMO soybeans and corn crops used to mass-produce additives and high-fructose syrup."

"That's impressive," Sam said with a glimmer of relief. "Maybe these conscious funds would be interested in supporting food currencies."

"One thing we know for sure," I said, "is nothing would make farmers more resilient and self-sufficient. Sam, did you see that Costco sold over $4 billion worth of organic produce last year?"

"Just in organic produce?" Sam qualified.

"Yes," I confirmed. "It's a huge number. They say they can't keep up with customer demand. They piloted a program to help farmers buy land and equipment to produce more organic food to meet demand. They have plans to expand the program to help farmers in other countries too."

"Look at how consumers' demand drives producers to collaborate and to use the power of their production—to get around the debt-money system."

"Sam, it makes me think there is a circle of opportunity here," I explained. "Costco or Whole Foods could offer their existing customers food credits at a discount. Anyone could buy $100 or up to $10,000 of these food credits (more if they wanted) perhaps for $90 or $9,000, then customers would receive 10% off the price of their food. This would allow Costco and Whole Foods to do a 'capital raise' or raise lots of cash from their customers in return for product and create a pile of money to invest in farmers, without interest, just by doing profit-sharing with customers."

"They could lend this money to farmers at low-interest rates or even 0% interest," added Sam.

"Right and farmers could repay in money or in...."

"In food!"

"This organic produce would fill the shelves," I added. "It would meet customers' demand—and they would buy it at a discount with their food credits."

"Not only that, Kristen," Sam agreed, "before the time they redeemed them for food, communities could circulate them as money like Anton-the-baker's vouchers circulated in the town."

"You read my mind!" I said with a smile.

"How interesting," Sam mused, "The failure imposed by the nature of debt-money, and its destructive imperatives, brings about innovation," Sam added. "Investors like Costco and socially conscious funds are helping farmers directly without traditional lending."

"You know," I suggested, "this idea could be used in other networks, or forums, where small producers sell their goods. Like Etsy, eBay? Or even Uber and Airbnb?"

"Yes," Sam agreed, "money raised by customers in return for credit, credits purchased at a discount to incentivize customers to take part in their services, and do some profit-sharing. Corporations can use the money raised to create low-interest or no-interest loans to help the entrepreneurs produce more of the services—and better services—these corporate platforms market and coordinate."

"When you think of it Sam, Uber and Airbnb could radically upgrade their business model by issuing their own producer credits. They could take the money they raised by issuing their credit and use it either to issue loans or direct payments to their top producing rental properties or drivers and help them upgrade their homes or their cars. Producer credits would give them an opportunity to do profit-sharing with their contractors and invest in the people who use their platform to do business."

"That would solve the image problem they have. This way they could integrate some kind of quality control, and also partner with property owners or drivers. Many criticize them for feeding off the profits that property owners or drivers create for them while the companies do not put any money into infrastructure."

"It's true, Sam. Just by creating producer-credits, backed in housing or ride credits, a loop is developed where all players support each other, and stabilize and even out the playing field. It is a core-abundance principle because it is built on the principle that producers and customers or buyers and sellers are connected."

"It's not a big leap to create abundance-money from these networks," Sam proposed. "It just takes some vision and understanding. We can come together building our connections and circles, strengthening each other and our societies."

"These are ways we can bring the idea in quietly through the back door."

"Like a Trojan horse," Sam smiled with a wink. "Most people will not notice that abundance-money principles have been introduced as these collaborative practices are a way to perform and compete better. Yet all the while abundance-money is sown, and as it takes root and spreads under the leaves it undoes scarcity and the need for pointless growth and sabotage."

"This is how forest fires start, right?" I added. "They smolder and burn with low intensity under the brush and cover. They work their way, blanketing vast distances unnoticed. Then suddenly, bam! they blaze. The fire is hot, and the flames so big, seemingly coming from nowhere. Now, they catch everyone's attention. Even though, they were there long before, working slowly and persistently—active, just unseen."

"Unseen by those who did not know what to look for," added Sam.

"Right, something hidden in plain sight so unexpected only those who know what to look for spot the new way to do money, and introduce it to others as the '100th monkey' principle grows and reaches its pinnacle. Then, all of society takes part in the new way of living."

"In a whole new way of being," Sam agreed, as he put his arm around my shoulder and smiled. "I think it's time we go meet some farmers."

We spent the next couple of hours perusing the market and talking with the local farmers. The afternoon was delightful as we engaged with others. By the time we left, we made some good contacts, and set up meetings to see how we might be able to establish a new money backed in food. We headed to Park Station to catch the Red Line to Harvard Square.

"Look at how many people are still enjoying the park!" Sam said as we looked at the people spread out on the lawn.

"Well, it's only October," I chuckled. "That means there are at least two months left before hearty New Englanders pack-up and spend city weekends inside."

"Boston has so many beautiful places to enjoy the city," Sam said as two squirrels scurried in front of us. "Debt-money creates a horrible noose on our lives with its seven destructive imperatives squeezing every ounce of living from our lives. I guess these same seven imperatives are driving us to change though."

I nodded. "Without the pressure, people wouldn't stop to question our money system. If things were comfortable, people would keep going, believing they needed a little more money or little more time... continuing to blame their frustration on others, like frogs slowly cooking in a pot of water, lulled by some sense of comfort, unable to see what is happening."

"The seven debt imperatives turn the heat on high," Sam said. "They make us willing to find out what's wrong and discover scarcity-money is making us poor and keeping us broke!"

I agreed. "I think without our suffering, we wouldn't wake up."

"Just like the growing chick finding an ever-troubling, unsolvable problem with its egg—the problem with the egg is the catalyst for it to grow—and go beyond its wildest imagination. It would never think the egg protecting it, giving it stability, was to become its greatest obstacle to living."

"Even requiring the chick to break it down," I continued. "This is the means by which life spurs us onto greater realities, onto new ways of seeing, being, and living. It's awe inspiring, like a divine hand prompting us to let go of what no longer serves us, even as we tremble it is, quietly there, preparing to catch us as we leap."

Sam and I went downstairs to the Park Street T-station and slid our trolley-cards through the turn-style gate and found the platform to catch our train to Harvard Square. While we waited, we discussed how our lives would change as the new money revolution emerged with abundance-money and how the seven destructive imperatives would naturally dissolve.

We saw the first imperative end, as the need for constant debt was gone. We were no longer on the endless cycle of creating and repaying debt. The second imperative vanished as the debt-clock no longer entrained an artificial and inhuman pace, robbing us of our ability to adjust our schedules. Instead, we lived in the natural rhythm of life, and had space to get in touch with our creativity and insights.

No longer run by the third imperative, there was no desperation to get a job, any job we could find. On our debt-money system whether we had a mortgage or rent to pay, every passing hour meant the deadline was closer to give the debt-machine its monthly dose of fuel. Instead, we were free. We did not sell our labor like a commodity, something separate from who we were. We gravitated to what we loved and what we were gifted to do. We lived for our heart's content to serve, create, and enjoy.

The fourth imperative ran out of steam with its requirement for mindless, addictive consumption and need to contaminate our lives with the idea that we were forever incomplete, to propel and compel us to buy more. Companies were not squeezed to produce the lowest quality, with the worst practices. Instead, we lived in a world where our innovations served people and the earth.

The need for bottomless, empty growth and reckless speculation that the fifth and sixth imperatives mandated stopped. Nor was there any desire to glorify the modern-day super rich, who used the financial markets to skim money from society and gain power acquiring the things others produced and required for themselves. They were no longer role models. Rather, those living in integrity, developing their talents, and bringing forth their gifts, were honored. Inspiring others to look for their own strengths and beauty, and to contribute from there.

The power of government returned to the people. As the seventh imperative no longer demanded that small groups controlled and created rules for everyone else. The steep, hierarchical pyramids structuring society dissolved as egalitarian frameworks emerged. Communities and companies were empowered to self-issue credit from the wealth of what they produced. They came together in independent circles, connected, and did business with each other. We thrived in the web of life, no longer trapped in the web of debt.

The neo-feudalist order constricting our lives also fell apart, as a new blueprint structuring society took its place. It took the shape of the flower of life, the most sacred geometric pattern of life, the configuration life follows as it begins when cells divide and form the miracle of our bodies. It was the way our institutions would now structure as we reorganized and harmonized with our rising empowerment. Producers formed circles of exchange directly with others. As we continued to come together, our circles would double and double, and form the pattern of the flower of life. Our institutions embodied our true nature—separate but connected. It only made sense that a liberating and life-promoting money system had the same framework of life itself.

The Red Line train to Harvard Square approached as it entered the tunnel. With a rush of warm wind, the heat of the subway swept us back. As the doors opened, we were pushed into the car as the crowd moved us forward. We scanned the train for two seats together and found a pair in the middle. We sat down just as the doors closed and the train sped off.

"What's that?" I asked.

"What?" Sam questioned.

"You're sitting on something, it looks like a magazine," I said as I tugged at the corner.

"It's a copy of *Brainstorm Magazine*," Sam said as he held it in his hand. "Hey, check out this article!"

"'Alternative Currencies are Coming,' written by Paul Furber," I said amazed. "Look at the subtitle: 'The nature of money itself will change, with sweeping consequences for society,' says a senior Gartner executive."

"The Gartner Group, that's a consulting group specializing in innovative technologies," said Sam. "Oh, interesting, the article highlights what David Furlonger, VP of the banking sector, says about how money is changing."

Sam handed the magazine to me as I skimmed the article. "He suggests that the amount of money in complementary currencies will exceed the amount of money people have in dollars by 2020—despite that most people don't have an idea what complementary currencies are. He suggests these new currencies could even be game tokens, cellphone minutes, or—customer loyalty reward points!"

"Let me see," Sam said as he took the magazine back, "Furlonger notes that for over the past one-thousand years the way money changed was tied to the way society changed. He says that since we are experiencing massive shifts in society today the nature and role of our money—is being challenged because these changes are making life as we know it unsustainable."

"He's right, Sam. He points to the fact that cities and regions are going bankrupt. Look at Puerto Rico or even the trouble the city of Chicago is in—societies are facing fundamental issues of scarcity and lack, with pensions to pay, healthcare, and infrastructure to fund. And while this is happening, people around the world are becoming millionaires—in points— that buy them things. They acquire these points by playing games or even with shopping rewards. Furlonger suggests that it doesn't matter how we store our wealth, be it in loyalty points, solar credits or food vouchers, these currencies are money because we can buy things we need with them."

Sam continued to share as he read on. "Debt, scarcity, and poverty in Europe have become a catastrophe. Furlonger questions how governments will fund pensions, pay for medical costs, and infrastructure improvements. He says there are massive economic shifts coming."

I interrupted, "Is he suggesting—what we are working on—a new form of money?"

"Pretty much. He suggests that financial institutions build exchange networks, so that loyalty points, airline miles, and other credits can be exchanged into one uniform credit that can be readily used as money anywhere."

I pulled the magazine closer. "Look at what he says next, Sam. That it is not in the interest of banks to allow these new currencies to come to the forefront because they own the monopolies over our current money system. If banks were able to stop them, they would, but we have the Internet now. So, we have tremendous connectivity and power that did not exist before."

"This is similar to what Paul Grignon says," Sam added. "We have the opportunity now, as never before in history, to create circles of exchange and create money far beyond anything we have done before."

"My mom told me about a program American Express offered for several years. Merchants offered loyalty points to customers called 'Plenti Rewards.' As customers shopped at participating stores, they 'earned' points and stocked up credits to use as 'money' within the network."

"Well, Kristen, these Plenti points *were* money. Money created without debt! Recorded in people's accounts as a credit on their statements—with no corresponding debt."

"American Express converted various merchant credits into a uniform credit that was redeemed at any of the participating stores. This was a mini-version of the network David Furlonger urges financial institutions to build, so that credits can be used as debt-money is now."

"Think about what Paul and Tsiporah told us about Canada Tire," Sam added, "the large Canadian retailer selling household goods. They issue more than $100 million a year in Canadian Tire money as customer rewards, and over a billion dollars of them have circulated to date."

"That's right. Interesting. People use them as money, just like Anton-the-baker's credits. One Canadian Tire dollar is equal to one Canadian government dollar."

"Money created without debt, and redeemable for real products at the store."

"What about the Plastic Bank, Sam?" I enthusiastically interjected. "David Katz, the CEO, had a grand vision for clearing plastic out of the oceans, inundating so many third world island nations. He set up local 'bank branches' where collected plastic is weighed and sent off to be recycled, and in return pickers receive digital tokens they can use as money. He is working with major retailers to use this recycled or 'social plastic' in their product lines. The quantity of the tokens are generated by the quantity of plastic collected!"

"That's truly inspiring. This is only a few iterations away from being a producer-credit. Are the tokens exchanged into local currencies?"

"Yes, they need to raise money to pay for the plastic collectors. If they evolve the tokens into 'plastic producer-credits' there would be no need for money. The act of delivering the plastic to the branches would create 'plastic producer-credits' worth a specified amount of money determined by the quantity and value of the plastic, but denominated in 'plastic producer-credits.' People would come to understand it was an additional—alternative currency and it would operate along side the national money."

"Then we have JP Morgan who surprised everyone with their own new digital coin, JPM coin, despite how openly negative they have been on Bitcoin. Again, not much of a producer-credit but it shows they are watching what's happening and taking it very seriously," shared Sam.

"And, Facebook?" I posed with hesitation, "They, too, are preparing their own coin to compete with fiat currencies. I have to say I have been imagining all these corporations would create coins, but it does make me more cautiously nervous than optimistic. Unless they issue coins as producer credits, it will be more of the old paradigm—and possibly, accelerating the old paradigm—on steroids. As they add new tokens, they create confusion and noise. They will encourage people to seek speculation, and issue their 'money' tokens with no corresponding value and mere arbitrary quantity all to maintain market share and dominance, and propel the old scarcity model."

"I think it is a positive development," gathered Sam, "Even if they don't understand the difference between scarcity and abundance money, they are priming the pump, helping people to see money as changeable, *something we can redesign*. The truth is, when we look, we see producer-credit like money already beginning to take shape in our world. Just as David Furlonger articulates there are many forms of wealth that are becoming usable credits now. We see abundance-money forming in society—and we can take it much further. This is the unstoppable coming revolution of money."

"Well, you're right, Sam, we can. We can, and we will, take it much further than anything we've seen so far, because these core principles of abundance-money must be integrated. This is how the real revolution is being born. Companies and producers of the actual things we need and want now have the ability to create the money that we all need, unencumbered. With the producer-credit model, ethical companies producing products and services aligned with the greater good will naturally succeed and rise, while others fail. We are stepping into a new world where our creativity and imagination is our wealth, and we no longer need to find political or powerful corporate monopolies to manage our money supply or distribute resources."

"No, we no longer need to wait for someone else to change our systems. We are discovering the power is ours, we hold it, and with the right money, we have the way to create our liberation."

The train pulled into Harvard Square, and we were at our stop. Sam put the magazine in my bag as we headed up the escalator to the street.

"Hey, we have at least an hour to spare," Sam said looking at his watch. "Let's go to the Harvard Museum of Natural History. It's one of my favorites."

"I don't think I've ever been there. Is it open on Sunday afternoons?"

"Every day except for major holidays," Sam said with a wink. "Come this way, ma'am. It's a short walk."

We crossed the street and headed to Harvard Yard. We walked down the path between the old, idyllic brick buildings as students rambled about. The museum was just a small distance away.

"This is beautiful, Sam," I said as I looked at the building. "I can't believe that I haven't been here before."

"It's one of the best-kept secrets in Massachusetts," he declared and opened the door. "You're going to love it."

"Earth sciences, giant amethyst geodes, and glass flowers. Where do you want to start?" I asked as we were surrounded by the endless beauty of the exhibits.

"Dinosaurs," Sam said without any hesitation.

"Survival of the Fittest," I said. "Have you ever thought about how Darwinism and its theory of evolution mirror the narrative of debt-money?"

"You mean how Darwinism explains why we compete," suggested Sam, "the process of Natural Selection secures that only the most-fit, the fiercest competitors survive the harsh, unrelenting battle of life to pass on their genes, ensuring that only the winners continue in life."

"Yes, that's it."

"I guess this narrative reinforces ruthless competition for money," Sam considered.

"Making it socially acceptable, Sam, as though ruthless competition is part of our nature, and nature itself. It is the unspoken permission to do whatever is necessary to win, or gain market share, and let the means justify the end."

"That's how the debt-money system operates, and what Darwinism suggests."

"The idea was taken from his book *Origin of Species,* published in 1869," I said. "It was used to mold our perspectives and indoctrinate us with an immoral code. The idea was used to encourage us to take high-stake risks, deal with devastating losses, and accept unforgiving punishment as part of our hero's journey. But Charles Darwin did not suggest 'Survival of the Fittest' and 'Natural Selection' applied to economics—or even nature, at all."

"Really?" Sam remarked. "Who did?"

"Herbert Spencer, English philosopher and political theorist," I answered. "He took these phrases from Darwin's writings to draw parallels with his own economic theories and views of society. Spencer construed and manipulated Darwin's observations as he framed seemingly scientific research to legitimize his philosophy of 'Social Darwinism.' He used this reasoning as a warrant to encourage and reinforce imperialistic pursuits—and dominance."

"What about Darwin's writings themselves?" asked Sam curiously. "Didn't he find nature operated on these principles?"

"David Loye, author, and visionary, reviewed Darwin's writings extensively," I explained. "He found Darwin's dominant themes focused on selflessness, love, and moral sensitivity. Darwin's research focused on interconnectedness, the web of life. Loye created 'The Darwin Project' to restore Darwin's original message and lost theories."

"Wow," Sam said shocked. "Did Darwin talk about survival of the fittest at all?"

"In his work, *The Descent of Man*, Darwin made only two references to it," I shared, "and yet, he made ninety-five observations about love and ninety-two about moral sensitivity. In fact, to Darwin, 'Survival of the Fittest' meant the most adaptable to the immediate environment, the one who understood how to get along with others, to live within a moral code of mutual love and connectedness."

"That blows my mind and gives me a new perspective on why species don't make it," Sam said as we looked at the massive skeleton of a Tyrannosaurus Rex suspended overhead.

"You know, altruism, caring about each other, is our true nature," I said. "We have a natural tendency to care about ourselves *and* each other. Not only do we feel better when we do, but science shows we are wired to care for each other."

"You mean we are wired for altruism, instead of selfishness?" Sam clarified.

"*Nature Communications* published a study," I answered, "that found evidence of this while scientists interacted with Capuchin monkeys. The monkeys watched one person either refuse or agree to help another person open a jar. Afterward, both people then offered a treat to the monkeys. When the person who declined to help the other offered a treat to the monkeys, all seven rejected it. Then the scientists tried a twist, the person acted busy and refused to help the other, and then monkeys showed no bias against him, taking the treat when he offered it to them. But when they saw a person unwilling and able to help, the monkeys didn't want to have anything to do with him or the treats he offered."

"That's amazing!" exclaimed Sam.

"Another study was done by researchers who observed students watching a film that showcased Mother Teresa's work helping the poor and sick in Calcutta, India. They found the students, just by watching the film, had a significant increase in the amount of immunoglobulin, a protective antibody found in blood and saliva, as compared to others who watched a neutral film, one without violence or acts of kindness."

"We've been brainwashed," Sam said as he shook his head, "with selective narratives to sell us a story of ruthless competition. When it is our nature to collaborate with each other—to contribute and help where we can."

"I agree," I said with a sigh. "Look, they have an African gallery. Let's go there. You have to think, Sam, that indigenous cultures have lost less of their connection to wisdom than we have. And we, in the more 'established' part of the world, depend on outside experts to tell us what we know. Instead of trusting ourselves to feel and know what is right and what is wrong."

"I haven't really thought about it."

"Have you heard the story of the Ubuntu children?" I asked. "Talk about wisdom!"

"No," Sam said. "Tell me what that is all about."

"There is a beautiful story of an anthropologist who came to live with them in Africa to understand their ways. Despite months of research and effort, he learned little until the last day. He proposed they play a game where he put a stash of candy in a basket under a tree and told them to all stand behind a line and race to it. The first one to get there would have the spoils all to themselves."

"What happened?"

"He shouted, 'Go!' and they unexpectedly held each other's hands and ran toward the basket—together! Then they shared the candy with each other."

"I bet the anthropologist did not expect that."

"No, he didn't," I affirmed. "He asked them why they ran together instead of trying to win the candy for themselves. A girl answered, 'How can one of us be happy if all the others are sad?' Ubuntu means, 'I am because we are.'"

"Wow, that is so beautiful," Sam said as his voice cracked a little. "That makes me long for what they have."

"The Archbishop Desmond Tutu shared what Ubuntu is and what it means," I added. "He said, *'Africans have a thing called Ubuntu. It is about the essence of being human; it is part of the gift Africa will give the world. It embraces hospitality, caring about others, being willing to go the extra mile for the sake of another. We believe that a person is a person through other persons, that my humanity is caught up, bound up, inextricably with yours. When I dehumanize you, I inexorably dehumanize myself. The solitary human being is a contradiction in terms. Therefore, you seek to work for the common good because your humanity comes into its own in community, in belonging.'* Yes. Beautiful, indeed."

"This is so humbling," shared Sam.

"It's the truth we all recognize, isn't it? The ever-present presence of unconditional love is the core of our being. We instantly know it's true, even when we capture the smallest glimpses of it," I said as we both fell silent for a moment.

"Let's check out the glass-flower exhibit," Sam said. "It is over there—to the left."

"Nature is amazing. I think this flower looks like the human heart," I said staring at the fine handblown ruby-colored glass. "My mom always had flowers like this in her garden, I think they were bleeding-heart plants. They were her favorite, along with lily-of-the-valley and violets."

"I want to have a big garden someday, filled with everything," Sam said. "Talk about making my heart happy."

"Sam, did you know that our hearts form before our brains? And our heart even starts to beat on its own! — The brain doesn't get it going. Even in heart transplants, doctors have to wait for the new heart to beat in the patient."

"That's astounding."

"The Heartmath Institute has done quite a bit of research in the past few years. As it turns out, heart cells of different people, in

Petrie dishes, actually sync together and beat in harmony. The cells find a matching resonance and beat in unison. This phenomenon happens across species too, dog, cat, human—you name it, hearts seek to beat in the same rhythm."

"Wow," Sam remarked. "I would never imagine that."

"They found the electromagnetic field of the heart is 5,000 times stronger than that of the brain. The field of one person affects another as it radiates in a 360-degree circular field. When we feel upset and stressed our hearts beat in a jagged frequency, or an incoherent pattern. As our hearts beats in discord a lower frequency is sent out which disables our brain's capacity to access higher thinking and seeing."

"What happens when we move out of frustration? Does the frequency change?"

"Yes, it does," I answered. "When we move into appreciation, and restore a feeling of well-being, our hearts beat in coherence and harmony again. This higher frequency activates our brain's neocortex, the center of higher perception and higher thinking. Appreciation and gratitude turn on the higher centers of our brain. We can make the switch and affect the body consciously, simply by moving into gratitude and appreciation."

"This is incredible," Sam said. "Think about it. Living in the mode of scarcity, we are immersed in lower emotions. These emotions prevent the brain from accessing its higher faculties of greater perception and modes of thinking. Our physiology traps us in the cycle of blame. We cannot see past our own suffering."

"That's right, we cannot imagine a solution or another way—a higher, more beautiful way. Because we are literally stuck in discord, sending out dissonant energy, hurting ourselves and each other, as we fight the harmony of life."

Just as we turned right to leave the exhibit, a storm of six and seven-year-olds charged out of the craft room. They yelled and cheered with all kinds of excitement, leaving the museum with their new artwork in hand. Each one had drawn a vibrantly colored butterfly. They were learning about the process of metamorphosis and finished by creating a butterfly of their own to take home.

"It is a swarm of butterflies! They look like they are ready to take flight. How much joy can one room hold?" I said as we laughed, backing up to make way for them.

"Perhaps it is true," Sam said, "the secret key might just lie within us, within our hearts. This may be why the universe keeps the same DNA code to create the butterfly's new heart in the cells of our hearts as well. It is the code that lets us take flight too. We are not wired for fear and greed, after all. We are wired for unconditional love and appreciation."

"As we stumble upon truth, we activate the code with appreciation," I said. "Launching the next stage of who we are by being grateful for all that has been, all that is, and for all the beauty yet to come." I stopped and placed my hand on his heart, "I think it's true, Sam. The key we are looking for is lying dormant in the dimly-lit parts of our hearts. As we are set free and come to experience our true nature, the light of joy ignites the key and activates what we are wired for...the joy of being alive."

Sam and I headed out of the museum and over toward Garden Street. As we walked across the campus, I couldn't help but reflect on the words of Dee Hock. With his prescient insight, he encouraged us to see that we were on the precipice of change, a beautiful and grand change. Everything was more than fine, and even in right order, all that was needed was for us to take a leap, a leap of faith into the unseen.

He conveyed that we were at the precise point when a four-hundred-year-old age rattled in its deathbed, and another struggled to be born. It was a coming shift in our culture, society, and institutions enormously greater than the world had yet to experience. Ahead, stood the possibility of the regeneration of individuality, liberty, community, and ethics such that the world had never known, and a harmony with nature, with one another and with the divine intelligence such as the world had ever yet come to dream. All this wisdom from a man who created a credit card company but who was in fact so much more. Since the time he spoke of these great ideas, our struggle had started to give way. The new paradigm had begun to unfurl from its chrysalis. Tightly woven into the fabric of its expansive wings, we, and all our ways of living rode upon its pulsating wave as we entered the next stage of our metamorphosis.

16

A WORLD OF PLENTY

"Ready to go?" Sam said as I opened the car door.

"Ready as ever. How long will it take us to get there?"

"About three-to-four hours. The whole drive will be through the mountains, and we should get to see some beautiful lakes. Maybe some snow, you never know."

We were off to Cabot, Vermont, to meet a group of people interested in starting a conversation about organizing a food currency.

"Hopefully, we can find a way to make the money redeemable for the cheese they make and better yet, Ben and Jerry's ice cream." Sam laughed.

"We should stop for some Ben and Jerry's on the way," I suggested. "You know, Sam, speaking of cheese, there is a bank in the Emilian Romagna region of northern Italy that gives low-interest loans to Parmigiano-Reggiano cheese producers using their cheese as collateral."

"Really?" asked Sam. "What's in the vault?"

"Cheese!" I said. "They keep it in refrigerated, humidified vaults. The cheese is worth over 200 million Euros. The bankers say it is worth more than gold."

"I could see where cheese would be worth more than gold."

"Well, the bankers are willing to make loans and at low rates, at 3% to 5% interest."

"So, if farmers can't pay the loans back," Sam suggested, "the banks sell their cheese?"

"Right," I answered. "Interesting as it may be, it is another sign of how confused we are. The cheesemakers producing cheese which is in high demand, and still have to go to a bank to get pieces of paper, Euros, in this case. They go into debt for that paper, and pay interest on that paper, just to buy what they need to produce their cheese. In turn, they have to sell the cheese at higher prices, and fast enough to get the pieces of paper back—to pay the bank."

"Otherwise, the bank keeps all the interest, fees—*and the cheese!*" Sam added, "The bank can sell the cheese while the cheesemakers go bankrupt."

"And, really, what did the bank do here? It just gave the cheesemakers pieces of paper that they agreed to use as money."

"Yes, just because they have the monopoly to issue money."

"All the cheesemakers need is a community, a circle of exchange, where they issue their credit-as-money backed by the promise to deliver cheese. They can raise the money they need to run their business directly from their customers and create new money to circulate like Anton-the-baker's credits—adding money into a society choked with too much debt."

"This way the cheesemakers get out from under-the-thumb of the debt-clock with its hard repayment schedule," Sam interjected. "They will have no interest to pay and could reward their customers by reducing the price of the cheese."

"Interesting, isn't it?" I said as I looked at him. "The cheese bank is only a step or two away from becoming producer-credit money."

"Speaking of interesting," Sam said, "I think producer-credit money needs a new name."

"What do you mean?"

"Something more interesting than 'producer-credits.'"

"Like Twitter?" I guessed.

"You read my mind. The name doesn't have to mean anything, but it needs to be called something that's more accessible, and, well, fun—without being so technical sounding. After all, money done right, money that liberates us, should have a good vibe. We don't need to be so serious."

"I love the idea, Sam. I think you're on to something. But what would we call it?"

"Well, we've got four hours of driving ahead of us," Sam said with a big grin. "Let's see if inspiration hits us. No pressure."

"Okay, but no promises," I said as my mind went blank. "Hey, why are you turning left? I-93 is right up the road."

"Oh, you didn't see it, did you?" Sam said as he took a hard left and sped up to get ahead of the oncoming traffic. "Look at this bakery. It is Portuguese. Come on, let's go inside and check out what they have."

Sam found a parking spot right outside. The small storefront window was lined with cakes, golden cakes, chocolate cakes, and vanilla cream cakes, filling every shelf. I wasn't sure how he even noticed the shop as we drove by, but I was starting to suspect he had some kind of inborn homing device. His instincts proved right yet again, as the cakes were among the most beautiful I had seen.

"Look at this one, Bolo de Labacha Maria," Sam pulled me in front of a butter-creamed cake topped with vanilla cookie crumbs and a circle of dark espresso beans.

"Bolo de Labacha Maria? What does that mean?" I asked the woman behind the counter.

"A Portuguese favorite, it is the Marie Biscuit Cake. We make it by stacking vanilla cookies soaked in espresso in between layers of rich, sweet buttercream. It is pure heaven."

"Did you hear that?" Sam poked me. "I bet this Bolo was good enough for Marie Antoinette. What do you say? Let's eat cake?!"

"Two pieces to go, please." I nodded to the woman waiting on us. "Marie Antoinette certainly understood the abundance that exists behind everything. The abundance begging to be celebrated with cake!"

"Her Bolos," Sam corrected me. "We're getting in touch with abundance, too. We are no longer willing to scrape by using scarcity-money and compete for crumbs as they fall from the table as our way of life."

"That's right abundance is coming!" I said smiling, "Abundance is our natural way of life...it is the joy and celebration of being alive."

"That's it!" Sam said loudly. "That's what the new money should be called, Bolos! No need to scrape by, cut back and try to make ends meet. Instead, we will eat cake every time we create and trade as we share our wealth with each other!"

"Sam, I love it. With our Bolos, we will create our cake and eat it too!" I said as a message chimed on my phone.

"What is it?"

"Wait—Oh, Sam! I can't believe it!" I said barely able to get the words out as I tried to reread the message. "Sam! How would you like to spend the holidays in India with me?"

"What?"

"My dear friends in Southern India, they want to try it, Sam! They want to try to create the producer-credit money system in their community of 155 villages! They want to increase their prosperity, and they think this is a wonderful way to do it."

"You mean with Bolos," Sam winked as he corrected me again.

"Right... Bolos, Sam!" I gasped.

"What an opportunity!" Sam said. "Yes, I say, let's go to India and see how the Bolo system can make way for a better world."

Then I thought to myself in astonishment, "Jai Bolo." In Sanskrit, 'Bolo' meant to speak, to offer praise and 'Jai' meant victory. As we honored and shared our divinely given gifts with each other, we empowered one another. We lifted ourselves up and our communities at the same time. We praised our victory as we returned home to a world we were meant to live in.

When I first came to terms with the fact that the unjust

scarcity and suffering in the world were created by the money we used and that no political, economic, or social change could ever solve our issues, I grew to have hope that life was up to something grand. After all, the debt-money system we used, with its seven destructive imperatives, was the perfect system for the way we lived and understood the world. We were a people lost in fear, believing in scarcity, conditioned to fight and compromise our highest ideals just to survive, let alone find some happiness. Our collective level of consciousness kept the money-as-debt system in place. And, the good news was that it could not last.

Every day I saw evidence of it fraying at the seams, revealing its hand that it was unsustainable and no matter how we tried to piece it together, it was *not meant* to last. A new way was meant to come as we collectively questioned and challenged what we previously accepted. As we inquired who we were as a people, what we valued and how we wanted to live, we let go of our mental enslavement believing in lack and suffering. As we embodied the abundance of our true nature, our hearts grew, and our consciousness rose, and we stumbled upon and discovered this new way to recreate our money systems to unleash life's natural flow.

In fact, abundance money was rising in all different places and in all different ways, and at a faster pace than I could note. At first, this idea of how to create money properly seemed difficult to grasp, let alone to describe how it worked, and to imagine how to create. Bitcoin was fast and furiously becoming a mainstream concept, but it was the technology of its decentralized, unchangeable accounting ledger called the *blockchain* that made this revolution possible. The blockchain technology allowed for the liberation of money to happen. Still, Bitcoin and other cryptocurrencies remained speculative bets as they did not meet the requirements of abundance money. Yet, each day abundance money emerged, right before my eyes, as many companies issued their own credit backed by the promises to deliver their own goods or services, just as a delivery contract or a product voucher. Ex-Uber drivers created their coin redeemable for rides, SolarCoin grew in leaps and bounds, even

Burger King Russia issued the WhopperCoin redeemable for food. Many retailers came together to issue their loyalty reward points in digital coins, as they took the concept of Plenti points further and closer to true abundance money. The money revolution had begun, and proper, life supporting forms of money entered society in the most simple and benign ways. The liberation of our money system was restoring our power. Perhaps without knowing it, we were gaining the ability to determine what kind of world we wanted to live in. Still this development was undetected by most, as the daily apprehension and confusion kept our attention on the world we knew falling apart rather than what began to emerge.

As the democratization of creating the money supply began to expand and abundance money continued to materialize, money was no longer centralized and controlled, kept neither too small or too large, at the expense of humanity, the planet, and freedom, itself. Instead, for the first time in human history, we found ourselves at the nexus where the knowledge of how to create money properly reemerged and the technological capacity to establish the required systems was at hand. We had never been here before. We were the first people in recorded history who had the opportunity to liberate our money systems, and ourselves, as we stepped out of the cracked, decaying shell from the crumbling money order that had sustained our world and kept the collective human imagination limited for thousands and thousands of years. In fact, this transformation was impossible to stop, gaining traction, as it was reinforced every minute of every day.

Money was once again valueless, able to play the key role of the equal sign in the mathematical equation as two equal goods were exchanged. It resumed its place as a neutral technology, a tool of exchange, simply here to help us express what we could dream up, produce, and contribute to one another. We as humans could embrace our full capacity as brilliant creators. Producers could issue the right amount of money at the right time, denominated in the supply of the product they delivered, determined by the demand of their customers. Money was certifiably legitimate again, as it represented the real stuff we wanted and needed. No one with worthy goods and services could be shut out from succeeding anymore, and, if wanting and willing to participate, no one could be left out from accessing money and remain stuck in the cycle of welfare dependency without social mobility. Freedom whispered through every crack and seeped in through the corners of our lives, as our power quietly reignited, liberating our true nature.

Not only was abundance money voluntary as we decided whose credit we accepted and practices we supported, but it was market verified. And, the markets returned to markets again because the money or the fuel they used was the right kind of money which eliminated the seven imperatives that drove self-sabotaging speculation into our lives. No longer run by the debt machine, building legacies of debt carried on from one generation to the next, we could not be manipulated and compelled to accept destructive political agendas or ideologies of the few. Instead, any debt created could be repaid in real product besides abundance money tokens, unlike our old money-as-debt system which perpetuated artificial scarcity as the undercurrent brewing beneath our lives. This money revolution was the true love revolution. The power to create and live as we chose. With the potential of creating the parity principle as these systems grew and matured, we had the possibility of simple, common sense, and self-correcting system aligning profitability and success with the greater good. It was not only straightforward but simple.

Now with this opportunity to help these communities in India build out their own system to take control of their destiny with the wealth, genius, and work they were willing to do was beyond my wildest imagination. I hoped that as we worked together we would create a tangible prototype for communities in the United States and other regions to model. Farmers would easily take their rightful place in the realm of the world. And, I knew it would only be a matter of time before we saw large corporate players begin to directly issue their own credit, fully embodying the principles of abundance-money, as viable alternatives to the debt-dollar. Though at first we might be skeptical of large corporations issuing their own money, being able to increase their dominance and power over others, as true producer-credits they would be harbingers of good, spreading stability throughout the world with the right kind of money and the parity principle guiding them as their ultimate compass. Sam and I had no time to waste; there was so much opportunity to act on and so much energy to harness. We had to find out what was needed to get started and the time was now.

I whispered under my breath, "Jai bolo, what a beautiful time is ready to come."

Sam and I looked at each other and smiled in silence. He opened the door as we left the bakery, and we were filled with a humbled sense of awe. We could both feel there was something much greater going on, enveloping not just the two of us on the journey of its unfoldment, but every one of us. It seemed when we first started our journey, often we felt too small and alone to find our way. But there was a greater wisdom at hand, quietly, steadily, and powerfully working all along, shepherding us as it slowly revealed its true nature of abundance within us.

I opened the car door as my ear caught the sweetest sound of sparrows singing overhead. The rustle of wind moved through the branches of the tree as two acorns came bouncing at my feet in quick staccato beats. I looked up at the tree rich with its canopy of fire crimson leaves, and I could see that nature simply couldn't help but give of herself. All she created, she created from the endless joy and out of the sheer love of what she was. She could not help but give, never with a thought of how much or to whom. She was the very being of abundance itself. All she gave she gave out of sheer ecstasy of the divine presence coursing through her veins. And, *this* was why she sang.

The time had come for us to join her. No longer would we tell our sad stories bemoaning our sagas of woe. The time had come for us to drop the discord in our hearts with all its bitter tones of clashing cacophony. We were ready. Ready to join in the harmony, the harmony enveloping the rest of the Earth. The time had come for humanity to join Creation singing its song. We now would sing too, a song so sweet, so beautiful, coming from the pure joy of being alive. Expressing and giving of ourselves in gratitude for life flowing through us, as our hearts pounded full and deep in the wonderment of a world filled with plenty.

ACKNOWLEDGEMENTS

Writing this book has been a life lived in love with the essence of this book. For more than a decade, almost two now, its love has moved me, driven me—obsessed me. I feel often, that this book wrote me. It certainly wrote through me as I attempted to be its diligent scribe and servant dedicated to harnessing its message and sharing it with others. Like a beacon of light, it emitted steady frequencies. As I tuned to them, I saw the possibilities for the highest expressions of humanity and the planet to be realized relatively effortlessly. I sought to translate its language and capture its images. Even as I grew weary, wondering if it would ever be ready—careening between too early and too late, I surrendered to its vision, tone, and vibration knowing the truth of its message and captured by the sovereignty it carries.

In that light, there is endless gratitude I owe to all who have been in my life during these years, as they have been patient and tolerant in their unwitting position of sounding boards receiving fragmented wisdom and insights that I could not contain—I extrapolated them to almost everything we experienced in daily life. Most importantly I want to thank my parents. My father started my journey exploring money and encouraged me throughout all his days. And especially my mother, she was my greatest champion; loving this idea and reading every iteration of this book without every seeming tired or impatient. She praised it and believed in it, saying to me, "You know, this book is so much more than a money book. It *Is* you."

I especially want to thank my sister Cynthia Ragusin Roden, my dear friends Marika and Eddie Ray, Anne Rockwell, Cintra Reeve, Melissa Price, Antonio Sordillo, Danielle Norsworthy who were among my early readers, provided steadfast encouragement and priceless feedback, as did my spiritual teachers in India. My dear friend David Stevens read the manuscript close to the final stages and during one of the most trying times of my life with my mother's passing, his precise feedback, reactions, and encouragement gave me the final wind needed beneath my wings to cross the finish line. As did the grace and cheers from Ashley James, Sanjay Bhagia, and my business partner of twenty years and dear friend, Richard Lynch Jr who listened to hours of discussion from the very beginning and never revealed any exhaustion—except for his concern about the rough travel schedule Sam Bailey was subjected to throughout the book. Many of my teachers over the years, especially Dr. Len, Dr. Donny Epstein, Phil Gruber, and Dr. Vikas, created frameworks that sustained my hope and determination for what is to reveal itself in the highest light.

There were many amazing people who were skilled and caring who entered on cue to assist with all the administration of publishing. Terry Smith edited multiple times, Maggie Lynch offered sage consulting advice, as did Robin Philips, who held my hand answering questions of critical importance. Alan Kaufman reviewed the usage of works and gave expert advice. As well as designers Maxwell Roth interpreting my first vision of the cover and talented Anthony Morais who completed it and helped me with additional requests. Missy Feldman who arrived just in time to update and streamline my website. Diago Larenas illustrated more than 100 cartoon images that are in support of this work to soon become a separate children's book with videos.

I studied many works over the years with endless hours of conversations with economists, money reformers and visionaries. I am especially grateful to friends Ellen H. Brown, Steve Keen, and Paul and Tsiporah Grignon. There are so many I have missed in this brief acknowledgment because almost everyone I've known since this passion ignited played a role in making this come alive. I am grateful for the journey so far, and pray it has a profound and positive impact for all of humanity as it inspires living in the awe and wonder of life.

NOTES

Chapter One

Modern Money Mechanics - a complete booklet published by the Federal Reserve Bank of Chicago. Explanation of the money multiplier or fractional reserve lending
   https://www.academia.edu/9121613

On the Myth of Fractional Reserve Lending
   http://www.debtdeflation.com/blogs/2009/01/31/therovingcavaliersofcredit/

Bank of England explanation of how commercial banks create our money by making loans
   https://www.bankofengland.co.uk/-/media/boe/files/quarterly-bulletin/2014/money-creation-in-the-modern-economy.pdf

How money is destroyed when loans are repaid
   https://positivemoney.org/how-money-works/advanced/how-money-is-destroyed/

Chapter Two

One in Six Americans on anti-depressants
http://time.com/4900248/antidepressants-depression-more-common/

Further commentary on being a citizen rather than a consumer. Juliet Schor's work on overconsumption and the over worked American.
https://www.goodreads.com/book/show/178930.The_Overworked_American

Sale of Picasso's "Garçon a la Pipe."
https://www.cbsnews.com/pictures/most-expensive-paintings-ever-sold-at-auction/10/

Chapter Three

Albert Einstein's quote on consciousness
https://www.goodreads.com/quotes/320600-we-can-not-solve-our-problems-with-the-same-level

Chapter Four

About Basil Moore, economist
https://newsletter.blogs.wesleyan.edu/2018/03/19/moore-remembered-for-contributions-to-monetary-economics/

History of Bimetallism in the United States
https://www.econlib.org/library/YPDBooks/Laughlin/lghHBM.html

History of William Jennings Bryan's famous speech "Cross of Gold."
http://historymatters.gmu.edu/d/5354/

Federal Reserve Private or Public?
  http://www.conservativetruth.org/article.php?id=6598

Chapter Five

About Dr. Steve Keen and how he saw the Great Recession of 2008 coming
  https://theconversation.com/i-predicted-the-last-financial-crisis-now-soaring-global-debt-levels-pose-risk-of-another-84136

Interview with Dr. Steve Keen and Chris Martenson
  https://www.valueinvestingworld.com/2012/06/chris-martenson-interviews-steve-keen.html

Professor Steve Keen's Patreon site
  https://www.patreon.com/ProfSteveKeen/overview

Professor Steve Keen's interview on HARDtalk
  http://www.debtdeflation.com/blogs/2011/12/03/my-hardtalk-interview-transcribed/

The Debt Manifesto - Dr. Steve Keen
  https://www.debtdeflation.com/blogs/manifesto/

Occupy Wall Street Movement
  http://occupywallst.org

Blind Mice Parable
  https://www.goodreads.com/book/show/31213526-six-blind-mice-and-an-elephant

Chapter Six

Who was AmbroseBierce?

https://www.goodreads.com/author/show/14403.
Ambrose_Bierce

Dr. Michael Hudson
    http://michael-hudson.com/

Interview with Dr. Michael Hudson and Chuck Mertz
    https://antidotezine.com/2015/09/27/history-debt-fiction/

About the movie *It's A Wonderful Life*
    https://www.imdb.com/title/tt0038650/

Chapter Seven

David Graeber
    https://www.goodreads.com/author/show/29101.David_Graeber

David Graeber's *Debt: The First 5000 years*.
    https://www.goodreads.com/book/show/6617037-debt?ac=1&from_search=true&qid=HMaUJOmMJ8&rank=1

David Graeber on Madagascar.
    https://vodeocatalog.com/en/video/CZIINXhGDcs

Dr. Michael Hudson on the Sanctity of Debt
    http://michael-hudson.com/2015/09/the-sanctity-of-debt/

GM bankruptcy
    https://www.theguardian.com/business/2009/jun/01/general-motors-bankruptcy-chapter-11
    https://www.reuters.com/article/us-autos-gm-treasury/u-s-government-says-it-lost-11-2-billion-on-gm-bailout-idUSBREA3T0MR20140430

David Graeber's speech

https://www.youtube.com/watch?v=CZIINXhGDcs

David Graeber's new book, *Bullshit Jobs: A Theory*.
https://www.goodreads.com/book/show/34466958-bullshit-jobs

JP Getty quote
https://www.goodreads.com/quotes/214064-if-you-owe-the-bank-100-that-s-your-problem-if

Nick Hanauer's article *The Pitchforks Are Coming...For Us Plutocrats*
https://www.politico.com/magazine/story/2014/06/the-pitchforks-are-coming-for-us-plutocrats-108014

Chapter Eight

F.A.O. Schwarz toy retailer
https://faoschwarz.com

More about the history of the monopoly game
https://www.theguardian.com/lifeandstyle/2015/apr/11/secret-history-monopoly-capitalist-game-leftwing-origins
https://www.goodreads.com/book/show/37542879-pass-go-and-collect-200

More on the Anti-Monopoly game and Professor Anspach
https://killscreen.com/articles/conversation-ralph-anspach-man-behind-anti-monopoly/

Understanding the Rule of 72
https://www.investopedia.com/ask/answers/what-is-the-rule-72/

The Debt Clock in Times Square
http://content.time.com/time/business/article/0,8599,1850269,00.html

Political Rhetoric about Government debt
    https://www.youtube.com/watch?v=d57M6ATPZIE

Paul Ryan and Alan Greenspan on can the government pay for social security
    https://www.youtube.com/watch?v=veCAN9Mmaws

Stephanie Kelton, MMT and the truth about government debt
    http://harryshearer.com/transcript-stephanie-kelton-interview/
    www.youtube.com/watch?v=WS9nP-BKa3M

David Walker former comptroller on deficits.
    https://www.npr.org/templates/story/story.php?storyId=122436097

Treasury bonds are the national debt
    https://www.investopedia.com/articles/04/011404.asp

Who owns the federal debt?
    https://www.thebalance.com/who-owns-the-u-s-national-debt-3306124
    http://ticdata.treasury.gov/Publish/mfh.txt

Franklin, Benjamin. *A Modest Enquiry into the Nature and Necessity of Paper Currency.*
    1729.
    https://www.goodreads.com/search?q=Franklin%2C+Benjamin.+A+Modest+Enquiry+into+the+Nature+and+Necessity+of+Paper+Currency.&qid=9jCmvrTppl

Currency Act or 1764 and the Stamp Act of 1765
    http://www.stamp-act-history.com/timeline/1764-currency-act/

More about how the Revolutionary war was paid for

https://allthingsliberty.com/2015/02/how-was-the-revolutionary-war-paid-for/

Copy of speeches of Senator Robert L. Owen
https://fraser.stlouisfed.org/title/5328/item/535718

Ellen Brown, *The Web of Debt*.
https://www.goodreads.com/book/show/19168428-web-of-debt?from_search=true&from_srp=true&qid=oXMoI2siPe&rank=1

Bankers reducing money supply; James Buel Letter 1877.
https://archive.org/details/BankingAndCurrencyAndTheMoneyTrust-ByCharlesA.Lindbergh

Thomas Edison
https://fraser.stlouisfed.org/title/5328/item/535718

Money supply reduction from Great Recession
http://www.economicpopulist.org/content/40-worlds-wealth-wiped-out-now-davos-super-rich-china-russia-blame-united-states

Money supply reduction in Great Depression
https://www.youtube.com/watch?v=ObiIp8TKaLs
https://press.princeton.edu/titles/746.html

Watch Bill Still's *Secret of Oz*
https://topdocumentaryfilms.com/the-secret-of-oz/
https://www.imdb.com/title/tt1954955/

Chapter Nine

Learn about Ralph Waldo Emerson and the "Shot Heard Round the World."
https://www.constitutionfacts.com/us-declaration-of-independence/the-shot-heard-round-the-world/

Roman Republic issued plentiful brass and copper coins, instead of limited gold
https://www.goodreads.com/book/show/8356550-the-american-plutocracy

More on Tally Sticks
https://www.bl.uk/collection-items/tally-sticks
http://unusualhistoricals.blogspot.com/2010/10/money-matter-tally-stick-system.html
https://www.maa.org/press/periodicals/convergence/mathematical-treasures-english-tally-sticks

Quoted story of the tour of the British Parliament and Westminster Hall
https://www.parliament.uk/about/podcasts/video-tours/

About the Bank of International Settlements, BIS
https://www.bis.org/about/

Dr. Carroll Quigley's book *Tragedy and Hope: A History of the World in Our Time*. 1966.
https://archive.org/details/TragedyAndHope_501

Ellen Brown's commentary on the Bank of North Dakota
http://www.webofdebt.com/articles/north_dakota.php

Bank of North Dakota
https://bnd.nd.gov
https://ilsr.org/rule/bank-of-north-dakota-2/

About the Public Banking Institute
http://www.publicbankinginstitute.org

More about the European Union
https://europa.eu/european-union/about-eu/history_en

Greece and Goldman Sachs
    http://america.aljazeera.com/blogs/scrutineer/2015/7/14/did-wall-street-enable-greek-debt-crisis.html

In search of the real Marie Antoinette
    https://www.npr.org/templates/story/story.php?storyId=6095949

Chapter Ten

The National Mall and Memorial Parks
    https://www.nps.gov/nama/index.htm

Abraham Lincoln's *Gettysburg Address*
    http://www.abrahamlincolnonline.org/lincoln/speeches/gettysburg.htm

John Quincy Adam's *Warning Against the Search for Monsters to Destroy speech*.
    https://www.mtholyoke.edu/acad/intrel/jqadams.htm

President Eisenhower's farewell address warning about Military Industrial Complex
    https://www.history.com/this-day-in-history/eisenhower-warns-of-military-industrial-complex

About the Peace Alliance
    https://peacealliance.org/issues-advocacy/department-of-peace/

Marianne Williamson
    https://myhero.com/Marianne_Williamson_2013

Marianne Williamson's speech at Department of Peace conference
    https://www.youtube.com/watch?v=My6BF8GZM2g

Deepak Chopra comments taken from live speech at the annual peace alliance conference in Washington, DC. 2007.
https://www.nwffacim.org/tgp/forums/thread-view.asp?tid=13702
https://chopra.com

Robert Frost on believing
https://funtaqa.wordpress.com/2013/09/02/%E2%80%8E%E2%80%8Bbelieve-it-in-samuel-onatuga-isichei/

Michael Bernard Beckwith.
http://www.michaelbernardbeckwith.com/

Comments from Dr. Beckwith given in person at the annual peace alliance conference. 2007 https://www.nwffacim.org/tgp/forums/thread-view.asp?tid=13702

Margaret Mead
http://www.famousquotes123.com/margaret-mead-quotes.html

Chapter Eleven

Ellen Brown on the US Postal Service talk
https://ellenbrown.com/2013/09/23/what-we-could-do-with-a-postal-savings-bank-infrastructure-that-doesnt-cost-taxpayers-a-dime/

More about the history of the Postal Savings System
https://slate.com/news-and-politics/2014/08/postal-banking-already-worked-in-the-usa-and-it-will-work-again.html

The Dodd-Frank Act and bail-ins
https://www.huffingtonpost.com/ellen-brown/bailout-is-out-bailin-is-_b_3178702.html

Ellen Brown on FDIC funding

https://usawatchdog.com/big-banks-will-take-depositors-money-in-next-crash-ellen-brown/

The unbanked and underbanked people
https://www.forbes.com/sites/ashoka/2013/06/14/banking-the-unbanked-a-how-to/#411772335727
https://thefinancialbrand.com/25140/fdic-research-study-unbanked-underbanked/

Ithaca Hours
https://money.cnn.com/galleries/2012/pf/1201/gallery.community-currencies/3.html
https://www.investopedia.com/terms/i/ithaca-hours.asp

Paul Glover and Hometown money
http://www.paulglover.org/currencybook.html

Paul Glover's talk
https://www.youtube.com/watch?v=tyCHw6WmyQk

What is Crowdfunding?
https://www.fundable.com/learn/resources/guides/crowdfunding/what-is-crowdfunding
What is Bitcoin?
https://bitcoinfoundation.org

What is the Blockchain?
https://blockgeeks.com/guides/what-is-blockchain-technology/

What is the Bengla-pesa?
https://borgenproject.org/tag/bangla-pesa/

More about Will Ruddick and the Bangla-pesa
https://beyondmoney.net/tag/will-ruddick/

Videos on Bengla-pesa
    https://www.youtube.com/watch?v=UaspBGmsdLE&list=PLPUExzwZAUpZgrTqH55aAV2tjlohT_qlD

More on Micro-lending
    https://www.investopedia.com/articles/personal-finance/040715/what-microlending-and-how-does-it-work.asp

More on Mohammed Yunus and the Grameen Bank
    https://milaap.org/stories/what-is-grameen-bank-and-who-is-muhammad-yunus

More on MFIs
    https://www.microworld.org/en/news-from-the-field/article/what-microfinance-institution

Liberty Bell tour
    http://www.ushistory.org/tour/liberty-bell.htm

Chapter Twelve

E.C. Riegel, *Private Enterprise Money*, 1944.
    https://freedom-school.com/money/intro.htm

The Basic Functions of Money
    https://beyondmoney.net/the-end-of-money-and-the-future-of-civilization/

Chapter Thirteen

Paul Grignon
    http://www.moneyasdebt.net

Detailed information on producer credits
    http://www.moneyasdebt.net

Capacity Credits
https://www.google.com/url?sa=t&rct=j&q=&esrc=s&source=web&cd=&ved=2ahUKEwiT0L3PqNP4AhURRzABHZ1HC48QFnoECAcQAQ&url=https%3A%2F%2Fwww.longfinance.net%2Fdocuments%2F1328%2FCapacity_Trade_and_Credit_Summary_Findings-2011.pdf&usg=AOvVaw0lro6X4DXC8j2rxNgJ8SYY

Rogers Commodity Index
https://etfdb.com/index/rogers-international-commodity-index---agriculture-total-return/

Chapter Fourteen

More on the student loan crisis
https://www.forbes.com/sites/zackfriedman/2018/06/13/student-loan-debt-statistics-2018/#dbae5de7310f

German excess solar power
http://fortune.com/2016/05/11/germany-excess-power/

More on SolarCoin
https://solarcoin.org/

Japanese Fureai Kippu caring currencies
https://monneta.org/en/fureai-kippu-caring-currencies-in-japan/

Dee Hock
http://www.deewhock.com
http://www.griequity.com/resources/integraltech/GRIBusinessModel/chaordism/chaordic.html

Chapter Fifteen

What is Slow Money?
https://slowmoney.org

More on who invests in Farmland
https://www.cnbc.com/2016/01/21/getting-your-plot-of-american-farmland-.html

The Oakland Institute
https://www.oaklandinstitute.org

Costco's pilot program with farmers
http://www.trueactivist.com/costco-is-selling-so-much-organic-produce-its-helping-farmers-grow-more/

Iroquois Valley Farms
https://iroquoisvalley.com

More on the Flower of Life
http://flower-of-life.net

Paul Furber's full article on *Alternative Currencies are Coming*.
http://www.brainstormmag.co.za/indepth/trends/10673-alternative-currencies-are-coming

History on Plenti rewards points program and notice of it ending
https://www.americanexpress.com/us/legal/plenti/terms.html
https://www.americanexpress.com/us/legal/plenti/the-plenti-program.html

More on Canada Tire money
https://www.canadiantire.ca/content/canadian-tire/en/my-canadian-tire-money.html

Mitsubishi Bank's own digital currency
https://news.bitcoin.com/japan-banking-giant-mitsubishi-goes-crypto-with-own-coin/
https://www.ft.com/content/20c10d58-8d9c-11e7-a352-e46f43c5825d

Harvard Museum of Natural History
https://hmnh.harvard.edu

The Darwin Project
http://www.thedarwinproject.com

More info on Capuchin monkey experiment
https://healthypets.mercola.com/sites/healthypets/archive/2013/07/31/capuchin-monkeys.aspx

More on the Mother Teresa Experiments
https://medium.com/becoming-you/amazing-healing-power-of-molecules-energy-and-the-mother-teresa-effect-8d17a0c9bbed

Ubuntu Children Story
https://www.givemetap.com/blogs/stories/an-anthropologist-proposed-a-game-to-the-kids-in-an-african

Archbishop Desmond Tutu on Ubuntu
https://www.youtube.com/watch?v=0wZtfqZ271w#t=162

Learn more about the power of the heart
http://www.heartmath.org

Chapter Sixteen

More about Credito Emiliano - bank which accepts cheese as collateral.
https://www.forbes.com/sites/hbsworkingknowledge/2015/07/01/a-bank-that-accepts-parmesan-as-collateral-the-cheese-stands-a-loan/#67eb36ba10a2

THE SEVEN DEBT STRINGS

1. The First Imperative is the unrelenting pressure to take on debt, as fast as we can.

2. The Second Imperative is our time does not belong to us. 'Time is money.' Chop! Chop! No time to lose with each tick of the clock, we move closer to when loan payments and bills are due. Hurry up, earn money in time pay off your debts and quick, start again, new debt must be created.

3. The Third Imperative of debt-money: 'Everyone must get a job, any job.' We need a job to keep the debt-machine rolling.

4. The Fourth Imperative: Debt-money drives us to non-stop overconsumption.

5. The Fifth Imperative is the growth imperative. The debt-money machine needs endless growth

6. The Sixth Imperative is a debt-money system requires big risk-taking, or what's called speculation.

7. The Seventh Imperative requires a small group of people hold the most meaningful power and control in our society. The real power is held by those who dictate policy about how easily our money flows and its quantity grows.

ABOUT THE AUTHOR

Interested in the empowerment and liberation of humanity, Kristen Ragusin has been curious about how we can realize the unique, creative expression of our divinity and contribute to the well-being of society. A perpetual pragmatic-optimist, Kristen believes that life is always working toward our highest good, even in the most difficult and trying times, shaping and evolving us to grow. As a child, she studied the stock market with her father to earn her allowance. She saw the markets as an integral part of realizing the American Dream, as an accessible way to create wealth, support the collective genius and productivity of our society. She earned her Bachelor of Arts degrees, in Political Science and Anthropology, as she studied how societies distribute power and resources.

After graduating, Kristen became a professional financial advisor with Merrill Lynch and built her practice helping clients invest for the last thirty years, and recently moved her practice to Raymond James & Associates. She enjoyed the special connection of working with clients and the autonomy of running her practice. For over a decade, she was a member of an elite training faculty teaching thousands of financial advisors at the Merrill Lynch Corporate Campus in Princeton, New Jersey. A professional speaker, she has given hundreds of public seminars on retirement planning and tax management strategies, as well as talks on reforming our money system at the Public Banking Institute, Pace University in New York City, and Peace Conferences in New England. She received her Masters Degree from the renowned

Fletcher School of Law and Diplomacy, Tufts University, Medford, Massachusetts.

In 2008, as she prepared to leave for Jordan to earn a certificate in conflict resolution from the United Nations Institute, she saw the coming financial crisis. Sensing something was not right with how she understood the markets, she found everything she knew about money was wrong. She uncovered the shocking revelation that today there is no money, that instead there is only debt masquerading as money, and the way our money is designed is the real cause of perpetual scarcity. Knowing that our money caused such havoc in our world, she was compelled to learn how we could create money the right way. It set her on a seven-year journey around the world as she researched and tracked down economists, money reformers, and brilliant new thinkers to solve this mystery. In the end, a solution so simple, elegant, and powerful emerged, one that enables companies and communities, big or small, to implement these new systems of exchange making it possible to create and sustain a life worth living. This led to her writing, The End of Scarcity: The Dawn of the New Abundant World, to share these insights with others. With more than thirty years of experience in the financial markets, more than ten years of intensive monetary reform research, and certified as a digital currency professional by the Digital Currency Council in New York City, she is uniquely positioned to shed light on our current financial system and the new developing systems. She also holds certificates in FinTech from the Massachusetts Institute of Technology and in Sustainable Exchange from the University of Cumbria, London.

Her many adventures include walking in the Sahara Desert, climbing Mt. Kilimanjaro, and studying at a spiritual school in the foothills of southern India. She is on her path living life and experiencing all that it has to offer.

Made in the USA
Columbia, SC
20 April 2023